#The Joyful Mother of Children

from the barren woman to...

#The Joyful Mother of Children

Mandi Windsor

Hillsboro, OR

#The Joyful Mother of Children

Copyright © 2022 by Mandi Windsor. All rights reserved.
No part of this book may be reproduced or transmitted in any form or by any means, electronic or mechanical, without permission in writing from the publisher.

Published by Inscribe Press, Hillsboro, OR
Cover by Logan Anderson

Printed in the United States of America

ISBN (print) 978-1-951611-41-5
ISBN (eBook) 978-1-951611-42-2

Scripture quotations marked AMP taken from the Amplified® Bible (AMP), Copyright © 2015 by The Lockman Foundation. Used by permission. www.lockman.org
Quotations marked NKJV taken from the New King James Version®. Copyright © 1982 by Thomas Nelson. Used by permission. All rights reserved.
Quotations marked NLT are taken from the Holy Bible, New Living Translation, copyright ©1996, 2004, 2015 by Tyndale House Foundation. Used by permission of Tyndale House Publishers, Carol Stream, Illinois 60188. All rights reserved.
Quotations marked NASB taken from the (NASB®) New American Standard Bible®, Copyright © 1960, 1971, 1977, 1995, 2020 by The Lockman Foundation. Used by permission. All rights reserved. www.lockman.org
Quotations marked TPT are from The Passion Translation®. Copyright © 2017, 2018, 2020 by Passion & Fire Ministries, Inc. Used by permission. All rights reserved. ThePassionTranslation.com.
Quotations marked MSG are taken from THE MESSAGE, copyright © 1993, 2002, 2018 by Eugene H. Peterson. Used by permission of NavPress, represented by Tyndale House Publishers. All rights reserved.

Dedication

To The Barren Woman, I am your biggest fan.
This book is for you.

CONTENTS

TESTIMONIALS / 1
ACKNOWLEDGMENTS / 11
ONCE UPON A TIME / 13
BEFORE YOU GET STARTED / 14
INTRODUCTION / 17
1 THE LIE / 23
2 THE TRUTH / 27
3 ABSOLUTES / 31
4 SPEAK LIFE / 37
5 SING, OH BARREN / 41
6 PREPARE YOUR TEMPLE / 51
7 WHEN AF STILL VISITS / 63
8 THE WILDERNESS / 79
9 THE PROCESS OF SURRENDER / 95

10 THE FAITH CHAPTER / 107
11 THE PROMISED LAND / 121
12 FIGHT FOR YOUR TESTIMONY / 137
13 LABOR INTO REST / 167
14 TELL YOUR STORY / 183
15 FRUIT THAT REMAINS / 191
16 IN THE DELAY / 207
17 NOW IS THE TIME / 219
18 THE SONG OF VICTORY / 227
19 YOU ARE WHAT YOU SEE / 233
20 YOU WILL HAVE WHAT YOU SAY / 249
21 BLESSED ARE THOSE WHO MOURN / 257
22 THE NEW MAN / 263
23 THE BIRTHING / 275
24 A WALKING ADVERTISEMENT / 333
THE CAPSTONE / 359
ABOUT THE AUTHOR / 369

TESTIMONIALS

Mandi Windsor's book *#The Joyful Mother of Children* is refreshingly written out of a place of honesty, passion and vulnerability. It is a timeless, specific book of instruction for those struggling with trying to conceive natural children, but it also is so much more, because it deals with the spiritual aspect of a life totally surrendered to Christ and how that surrendered life will lead to a fulfilled life, which can be applied to any area of struggle in you might be dealing with. As a counselor to women, I have worked with, as well as personally experienced, the pain and sometimes debilitating issue of infertility. As I read, my mind kept going to other women that I know who could use this guide to help them with their struggle. I wished I had this book when I was silently living my own struggle with infertility many years ago; what a difference it would have made for me. Mandi has written out of her own journey and she leads the reader through the process of how to use scripture to change our mindset, how to surrender, and how to align our life more perfectly with God. Although the book is written from her journey with infertility, it is just as useful with any other area of weakness or struggle the reader might be experiencing.

    MARSHA CROWDER, Counselor, lead pastor's wife and director of Women's Ministry at Christian Life Center, Layton, Utah

I had the pleasure of meeting Mandi at a woman's retreat in Midland, Texas. A mutual friend got us together and Mandi prayed for my heart. I fought with infertility for seven plus years. After Mandi prayed with me my life changed in ways I never thought it would. After that day my heart felt different. The only thing I ever desired was to be a mommy – the same desire of every married middle-aged woman.

Each chapter is filled with content that truly spoke straight to my heart. This book brought me closer to God and helped me to understand that I was not alone. Sometimes, struggling with infertility you feel completely alone and wonder what you did wrong for God to punish you. After reading the multiple chapters of *#The Joyful Mother of Children* I soon realized that God's plan for each person is completely different. I never thought that choosing fertility treatments was the way I would become a mom. God's plan for me is not the same as it will be for you, or anyone else. After reading this book, I began to pray and ask *what is your plan for me God?* He spoke clearly to me one day. He said, "My plan for you is to be a joyful mother of children with the help of fertility specialists." So that is exactly what we did. My husband and I began our IVF journey in January of 2021. In October, 2021 we got our very first positive pregnancy test. While writing this review I am twenty-four weeks pregnant with our first blessing. Fertility treatments were never an option because – let's be real – they are extremely expensive. After the talk I had with God the financial assistance came raining down on us. He truly blessed us with amazing family and friends that helped us the entire way. God is amazing and he hears our cries.

This book truly helped me get closer to God in ways that I did not know were possible. It is never the plan you have for yourself but the greater plan that God has for you. Dealing with infertility is one of the hardest things anyone should ever have to go through. This book gives you hope, and the content speaks straight to your heart. I pray every day for every single barren woman that wishes so dearly to have a baby of their own. YOU ARE NOT ALONE!

Danlee Mata

This book will build your faith and bring you such hope and peace. You will laugh and cry, and your life will be transformed by the powerful truths on every page. Mandi is a gifted writer and a trusted friend who will guide you to a rock-solid understanding of your identity in Jesus and as #*The Joyful Mother of Children*.

PATTY NOEL, author of *Momistry*, and mom, grandma, Pattymom, foster mom, teacher, speaker, and daughter of the King

This book is solid truth and I love it! Mandi doesn't tip-toe around any hard truths or religious beliefs that keep people stuck. Instead, she lovingly calls them to a higher place of believing in a God who is good and does good.

Every woman struggling to conceive needs to read Mandi Windsor's new book, #*TheJoyfulMotherofChildren*. Her God-inspired words make this resource packed full of truth that will leave you encouraged and empowered with hope to believe for the impossible.

ELISHA KEARNS, author of the blog, *Waiting for Baby Bird* and founder of Waiting for Baby Bird Ministries

Mandi has been in my life since we were both in kindergarten and we have been friends through all of life's seasons. When she asked me to review chapters from her book she was writing I was honored but also felt totally unqualified to give voice to my opinions.

I was actually sitting in my new OBGYN doctor's office waiting to meet my new doctor when I started to read the first few chapters of this book. The words that convicted me the most when I started reading were the words that the lord used to convict Mandi's heart too, and those words were "The Entirety of His Word is Truth." The Lord had started to speak to me about this and had been calling me to this truth for a little while I had just become very good at ignoring it. Sitting in that doctor's office waiting anxiously to be diagnosed with yet another ailment and reading those words brought me to tears. That was the beginning of my transformation and what catapulted me into obedience and following the Lord without question with my whole heart.

Let's go back a few years...

I met my amazing husband when we were nineteen years old. We were married a couple years later when I was twenty-two and he was twenty-one. I always told him I wasn't sure we could ever have kids naturally because I believed that I couldn't have kids. I had been diagnosed with PCOS when I was sixteen years old shortly after finding out that I had diabetes. I was on birth control pills to regulate my cycles and believed I couldn't have one on my own because I was sick. I had partnered with my sicknesses. Despite that, we decided to start trying about two years into our marriage I went off the pill and we started trying. My cycle was irregular and my OBGYN at that time put me on meds to help us to conceive; a little over a year of trying that way we decided to see a specialist and started infertility meds. We did several rounds of medication followed by IUI'S (intrauterine insemination); after several failed attempts we decided to stop and give it a break. The emotional rollercoaster was just too much. I had pretty much given up hope but I still wanted to be a mom. It was really the only thing I've ever wanted besides being a wife; I really felt like I was supposed to be a mom. We started talking about adoption and foster care but my husband wasn't really open to either of those options at that time and so time marched on...

A couple of years ago we were talking about how we were okay if it was just the two of us and we could be happy just being a aunt and uncle to our eleven nieces and nephews. We were in our late thirties at the time and felt like our time to be parents had passed us by, but God had a different plan.

I couldn't find peace with that destiny; see I still desperately wanted to be a mom deep down I couldn't let it go. Reading Mandi's book gave me hope for the first time that that could still be a possibility for us all with the simple truth that "The Entirety of His Word is Truth." I started praying and asking the Lord to lead us in the direction that he wanted us to go, and for the first time I truly meant those words, and we laid it all down for him to transform in whatever way he wanted. I woke up one morning with a name on repeat in my head. It was so annoying that I called out about mid-day *what does this mean?* and I heard "You know what this means; she's yours." It was our first daughter's name that the Lord had given me and I knew it; I just wasn't sure how that was going to happen, but I believed his word and I stood on it. I told my husband that we were going to have a baby and the Lord had given me her name, and surprisingly he jumped headfirst into believing with me (it was truly all a God thing) and we started contending together for our children and our promises. The Lord surprised us several times with dreams and visions of our future children and we knew he was giving us little glimpses into the future, where he already was, and we knew without a shadow of a doubt that they were real and we would be standing in that future place with those blessings very soon. We started thanking him for them and praying for and over them as if they were already here (because to us they are real and very much already here with us.) And we kept receiving words, dreams, and visions about his plans for us – each one leading us into his will for our lives.

I believed that I was going to be pregnant soon and had started to take my health seriously; the Lord had begun leading me to take care of my temple and that meant I needed to obey and started working on my physical and mental health with him. I was able to go off birth control pills again and started to have my cycles on my own. They showed up every twenty-eight to twenty-nine days like clockwork and I was amazed at the healing I was witnessing. We started trying again to actively get pregnant in April 2021 and our first pregnancy happened at the end of July 2021. We found out we were pregnant in August and we were so excited! I had a normal first trimester, but when we went in for our eleven-week ultrasound our hearts were broken to find out our baby was no longer growing and it's heart had stopped beating. We were in shock and so very heartbroken; this was not supposed to happen. We started to declare in that office at that moment that we were not going to give up and that this was not how this story would end for us. We had promises from God to stand on, after all! The enemy was not going to win this and we started repenting of any strongholds and rebuking any plans the enemy was forming against us. We started to rebuild our faith and confidence in what the Lord had promised us and that's what we were standing on. After I had to have an emergency procedure done to remove the remaining tissue leftover from that pregnancy, my husband told my doctor that we would be back and pregnant again in three months (I was out of it and don't remember this but oh my goodness I really love this man!).

We celebrated seventeen years of marriage in April 2022; we would have been bringing our first baby home in April as well. What the enemy meant for destruction the Lord has redeemed fully and is restoring us completely.

My husband was correct in his declaration to the doctor – we were back in three months! We conceived at the beginning of January 2022 and we are expecting our miracle baby September 30th! God is so good!

The Entirety of His Word is Truth! If he said it he's going to do it, he will finish what he started. You can rest fully in this knowledge and stand fully in your victory because he's already conquered everything, and he's just waiting for you to show up and give your whole life over to him so he can show you the wonderful and amazing things he has planned for you.

Thank you Mandi for always being there throughout my life and calling me higher. I'm so incredibly thankful God gave us this lifelong friendship and that we get to walk this life together as sisters in Christ. This book is truly going to bless so many who, like me, had given up. Once they get ahold of the fundamental truths of Christ's finished work, and fully understand how that translates into their own lives and what they are contending for, lives will be changed from The Barren Woman to *The Joyful Mother of Children*!

Forever grateful,
CHRISTY WICKMAN

Mandi,

What a privilege it has been to read your book! I look forward to the impact it will have.

Here's my endorsement:

#The Joyful Mother of Children by Mandi Windsor will encourage anyone dealing with infertility. Her transparency and use of humor and Scripture throughout the book will offer a firm foundation of hope. As an overcomer of infertility myself, my favorite thought that she shared was, "I had reached a place where I wanted to be in His presence more than I wanted a baby." If you're looking for a godly source of peace and joy as you navigate infertility, this book is for you!

Wishing you much success with this book!

EVANGELINE COLBERT
Author of *A Seed of Hope: God's Promises of Fertility*
www.BooksByEvangeline.com

This book is a beautiful guide of how to practically give God's Word first place into the very depths and longings of your heart. This is not just a "how-to" or "faith-inspiring" book of principles to apply later. It is a "let's encounter Jesus now" (as you read through, His healing, love, faith, joy... follow along) kind of book.

Knowing the pain and joy of my own history with infertility, this book truly takes you on a journey of capturing God's perspectives and truths, igniting your faith and contending for God's promises!

Mandi's personal journey of raw faith and passion for Jesus and motherhood is absolutely spiritually invigorating.

LISA APKING
Pastor, Blue Springs MO
Mother of three! So glad I didn't give up! Jesus answers prayers!

Let's say you face a situation or difficulty that seems way bigger than you. So debilitating that it may drive you to desperation, isolation from society, panic attacks. The fears in your head are shouting so loudly that you can't hear the voice of wisdom and joy, the voice of God. You have turned to people, specialists but they can't help. What do you do?

When Mandi faced such a situation she was led by her heavenly Father to take a pen and study the Word as truth. Her journal, this book, became a spring of life for her and her readers, as it contains the Word of life. It definitely helped her childhood friend who had been struggling with infertility for eleven years. Her relationship with her Saviour Jesus Christ changed and out of this intimate relationship based on true, unconditional love, life sprang up! Nine months after conception she gave birth to her healthy baby. In this book you can read this friend's testimony and how Mandi's new understanding of Jesus' love transformed her whole life, faith, marriage, family life, friendships, ministry, finances ,and self-image.

While reading Mandi's revelations, her amazingly enriching godly dreams, I was led to deep conversations with Holy Spirit and received several confirmations, new revelations, godly dreams. I believe the Word (seed) and the intimate relationship with Jesus do not return void and bear fruit in all readers' lives: in Mandi's, yours, and ours. Amen.

So I recommend this book to all of you. Run with Mandi like David towards Goliath, shouting the Word, the name of Jesus the Lord of Hosts, and embrace your victory.

Marianna Koncz

Acknowledgments

I'd first like to thank my husband, Jonathan. Thank you for making all my dreams come true. Like I tell you often, you are my greatest gift and I love you more today than I did when we took our leap of faith. Oh, how far we've come! And we are just getting started.

To the beloved son of my heart, Jonathan Jr. Thank you for loving me as though I bore you myself. I chose you and I would choose you again every single time. I love you, I love you more, I love you mostest!

To my parents, thank you for loving me unconditionally and training me in the way I should go. It's because of you and the choices you made to change our family heritage, that I am so in love with Jesus today and can't stop talking about Him. I love you both so much!

To my Grandma, Melvina Jean Gerth. You have the best seat in the house to witness the events that are transpiring. Oh, how I wish you were here so I could see your joy, but I know I will see you again and we will have even more to rejoice about when I do. I love you and miss you.

To the numerous family and friends who have believed in me and prayed for me throughout this journey. You know who you are and I love you.

To Marguex Sigafus for her help editing and proofreading in the early days.

To the amazing people who rallied around me to get this book off the ground. Thank you for partnering with me in this endeavor and believing in this message.

To the many pastors, teachers, apostles, prophets, and evangelists, thank you for speaking truth into my heart throughout these many years. Thank you for your continuous boldness and bravery to teach and speak the Word of God.

Lastly and most importantly, thank you to my Beloved, Jesus Christ. May I fully represent your transforming power and truth that you have exhibited in my life. To You be the glory.

Once upon a time...

In the late 1980s and early 90s, in the middle-class suburbs, lived a little brown-eyed, curly-headed girl. This little girl had dreams. She had dreams of being a wife. She had dreams of being a mommy. She had dreams of a large family with a husband who loved and adored her. She lived in her own perfect little world of dolls, Barbies®, and animal critters. With these toys, she created families – large families. Families with a mom, a dad, and a multitude of sons and daughters. She never went anywhere without her favorite doll; accompanied by a diaper bag, bottles, and other baby accessories. This little girl so wanted to be a mommy, she even dressed her cats up in baby clothes and pushed them around in strollers!

As this little girl grew up, and grew out of playing with toys, she continued to dream. Her dreaming turned into writing about those desires. She wrote fiction stories of love and happily-ever-afters. Her dreams turned into fantasies of what it would be like to get married, become pregnant, and hold a precious baby born out of love. Her dreams sustained her through her high school years.

After high school, she began searching for the right man to make these dreams come true. And one day, she was full of hope, joy, and excitement, knowing that all her dreams were now coming into existence; for she had found her prince. And now, it was time to create the family for which she'd always dreamed; the family she had always desired in her play with toys, and in her writing and fantasies.

But with every fairytale there must be a villain or a heartbreaking plot. So eventually, her dreams led to a reality so utterly and disastrously unexpected that it changed the course of her present and future. Because this little girl, who had become a woman, faced what no woman who desires a family ever wants to face; something so horrific that can only bring pain and heartache. She was barren. Infertile. Not able to conceive. For this little girl, now a grown woman, this was the worst thing that could happen to her. Her dreams were shattered. She felt like a failure. What was she to do now? Read on to find out, because her shattered dreams were simply just the beginning of the greatest journey of her life.

Before You Get Started...

If you have picked up this book and are reading these words right now, it's probably because you are curious or have experienced or are experiencing the following feelings: shame, humiliation, brokenness, hurt, disappointment, worthlessness, inadequacy, depression, embarrassment; and the list goes on. Am I right? I don't have to explain to you why you're feeling this way; the reason why is spelled out on the front cover of this book. The Barren Woman. This is also called "infertility." The Infertile Woman. Isn't that why you picked it up? You can relate to those three small but profound words; those three words that have shamefully defined you for x number of years.

I am one of those: a barren or infertile woman. I am simply a woman – shamefully, a barren woman – who has a story. Do you mind if I'm real with you? I mean, like open, honest, gritty, I-can't-believe-she-just-said-that real? Do you mind if I'm vulnerable? I hope so. You will also need to have patience with me when I go off on my rabbit trails every once in a while. After all, I am somewhat writing this book in journal format. So stick with me. I promise you that I have a story to tell. It may be a little radical and a little uncomfortable and definitely supernatural at times. By the time you reach the end, however, you will have renewed hope like never before.

At least, that's my intention. You see, I have written this book in faith. I began this journey in 2014, not knowing what would lie ahead. You'll observe that in my writing. Please bear with me as you witness my healing, spiritual growth, and maturity throughout this extended journey (pretty please).

At the end of each chapter, I have included a section called "Going Deeper." In these sections, you will have the opportunity to answer some questions and study the scriptures I used more in depth. I encourage you to invest in a journal for this process, because, as you will see, I am all about journaling through anything we endure; whether it be growth or hardship.

Another thing to inform you of (and it may even annoy you), are the hashtags (#). For those of you who have no clue what that word even means (seriously, where have you been?), it's the little pound sign that allows people to follow that hashtag on their favorite social media site. Do I want you to follow all my hashtags? Umm, no. Why do I have them in my book? Because I want you to hear my "voice." I want you to feel like I'm speaking directly to you as though we're sitting down for a cup of coffee, having a regular conversation. I have these funny, sometimes witty sayings (at least in my head), that only makes sense and serves its purpose if I do the whole hashtag thing.

I realize that if you're barren and dealing with the humiliation and shame that accompany it, joking or even laughing can feel like a slap in the face. However, as you will eventually see by reading this book, it is still important to God and everyone around us that we live life to the fullest. Barrenness is no laughing matter, I assure you. It can drown us in depression like nobody's business. I get that. My little hashtags simply serve to break up the despair every now and again. If, or when, you get distracted by one, let that be a moment to take a breath and re-read the previous sentence. Maybe it will even make you laugh a bit, or, if nothing else, roll your eyes (#enoughwiththeramblings #nohatersplease #barrenwomensticktogether).

Introduction

#SIGH: The Barren Woman. Shame. Humiliation. Embarrassment. Emptiness. People say that to be a barren woman back in the Bible days was a horrific ordeal. According to everyone else, it was essentially a curse from God. So much so, The Barren Woman was ostracized from society. Even today, some pastors and teachers purport barrenness as an "ancient problem," as if women who still suffer from barrenness don't feel this way today. Umm, really? These feelings are still very real and alive in today's barren woman:

- Only The Barren Woman knows what it's like to put all her hopes and dreams onto a plastic-urine-coated-stick; then to be sobbing on the bathroom floor three minutes later. This is not just a one-time occurrence, but this cycle repeats every month for years (#icanseeyounoddingyourhead)
- Only The Barren Woman knows what it's like when she gets asked for the 100th time if she plans to start having children (#yep)
- Only The Barren Woman knows what it's like sitting through another baby shower for the fourth friend that year (#istilllovethembutithurts)
- Only The Barren Woman's eyes fill up with tears of despair when she sees another pregnancy announcement on her regular social media site (#thankfullytheycantseemecry)

- Only The Barren Woman admits that her least favorite holiday is Mother's Day (#ouch)

Maybe you were so desperate to find a solution that you tried everything out there on the market and wasted tens of thousands of dollars. Maybe you tried everything on the market, spent tons of money, and are reading this book holding your little miracle. But maybe, just maybe, something about spending all that money and feeling like a lab experiment didn't quite sit well with you. Maybe, through all the infertility procedures and "experiments," you faced a barrage of roller coaster emotions that left a queasiness in your stomach. In fact, maybe you're still recovering from that experience. Maybe, like me, you now have excess baggage and deep-seated issues because you tried to take your desires into your own hands and do things your way since God wouldn't do it for you.

Dear reader, your deepest heart's desire for a baby is not just because "everyone else is doing it." It is not just because you want the cute little family in the cute little house with the cute little white picket fence. It is not the American dream. It is God's dream.

In your mother's womb, you were divinely wired to have the desire for motherhood. It is in all of us no matter how many of us try to bury it. So what happens when we can't fulfill that desire? You guessed it. Shame; embarrassment; bitterness. Here is an "ancient" explanation for this:

> *There are three things that are never satisfied – no, four*
> *that never say, "Enough!":*
> *the grave,*
> *the barren womb,*
> *the thirsty desert,*
> *the blazing fire.*
> *Proverbs 30:15-16, NLT*

What you are struggling with, dear friend, is a circumstance that is never satisfied; a void that is never filled; a thirst that is never quenched; a hunger that is never sated. Have you ever looked up the definitions of barren? It is generally defined as the following: not producing or useful, unproductive, fruitless, empty, unprofitable, sterile, idle, inactive, isolated, cut off, desolate, deserted area, solitary, robbed of children, childless, oppression, dry land, wilderness, drought, deprived.

Umm, hello! Is that how you've felt or are feeling today? Look at those words! If you are infertile, you are considered a barren woman. If this is the modern-day definition of barren then this is clearly not an ancient problem! Shame and humiliation a thing of the past? Heck no!

Along with your exhausting monthly-snot-filled-tears, maybe you've questioned God about this very topic. Maybe you've even asked these same questions: *Why do women who don't even want to be moms pop up pregnant so easily? Why are there so many babies being aborted, up for adoption or in foster care and God can't even give ME a child? How come SHE can keep getting pregnant and I can't?* These are the universal questions most likely every woman who has struggled with barrenness has asked or pondered.

Maybe you've argued with God. *I thought you wanted to give me the desires of my heart! Why won't you answer my prayer? Am I even worthy to be a mother? Do you even love me, God? Do you even hear me?* Notice that doesn't begin to encompass the questions a miscarriage or infant death must bring about; because, alas, I've never even conceived. I am speaking from having a strictly barren, never-even-had-a-positive-pregnancy-test, womb (#dryandbarrenland).

Technically, I have been trying to conceive for over fifteen years. I was one of the ones who decided to play God and speed things along. I married the wrong man at the wrong time and continued down the wrong path (#wrongwrongwrong). I desperately wanted to be a mom so I tried to do it my way. The only thing conceived out of that forced marriage was the spirit of fear; and it continued to grow and fester within me from that point on.

Eventually, I found my escape; an escape to start over and try getting pregnant with someone else. Vulgar, yes. But like I said, I'm keeping it real. I was a horribly selfish human being on a mission to do things my way. I had my fun for the next two years. Living the dream; being wild and crazy; a fun-loving young lady in her mid-twenties with the whole world ahead of her. And then, I had hope for a new beginning with a new man. However, my hope was quickly squashed. I lost my boyfriend, I lost my job, I lost my house, I lost who I was, I lost my mind. I was broken. The only thing I found at this point was the fear within, growing rampantly and thriving inside of me.

Being at rock bottom, the best decision I made at that time was to pack up my pug, move back in with my parents, and complete my college degree. Thus, the healing began. Thank God my parents trained me up in the way a child should go! I grew up in church, you see. I considered myself a Christian my whole life but it wasn't until I could no longer hear Him or feel Him that I came back to Him. I now truly know what redemption is, although, that's a story for another book. I was redeemed. God healed me. But I needed the tools to combat my weaknesses and excess baggage.

God answered that need one Sunday morning in a teaching from my local pastor. The title of the message was "How to Battle the Storms of Life." My pastor encouraged the church to write down our weaknesses or struggles, and then research specific passages in the Bible to combat those weaknesses. This way of Bible study completely changed my life! I still have those note cards I used during this time of healing. In fact, I still do this same process for any sort of struggle I'm going through.

Yes, just because I'm a born-again believer does not mean that I don't go through struggles. God never promised we wouldn't have trials on this earth, but He did give us a way out (#Jesus).

Not too long after, I had my hallelujah moment. I wish I could add sound effects onto this page! I would add the "Hallelujah" chorus so you could truly understand this momentous event. But, since I can't add sound effects, how about we take a small musical break so you can hum the wonderful tune to yourself.

Musical Break...

In all honesty, it's not that momentous. It was simply a verse God revealed to me that rocked my world, "The entirety of Your Word is truth." (Psalm 119:160, NKJV) What is so momentous about this verse? Read that sentence again. The entirety of God's Word is truth; not just the small bits and pieces; not just the parts we like or that make us feel all warm and fuzzy; not just the parts that make sense to our earthly minds. The entirety of His Word is truth. Here are some synonyms for entirety: sum-total, wholeness, absoluteness, completeness, fullness, and perfectness. Say that sentence again and plug one of these synonyms in here:

THE _____ OF YOUR WORD IS TRUTH.

After reading this verse, the Holy Spirit asked me, "Do you believe this?" It was then I sang Ahhhhh picturing the light of God's glory shining upon those words. Here was the momentous event. Here was the defining moment of my faith. Did I truly believe the entirety of God's Word is true? Did I believe it as fact? Did I believe it as truth even in my own imperfect way? Why, yes, yes I did.

Thus began the journey from single woman to married-to-the-right-husband woman (again, another story for another book; #ilovemyhusband). And thus began the journey from The Barren Woman to The Joyful Mother of children. Won't you join me?

Going Deeper:
- What is your favorite childhood memory of pretending to be a mommy?
- List some of the emotions and feelings you've experienced with being barren.
- What other universal questions do you have that are not listed?
- Scripture to study: Ps. 119:160.

Chapter One
THE LIE

Now I could have named the title of this chapter "The Myth" because it's a bit more comfortable to the ears (and eyes). But I agreed to be real with you and sometimes being real is not always comfortable. So what is The Lie? Drum roll please...

THE LIE IS BARRENNESS = GOD'S WILL

Read it again. Focus on the words. Barrenness equals God's will. Maybe you need to use the word "infertility" in place of barrenness to help you grasp it. Infertility equals God's will. Now recognize those words as a...

BIG.
FAT.
LIE.

When a voice in your head tells you, *Maybe it's just not God's will for me to get pregnant*, then you have believed The Lie. When you have accepted barrenness in your friend's or family member's lives, then you have believed The Lie. If you are overcome by hopelessness, shame and humiliation at this very moment, you have believed The Lie. If you are angry at God, then you, my friend, have believed The Lie. How do I know it's a lie? Because, the Bible tells me that the entirety of His Word is truth.

If you are a Christian, having confessed Jesus as your Lord, then most likely you have felt the same confusion and bewilderment that I have upon accepting this lie. Conflicted and torn, your faith is shaken. Think about it. Step back. Pause for a moment; really dig deep into your heart. Be honest with yourself. Be honest with God. Be real. What have you felt within your heart as you believe this lie? Some of you may not have even known you believed it in the first place. If you're one of those, take a moment to pause and reflect.

When the doctor told you that you couldn't get pregnant, did you have conflicting emotions? Yes, you were probably devastated. But that devastation surely accompanied confusion, right? When the doctor told you that your husband was "shooting blanks" (#keepinitreal), what did you feel after the deep grief and sadness? Was there bewilderment? Did the deepest part of your soul experience turmoil? Fear? Depression? When you thought, *Third time's a charm for the IUI, and it still didn't "take,"* did you think, *maybe I'm just not meant to be a mother? Why do I even have the desire to be a mom if I'm not allowed to be one?*

I can answer yes to all of the above. Being barren just didn't make sense to me! It conflicted with my soul and made me question my faith. God brought my husband and me together. He truly did. Our experience was one of stepping out in total, radical faith. Why would He bring us together for His purposes if we couldn't get pregnant and pass on that heritage of faith? It just didn't make sense. Barrenness didn't line up to the miraculous God I knew as my Savior. I questioned my faith. I was tormented. I lived in fear. No wonder my soul was conflicted and confused!

So after surviving a week-long depression from the results of another negative pregnancy test, I began to research every verse ever written about pregnancy and barrenness. I was hungry and desperate to find The Truth. I was desperate to shut up the confusion and turmoil within my soul. I was tired of living in self-condemnation because I wasn't walking in faith and pleasing God (Hebrews 11:6). I was so fed up. I wanted to have faith in every area of my life. I was sick and tired of being depressed every month. I was weary and exhausted from putting my life on hold until I got pregnant. I was sick of despising my body. I was tired of hating Mother's Day. Something had to change!

So then, throughout this season of research and study, I soon learned that it is my responsibility to discover the heart of God. This is where I will find the will of God. His Word is a treasure trove of what God wants to do for us, but until we know what it says, there is nothing on which to base our faith. In other words, we must understand what the scriptures plainly teach regarding every area of our lives. This is where we will discover His heart and His will. However, if we don't take the time to renew our minds in His Word, we miss out on the truth of God's desires for us here on earth. And friend, if we miss out on His desires for us, we can even miss out on His love!

So, what does God's Word say about barrenness? What is God's heart concerning pregnancy? What is His will? If barrenness and infertility is The Lie, what is The Truth? Are you ready to make a discovery? Are you ready to be rid of the confusion and unrest (#yesplease)?

Going Deeper:
- Have you believed The Lie? Record how believing The Lie has affected your life.
- What other lies have you believed?
- What do you think God's will is for conception and pregnancy?

Chapter two
The Truth

Before we get radical, let me throw out a little disclaimer so you can't say that I didn't warn you (#alertalert). I don't know where your level of faith is as you spend time in this text. Maybe you are a new believer eager to strengthen your faith; maybe you are not technically a Christian but are desperate for a baby; maybe you believe there's a God and don't gather with other believers; maybe your heart is hardened against Christians or even God; maybe, like me, you've been doing church your whole life. Whether Christian or non-Christian, atheist or agnostic, I have learned that we can all get set in our ways.

We can get locked into a particular belief and accept that belief as opposed to what the Word of God says. We can get so comfortable in church, expecting the pastor to hand-feed us the "absolute truth" instead of discovering it for ourselves. We can pick and choose which scriptures to believe. And we can have faith in one area but not in another.

However, these next two chapters that I share with you will take some revelation by none other than my Main Man, Jesus Christ (#ithinkJesuslookslikerockybalboa). I can picture Him running through the streets and dancing in victory on the top of the stairs (#cueRockysoundtrack). I really wish I could have made this an interactive book.

Anyhow, no matter where you are in your level of faith, the Holy Spirit is the only one who can make these truths come alive in your heart and mind. What I'm about to share with you doesn't make sense. It might make you uncomfortable or utter the phrase, "Say what?" However, if you've come this far and haven't closed the book and donated it to charity, then we are probably good. But just in case, here is a scripture reference to back up The Truth. And remember, the entirety of God's Word is truth:

> *Do not be conformed to this world (this age), [fashioned after and adapted to its external, superficial customs], but be transformed (changed) by the [entire] renewal of your mind [by its new ideals and its new attitude], so that you may prove [for yourselves] what is the good and acceptable and perfect will of God, even the thing which is good and acceptable and perfect [in His sight for you].*
> Romans 12:2, AMP

There it is. We allow our minds to be renewed so we can prove for ourselves what is the good and acceptable and perfect will of God. Before we get to The Truth, take a minute and ponder this passage above and pray the following prayer. I know, I know. It seems like I'm stalling. However, dear friend, you must allow the Holy Spirit to renew your mind and give you your own hallelujah moment.

> Dear Abba Father,
> As I dig deeper to discover Your perfect will for me, I ask that You would prepare my heart to receive it. Renew my mind with Your truth and transform my previous ideas and thinking where I lack your Biblical truth. I open my heart and mind to receive my hallelujah moment that will forever change my thinking and strengthen my faith. Amen!

THE TRUTH = IF HEALING IS FOR ALL; THEN BARRENNESS IS FOR NONE

Please hear me out. Surely, you're now wondering what God's will is concerning healing. Surely, you want to know the correlation between healing and barrenness. Well, we're on our way there, so keep reading (#fastenyourseatbelts)!

Going Deeper:
- Record your first reaction to learning The Truth.
- Just for fun: How do you picture Jesus?
- Scripture to study: Rom. 12:2.

Chapter three
ABSOLUTES

I'll get right to the point. In the Word, we can see that there is a direct correlation between salvation and healing. Take a look at these two scriptures:

> *Bless and affectionately praise the Lord, O my soul, And do not forget any of His benefits;* **Who forgives all your sins, Who heals all your diseases**. *(emphasis added)*
> Psalm 103:2-3, AMP

> *But He was wounded for our transgressions, He was crushed for our wickedness [our sin, our injustice, our wrongdoing]; The punishment [required] for our well-being fell on Him,* **And by His stripes (wounds) we are healed**. *(emphasis added)*
> Isaiah 53:5, AMP

Both of these verses prove our salvation through the death and resurrection of Jesus. They also prove our physical, bodily healing, right? Right. So, the first Absolute is:

1. It is God's will to heal all.

Even before Jesus walked the earth, God revealed a divine healing covenant. Here, God reveals Himself as our Great Physician, Jehovah-Rapha, saying:

> *If you will diligently listen and pay attention to the voice of the* LORD *your God, and do what is right in His sight, and listen to His commandments, and keep [foremost in your thoughts and actively obey] all His precepts and statutes, then I will not put on you any of the diseases which I have put on the Egyptians;* **for I am the** LORD **who heals you.** *(emphasis added)*
> Exodus 15:26, AMP

Furthermore, when Jesus walked the earth, He *always* demonstrated His Father's will by healing those brought to Him. I mean, seriously. We can look at His life; see how He lived and loved, and; we *will* see the Father's heart.

So, if we search the scriptures, the obvious truth is: God desires to heal *every* disease and *every* sickness.

> *He went about all Galilee, teaching in their synagogues and preaching the good news (Gospel) of the kingdom, and healing every disease and every weakness and infirmity among the people.*
> Matthew 4:23, AMP

Now, these are just a few examples. I am not a Bible scholar or theologian. So, before all the critics come out, please remember, I am just a broken woman who has dug into the Word to find out who this Jesus really is. And if this makes you uncomfortable, then search the scriptures for yourself. Ask the Holy Spirit to reveal The Truth to you. But seriously, if the same Spirit lives in us who raised Christ from the dead, I'm pretty sure, based on that verse alone, that healing is also for today (Romans 8:11).

The entirety of His Word is truth, no matter if it makes sense or not. Yes, friend, I will keep saying that over and over again (#brokenrecord). So, what else do the scriptures say? Here's another shocker for you:

2. Just as it is God's desire for all to be healed, He desires that no one die prematurely

#pleasenote: This is clearly a sensitive subject. Unfortunately, we all know of someone who has died prematurely. It is utterly tragic and devastating. It is one of the mysteries we may never understand. It is so very easy to partner with unbelief when we have experienced such tragedy. BUT, BUT, BUT! In the face of such tragedy, we must ask ourselves, *What do I believe?*

To find this answer, we need to search God's Word and learn His heart. His Word is truth. He is a good God, and His mercy and goodness endures forever (Psalm 136:1); I believe, in spite of the grief and heartache, He will create beauty from ashes (Isaiah 61:3); He will make everything work together for our good (Romans 8:28); He is faithful, and He will complete what He began (Philippians 1:6). This is what I believe. This is the God I know. I don't understand why some people receive supernatural healing, and some do not. When faced with praying for someone to be healed, however, I choose to believe God wants their healing and that they *can* be healed because of what His Word says.

But don't just take my word for it, "with a long life [length of days] I will satisfy him." (Psalm 91:16, AMP) And "I will fulfill the number of your days." (Exodus 23:26, NASB) I also love this promise, "The Lord shall preserve you from all evil; He shall preserve your soul. The Lord shall preserve your going out and your coming in from this time forth, and even forevermore." (Psalm 121:7-8, NKJV) No matter our level of faith, we should confidently walk in this covenant blessing of supernatural protection and preservation, for this is God's will for us.

So, what else does God say? What else is the Absolute Truth? What other promises go into His perfect will for us? And what on earth does this have to do with getting pregnant? Most likely, you are either getting excited or freaked out (#orboth). Either way, I pray you find your hallelujah moment in these next few paragraphs.

3. If healing is for all, then barrenness is for none

#hearmeout: As I said previously in my research, I've seen a correlation between salvation and healing scriptures. I've also seen a correlation between healing scriptures and scriptures on barrenness. There are even correlations between a long life and miscarriage as well, "There shall be no one miscarrying or barren in your land; I will fulfill the number of your days." (Exodus 23:26, NASB) And here is a covenant promise for fertility and healing:

> *He will love you and bless you and multiply you; He will also bless the fruit of your womb and the fruit of your land... You shall be blessed above all peoples; there will be no male or female barren (childless, infertile) among you or among your cattle. The* L<small>ORD</small> *will take away from you all sickness.*
> *Deuteronomy 7:13-15, AMP*

We can see the heart of God in those two scriptures alone. It is *not* His will for couples to struggle with getting pregnant or struggle to keep their pregnancy (#truth). Why, then, do we so readily accept infertility? Why do we fear having miscarriages? Why does it still happen? Why are people still sick? These mysteries scholars and theologians can't even fully answer; other than we live in a fallen world where sin, sickness, and disease run rampant. But we still must ask ourselves, *What do I believe?*

If we make the choice to walk a life of belief in healing, we must also choose to believe that it is God's desire to give every woman a child who wants one. Our Father has desired to bless us and even multiply us since the beginning of man, "Then God blessed them and God said to them, 'be fruitful and multiply.'" (Genesis 1:28, NKJV) If God's heart was for man to be fruitful and multiply in the Garden of Eden, then we can be certain it is still His desire for us today (#Heneverchanges).

Okay, selah moment; sit and process. I'll hum the Jeopardy tune in my head for a second while I wait. Deep breaths! There it is. The Truth. Hopefully, your hallelujah moment is being revealed (#lightbulb). Do you see now that the acceptance of barrenness is an utter lie? It is *The* Lie designed by the enemy to steal our joy and to rob us of our faith.

If you choose to believe these three absolutes, acknowledging the entirety of God's Word is truth, then keep on keepin' on! Continue with me from The Barren Woman to Joyful Mother of children (#hallelujah)!

GOING DEEPER:

- Make a list of what you know and believe about God's nature and character.
- Have you ever experienced the premature death of a friend or loved one? Record your experience.
- Even in the face of disaster and tragedy, what do you choose to believe?
- Scriptures to study: Ps. 103:2-3; Is. 53:5; Ex. 15:26; Matt. 4:23; Rom. 8:11; Ps. 136:1; Is. 61:3; Rom. 8:28; Phil. 1:6; Ps. 91:16; Ex. 23:26; Ps. 121:7-8; Deut. 7:13-15; Prov. 4:22; Ps. 113:9; Gen. 1:28; Ps. 127:3.

Chapter four

SPEAK LIFE

Hopefully, you are starting this chapter at least a couple of hours after the last one. I hope you had some time to take a selah moment and absorb The Truth and Absolutes. I pray that you searched the scriptures for yourself, that your mind is being renewed, your faith strengthened, and you had your hallelujah moment. Can you feel seeds of hope beginning to sprout within your broken spirit? I hope so! Because God wants to bring hope, joy, faith, and power back to The Barren Woman, to awaken The Barren Woman's soul. We have believed the lies long enough (#amen)!

With that said, God's Word is "life to those who find them and health to all their body." (Proverbs 4:22, NASB) But, in order to appropriate this healing, one takes the Word as though it is medicine. Coincidentally, in order to appropriate conception, one takes the Word, confesses with her mouth, and believes in her heart that she is The Joyful Mother of children. After all, that's what the Bible says, "He makes the barren woman abide in the house as a joyful mother of children. Praise the Lord!" (Psalms 113:9, NASB #myfavoriteverse)

So, to appropriate conception (#orhealing), we must take the Word as though it were medicine. However, I hate taking medicine but have no issues with chocolate. So then, we take the Word as medicine, or if you're like me, feed on the Word as though it is chocolate. Why? Because "faith comes by hearing [what is told], and what is heard comes by the preaching [of the message that came from the lips] of Christ (the Messiah Himself)." (Romans 10:17, AMP) The Message translation says it like this: "The point is: Before you trust, you have to listen. But unless Christ's Word is preached, there's nothing to listen to." In other words, preaching comes before hearing; from hearing, comes faith (#readthatagain).

Furthermore, "if you acknowledge and confess with your lips that Jesus is Lord and in your heart believe (adhere to, trust in, and rely on the truth) that God raised Him from the dead, you will be saved." (Romans 10:9, AMP) So, even before I can be saved, I must confess with my lips that Jesus is Lord, then believe in my heart. Likewise, I must first hear preaching, speaking, or what is told before I can have faith. Hmm. Very interesting.

Let's go even further.

Death and life are in the power of the tongue, And those who love it will eat its fruit. Proverbs 18:21, NASB

So, not only is my confession of the lips that Jesus is Lord vital to my soul; not only is it crucial for my faith to hear preaching or speaking of the Word, but whatever I speak from my tongue has the power to create fruit; either life or death (#whoa).

So, do I speak Life or death? When strengthening my faith by the hearing of the Word, do I have to listen to preaching solely? No. Instead, I can speak His Word to appropriate faith which means, I can speak Life, His Word, over *every* circumstance and the result will be fruitful. "Hallelujah" chorus moment!

Previously, I challenged you with the three Absolutes. Now it is time to speak Life. We believe in our hearts what His Word says is true, so we must also release the power of His Word through the confession of our mouths:

For the Word that God speaks is alive and full of power [making it active, operative, energizing, and effective]; it is sharper than any

two-edged sword, penetrating to the dividing line of the breath of life (soul) and [the immortal] spirit, and of joints and marrow [of the deepest parts of our nature], exposing and sifting and analyzing and judging the very thoughts and purposes of the heart.
Hebrews 4:12, AMP

If God's Word is so powerful that it can penetrate to our souls and even into the deepest parts of our bones, do you believe His Word can also reach our wombs? Friends, this is how healing occurs! Bodily and emotional healings occur from speaking His Word and taking it like a dose of medicine. Therefore, we can believe that conception will occur as we feed on His Word like a girl with PMS eating chocolate (#dovechocolateisthebomb)!

If you're anything like me, however, you need a simplified version or something that looks like a formula (#nerdalert). So, this is what it looks like to speak Life:

$$\frac{\text{HEAR (listen/feed)} \dashrightarrow \text{FAITH (trust/believe)} \dashrightarrow \text{CONFESS (speak/acknowledge)}}{\text{healing, conception, protection, etc.}}$$

- Hear, listen, and feed on the Word
- Have faith, belief, and trust in the Word
- Confess, speak, and acknowledge the Word with your lips
- All of the above in that order results in healing, conception, protection, etc.

How do we know that confession will lead to answered prayers? Because God's Word says so:

Since we have this confidence, we can also have great boldness before him, for if we present any request agreeable to his will, he will hear us. And if we know that he hears us in whatever we ask,

we also know that we have obtained the requests we ask of him.
1 John 5:14-15, TPT

Wow! I just love the Word of God! Isn't it just so good? If I hadn't already had my hallelujah moment, I would've had one right there after reading that verse (#lightbulb)! I hope you realize that when you ask for a child and confess His Word, you are truly praying according to His will. In the same way, when you pray and ask for healing based on a healing confession, you are simply agreeing with His own plan for you. So why wouldn't He answer your requests? Especially if you are simply agreeing with His own Word?

Furthermore, "Truly I say to you, whoever says to this mountain, 'Be taken up and cast into the sea,' and does not doubt in his heart, but believes that what he says is going to happen, it will be granted him." (Mark 11:23, NASB) Faith and belief are the key. It is one thing to hear and confess the truth; it is quite another to have utter faith and belief that His promises will come to fruition (#doyoubelieve #moreonthiscomingsoon).

So, what will we do? Do we choose to believe that the entirety of His Word is truth? Do we accept it for ourselves? Do we choose to speak Life? I challenge you to begin today if this is something new for you. What have you got to lose? Moreover, what have you got to gain (#babies)?

Going Deeper:

- What are your top three needs/weaknesses you want to change?
- Search for scriptures that bring life to those needs/weaknesses. Then, begin feeding on those scriptures to renew your mind and start speaking life.
- Scriptures to study: Prov. 18:21; Heb. 4:12; 1 Jn. 5:14-15; Mk. 11:23.

Chapter five
Sing, Oh Barren

#RABBITTRAIL:

I may sound a little crazy right now because what I say may not make sense to you. But I told you that I would be real. If I asked you to come over to chat, I would be telling you this same thing, annoying you with my sound effects and hashtags.

So here it is… for the past few months, I have been refusing to write. I have been stubborn (#sorrytodisappoint). This book is about my journey from The Barren Woman to The Joyful Mother of children, but I'm still barren. I have to admit I feel crazy when I think of how God called me from work to stay home and write. Now, I don't spend all my time writing. In fact, I've managed to keep myself quite busy. But, I have been stubborn, actually, acting like a spoiled brat, refusing to obey my Father's purpose for me during this season in my life.

It's funny how the enemy distorts things. He likes to get us thinking about ourselves. You see, I had forgotten about you; ashamed and possibly depressed. I forgot that there are other women out there who need to hear these words; The Truth; The Truth that comes from the Word of God. Forgive me, dear sister, for wasting several months of my time. Forgive me for momentarily getting stuck inside of myself and forgetting your pain (#Godstilllovesmeevenwheniactlikea2yearold) (#rabbittrailcompleted).

So, we have stopped believing The Lie. We are seeking The Truth. We have been renewing our minds. We have been eating God's Word like chocolate and confessing. But still no positive pregnancy test. So, what do we do now? (#donotfeartheHolySpiritishere)

Now... we sing! Lalalalala...

I love music. I grew up with parents who loved singing and listening to music. Church hymns with mom, her friends, or sisters, singing in three-part harmony. Dad blasting Carman to wake us up on Sunday mornings (#lazaruscomeforth). We listened to Alabama's Christmas album during the holidays to Billy Ocean's "When the Going Gets Tough" on my way to basketball games. Later, in high school, I fell in love with the sound of Frank Sinatra through listening to my brother's jazz band; and I sang on the worship team in Youth Group at church. Today, as I have my own house and family, I find myself blasting the music Sunday mornings before church, and it's either Frank Sinatra or Christmas music as I cook (#yesilistentochristmasmusicallyyearlong #OCD #ObssessiveChristmasDisorder).

God loves music too. That's what this chapter is all about. Singing. Not about whether our voice is good or bad. Rather, it's about singing praises that please God and win battles. Just what does this have to do with getting pregnant? Quite a bit, apparently. The Great Teacher told me to include it (#dontshootthemessenger).

From what little Bible scholaring I've done (#iliketomakeupwords), I believe there are three types of songs:

1. The song of praise
2. The song of battle
3. The song of victory

For now, I will be focusing on the Songs of Praise and Battle. Why you ask? Has getting pregnant been a battle for you? It has literally been the most difficult battle of my life. However, in my weakest moments of depression and doubt, God still desired for me to praise Him. During these moments, I've actually felt His love the most. In fact, He calls *each*

Barren Woman to sing:

> *Sing, barren woman, who has never had a baby. Fill the air with song, you who've never experienced childbirth! You're ending up with far more children than all those childbearing women. God says so! Clear lots of ground for your tents! Make your tents large. Spread out! Think big! Use plenty of rope, drive the tent pegs deep. You're going to need lots of elbow room for your growing family.*
> Isaiah 54:1-3, MSG

I'm sure Bible scholars would rip me a new one because the rest of these verses don't apply to The Barren Woman. But, the Holy Spirit gave me this outline. He has a purpose for these scriptures on our journey to become The Joyful Mother of children. Read through that passage again. I love those words – clear lots of ground, make your tents large, spread out, think big, use plenty of rope. It sure sounds like a pregnant belly to me!

1. The Song of Praise

In my research of this passage, I learned that a captive Israel was being compared to The Barren Woman, an object of disappointment and shame. Israel definitely would not have been singing and rejoicing while captive. But Isaiah encourages her to deal with her barrenness through worship, enthroning God in song, and releasing His miraculous power.

So, if Israel, a captive barren land, metaphorically a barren womb, can be commanded to sing in the face of such a state; can be commanded to prepare and spread out, can we also apply this to The Barren Woman? Can *we* sing and worship and open up the heavens to receive miraculous power? I believe we can. I believe that He desires for us, The Barren Woman, to worship Him in the state of such shame, humiliation, and disappointment. It is powerful, friend, but oh so hard.

After the nth negative pregnancy test, when your heart is breaking, and you're crying so hard that all you can do is lay prostrate on the ground, that is the time to sing. Something happens when you sing in the face of such grief and heartache; something powerful in the supernatural realm; in the unseen. When your heart is in pieces, and you are sobbing with disappointment, I encourage you to lift your eyes to your Abba. Cry out and sing! Sing praises to Him. The Bible tells us that the Lord is close to the brokenhearted. He sees and knows your broken heart. He is so near in those moments. But *what* are we supposed to sing if we have nothing to celebrate? I hear ya, dear sister. We'll get to that in a minute.

For now, here is *why* to sing: if *we* don't praise our Father, the rocks *will*, "As soon as He [Jesus] was approaching… The whole crowd of the disciples began to praise God joyfully with a loud voice for all the miracles which they had seen…Some of the Pharisees in the crowd said to Him, 'Teacher, rebuke Your disciples.' But Jesus answered, 'I tell you, if these become silent, the stones will cry out!'" (Luke 19:37-40, NASB)

Now, if this is new to you and it is your first-time studying praise and worship, stick with me for a bit. Have you ever wondered why we sing at church? Why do we have a time of music – not just music, but actual words sung? Some denominations don't use instruments, just their voices. Why do we do this? Simply stated, we are instructed to do so. In fact, the book of Psalm was actually the songbook for worship in the temple at Jerusalem. The songbook was designed specifically for singing. But when our greatest desires have yet to come to pass, when we are at our lowest of lows, *what* do we sing?

> *O come, let us sing to the Lord; let us make a joyful noise to the Rock of our salvation! Let us come before His presence with thanksgiving; let us make a joyful noise to Him with songs of praise! For the Lord is a great God, and a great King above all gods. In His hand are the deep places of the earth; the heights and strength of the hills are His also. The sea is His, for He made it; and His hands formed the dry land. O come, let us worship and bow down, let us kneel before the Lord our Maker [in reverent praise and supplication]. For He is our God and we are the people of His pasture and the sheep of His hand.*
> *Psalm 95:1-6, AMP*

We don't just sing for what He's done for us individually; we sing about *who* He is! Seriously though, did you know that He specifically called you to be His daughter? We are His children. He becomes a Father to the Fatherless; He is good; He is full of mercy and loving-kindness; He heals our sickness and disease; He comforts those who mourn; He never changes. Really. He could strike us dead at any minute. Laugh all you want, but that stuff really happened in the Old Testament.

But thankfully, He sent Jesus, His only Son, to take the punishment for us. He doesn't want to strike us dead. He doesn't want *anyone* to perish! He gave us His precious Word and left us with the greatest gift of all, the Holy Spirit. We carry God around within us wherever we go. We are never alone. He is faithful; He is full of truth; He is so worthy to be praised simply for whom He is.

Now that you know *why* we praise Him and *what* we praise Him for. Let me tell you what naturally (#orsupernaturally) *results* from praise and worship, "Yet You are holy, O You who are enthroned upon the praises of Israel." (Psalm 22:3, NASB) When God is enthroned upon our praises, we exalt His name and make Him ruler above any situation or circumstance. Without even knowing it, we have invited Him and His power to manifest in our lives resulting in "Thy kingdom come, and Thy will be done".

How do we know His will? Remember, it is His Word, the Bible. And what does the Bible say about barrenness and children? Oh yeah (#noneshallbebarren)! So, are you kind of getting it yet? Are you seeing the power that can occur when The Barren Woman sings, when she praises and enthrones her Father in Heaven? If you're still not convinced, keep reading. Psalm 34 is one of my favorites (#sorryitslong):

> *I will bless the Lord at all times; His praise shall continually be in my mouth. My life makes its boast in the Lord; let the humble and afflicted hear and be glad. O magnify the Lord with me, and let us exalt His name together. I sought (inquired of) the Lord and required Him [of necessity and on the authority of His Word], and He heard me, and delivered me from all my fears. They looked to Him and were*

> *radiant; their faces shall never blush for shame or be confused. This poor man cried, and the Lord heard him, and saved him out of all his troubles. The Angel of the Lord encamps around those who fear Him [who revere and worship Him with awe] and each of them He delivers. O taste and see that the Lord [our God] is good! Blessed (happy, fortunate, to be envied) is the man who trusts and takes refuge in Him. O fear the Lord, you His saints [revere and worship Him]! For there is no want to those who truly revere and worship Him with godly fear. The young lions lack food and suffer hunger, but they who seek (inquire of and require) the Lord [by right of their need and on the authority of His Word], none of them shall lack any beneficial thing....*
>
> *The eyes of the Lord are toward the [uncompromisingly] righteous and His ears are open to their cry.... When the righteous cry for help, the Lord hears, and delivers them out of all their distress and troubles. The Lord is close to those who are of a broken heart and saves such as are crushed with sorrow for sin and are humbly and thoroughly penitent. Many evils confront the [consistently] righteous, but the Lord delivers him out of them all. He keeps all his bones; not one of them is broken... The Lord redeems the lives of His servants, and none of those who take refuge and trust in Him shall be condemned or held guilty.*
> Psalms 34:1-10, 15, 17-19, 20, 22, AMP

Wow! I just love that. When we continually praise and sing to God, no matter how we feel, we encourage others to do the same; we are delivered from our fears, and we are delivered from our troubles. Now, these results are simply from this passage. There are so many other passages on this topic. We are not even scratching the surface. Praise and worship also bring peace, renewed strength, joy, new revelation, comfort, intercession, creative gifts, freedom, etc. I could keep going and going and going.

When in my weakest moments, I sing praises to my Abba. It is then that I am made strong. My eyes get off of my heartache and negative pregnancy test, and I'm able to look up. I look to a God who sees me hears me, and loves me. I get Biblical perspective – The Truth – instead of looking at and dwelling on the negative, The Lie. Though I stumble, I do not fall. He frees me from my fear, and I am able to get off that bathroom floor, dry my tears, and go on with my day.

What have we got to lose if we begin singing praises to our Savior? Nothing! In fact, we have a whole lot to gain! If you're not already experienced in praising and singing to our God, then now is the time to start. It's never too late. He will be so pleased by whatever comes from your heart and out of your lips. If you're already singing praises, then keep it up. And, don't forget to do it when you have a broken heart. It can be so very difficult, but *so very worth it.*

2. The Song of Battle

I can hear the "Rocky" theme music again as I gear up to talk about the Song of Battle. But don't worry, I won't make you stop and sing the music this time. There is so much encompassing praise and specifically the Song of Battle (#akawarfare). However, I'm only going to cover a couple of examples of this type of song. If you get nothing else out of this section, I pray for you to get this: praise is powerful; praise can defeat the enemy.

#timeforsundayschool: Let me tell you a story about a man named Gideon. Because the Israelites did evil in the Lord's sight, they were handed over to the Midianites for seven years. And during those seven years, the Midianites attacked Israel, took everything from them, and left them to starve. When they eventually cried out to the Lord for help, God raised up Gideon as the leader to fight and destroy the Midianites. However, He informed Gideon that he had too many warriors, so before he could go into battle, he had to diminish his numbers to just 300 (#yikes). He split the 300 men into three groups and gave each man a trumpet and a clay pitcher containing a torch and told them to shout, "For the Lord and for Gideon!" Here is what happened next:

> *And the three companies blew the trumpets and shattered the pitchers, holding the torches in their left hands, and in their right hands the trum-*

> *pets to blow [leaving no chance to use swords], and they cried, The sword for the Lord and Gideon! They stood every man in his place round about the camp, and all the [Midianite] army ran – they cried out and fled.*
> *Judges 7:20-21, AMP*

Do you see that? The enemy ran away! Here's a similar story about a man named Jehoshaphat. Instead of using an instrument for his Song of Battle, this man appointed his worship leaders to go before the army. Check it out:

> *When he had consulted with the people, he appointed singers to sing to the Lord and praise Him in their holy [priestly] garments as they went out before the army, saying, Give thanks to the Lord, for His mercy and loving-kindness endure forever! And when they began to sing and to praise, the Lord set ambushments against the men of Ammon, Moab, and Mount Seir who had come against Judah, and they were [self-] slaughtered.*
> *2 Chronicles 20:21-22, AMP*

In these two stories, we see how God defeated the enemy through praise. First, we see praise through musical instruments and shouting; and now we see praise through vocal singing. What does this have to do with getting pregnant? Well, we already established that getting pregnant *is* the battle! We are in a battle right now. When you are barren, you are battling for your joy daily, if not hourly. So, we praise our Father in Heaven because He deserves it; we praise our Savior because it allows His power to come into the natural, and we praise our Daddy-God so He can go before us and fight our battles.

GOING DEEPER:

- Get out your list from Chapter 3 of what you believe about the nature of God. Compare your list with what you just learned and edit or add to it if possible.
- Make a new list about what He has done for you individually.
- Sing a Song of Praise based on your lists.
- Scriptures to study: Is. 54:1-3; Ps. 100:1-5; Ps. 34; Jdg. 7; 2 Chr. 20.

Chapter six
Prepare Your Temple

Jesus loves us unconditionally. We can come as we are, we are loved and accepted. We do not have to look a certain way. He doesn't show favoritism, and what He has done for one person, He can do for another (Acts 10:34). Likewise, you do not have to achieve a certain amount of steps in order to conceive. This book is simply my story and journey. These are principles I've learned along the way to strengthen my faith and get my joy back in hopes that other barren women will receive, know the truth, and be set free. Open your heart, keep reading, and let's see if we can experience some more hallelujah moments!

What is our temple? Based on the following passage, our temple is our physical bodies, "Do you not know that your body is the temple (the very sanctuary) of the Holy Spirit Who lives within you, Whom you have received [as a Gift] from God?" (1 Corinthians 6:19, AMP) As I have journeyed through this season, the Holy Spirit showed me two ways in which to prepare our temples for conception:

PHYSICAL PREPARATION
Let's get physical, physical! Let's get physical (#singitladies)! No seriously. I will be real with you. I have hated my body for a very long time. Not because of the accumulating cellulite over the years, or the laugh lines around my eyes since I turned thirty, or the back pain I've endured, or even the newfound flab around my midsection. I have hated my body because it has completely and utterly failed me. It has failed to produce

or even conceive a baby. It has failed its purpose in making me a mother. In my eyes, I see nothing to love about my body. But according to the Word, there is quite a lot to love.

You see, this body houses the Creator of the Universe! As believers, our bodies are homes to the living and powerful God. Shortly before Jesus was crucified on the cross, He had this conversation with His disciples:

And I will ask the Father, and He will give you another Comforter (Counselor, Helper, Intercessor, Advocate, Strengthener, and Standby), that He may remain with you forever –... But the Comforter (Counselor, Helper, Intercessor, Advocate, Strengthener, Standby), the Holy Spirit, Whom the Father will send in My name [in My place, to represent Me and act on My behalf], He will teach you all things. And He will cause you to recall (will remind you of, bring to your remembrance) everything I have told you...John 14: 16, 26, AMP

Jesus is with us forever! He even said it was good for us that He went away so that the Holy Spirit would come to us (John 16)! Think about that. Jesus said it was the best thing for us that He die on the cross and rise again so that all of us may have the Holy Spirit dwelling within us. How special is that? Jesus is right on the inside of us, comforting us, helping us, interceding for us, advocating for us, strengthening us, standing by us, and teaching us! He lives within us. Our body is not just an outer shell of our spirit, but it's literally a home for the Holy Spirit.

Let's look at this verse again, "Do you not know that your body is the temple (the very sanctuary) of the Holy Spirit Who lives within you, Whom you have received [as a Gift] from God? You are not your own..." (1 Corinthians 6:19, AMP) My body is not just my own to despise. If it actually belongs to the perfect God of the universe, then I must learn to be a good steward of said body.

A steward? What kind of ancient word is that? I know, right. Here are some modern synonyms: to administer, direct, govern, guide, keep, manage, operate, overlook, oversee, preside over, run, supervise, and tend. A steward is not the owner but the operator. So yeah, I couldn't hate my body anymore even if I tried! Not when it houses my faithful Abba Father. Especially not because He actually owns my body. It is very clear to me that I have a responsibility, dare I say, mandate, to be a good steward/operator of this body.

In the following passage, Paul speaks to the church at Corinth and to us. We are to flee from sexual immorality. However, I believe this scripture is not just related to sexual sins (#dontputGodinabox), "You were bought with a price [purchased with a preciousness and paid for, made His own]. So then, honor God and bring glory to Him in your body." (1 Corinthians 6:20, AMP) Hmm. Be a good steward of my body and bring glory to Him in my body? How do I do that?

Simply put, love my body (#shortandsweet).

I am going to list some practical steps to love our bodies and physically prepare our temples at the same time. For each step, I have an actual testimony of how the Holy Spirit guided me. You will see how practical our Helper is when we seek His wisdom:

1. Just do it

No more ifs, ands, or buts! No more excuses. Make being physically healthy a priority. Make time in your schedule to walk, workout, exercise, etc. Not only are you showing obedience in taking care of your temple, but it will reward you as well. Any time we obey the Word of God, it is for our good. I mean, seriously. Who doesn't feel amazing after a good workout (#word)?

Testimony: I took being active and athletic for granted. I was one of those skinny stick girls my whole childhood, all arms and legs. I played basketball and remained athletic. It wasn't until my late 20's that I stopped being active. I just stopped making it a priority. And I paid for it. My muscles eventually weakened, and I started having severe back issues, where I had to ice my back every night when I got home from work. I even missed some work because of it! However, eventually, chiropractic care and exercise greatly diminished my pain to where I am almost pain-free. And I am fully expecting to be completely pain-free by the end of this book! So, make your physical health a priority today.

2. Get checked out

Don't be afraid to see your general practitioner and your OB/GYN to check for any core physical issues. Get a physical and lab work done. If there are changes to be made, make them. Use wisdom and listen to your doctors but bring any decision to God first. Make His wisdom your final authority. If you've done this and tried all the testing and even your doctor's advice, then seek the Holy Spirit for His solution. The main thing is that you don't waste time wondering if something is wrong with you (#guiltyascharged #yesididthis).

Testimony: I hate going to the doctor (#nooffense). The reason I use the word hate is that any kind of doctor visit would strike fear within me (outside of the chiropractor). Since my body has failed in producing children, I have allowed this shame to morph into the fear that something is wrong with my body. I was scared to get it checked out. When you do get checked out and if you discover something is off (i.e., vitamin D deficiency, thyroid issues, blocked fallopian tubes, anovulatory, etc.), make a conscious choice not to partner with fear. I am thankful for doctors and modern medicine. However, they are not our final authority. *We do not become their diagnosis.* We use wisdom and listen with respect to their advice, but we remember what God's Word says about us. Don't make decisions out of fear but out of wisdom. Seek God for the direction to take and trust in His treatment plan. Doctors are not God. They are resources. God is the Source. Miracles can happen.

3. Get your sexy back

As much as I would love to encourage you to get your sexy back for your husbands, that's not what this step is about (#sadface). I just wanted to keep your attention. Getting your sexy back is simply stated: eliminate bad habits and abuse of your physical body. In other words, let the Healer restore your strength and health.

Testimony: Along with suffering from back issues for the past few years, I have also suffered from chronic sinus infections. I probably had one every month and, even after taking multiple antibiotics, I lived with the infection in my body. I was miserable, fuzzy-headed, fatigued, weak, etc. I just felt yucky *all* the time. I finally saw an allergist to see if they resulted from allergies. Sure enough, it turns out I'm allergic to everything! I tried allergy shots for a while, but still felt yucky. Eventually, I sought God for a natural solution and He opened my eyes to essential oils. My health is better in every area! I no longer have to take allergy shots, I rarely have sinus infections, and I have a lot more energy (#healthiestfamilyontheblock)! As if that wasn't enough, not only did He show me the essential oils, but He also revealed to me how stressful my life had become. So I eliminated any extra stress and commitments. Lastly, He showed me I needed to change my family's diet, so we began a cleaner eating approach within our home (#notperfect #westillhavepizzanights).

#whoa: That was a lot, I know. I'm not saying you need to make these same choices. But I do believe God will show you what things to change if you ask Him for help. He desires to restore and heal us. But He's such a Gentleman that He won't do it unless we ask Him.

4. Step out in faith

This can be a fun one! Simply put, step out in faith by participating in a physical activity you've been too scared to do (#iamnotresponsibleforanydeaths #orsoremuscles). Your step of faith could be as simple as joining the gym, walking your neighborhood every day, attempting push-ups, joining a co-ed softball league, skydiving, running a 5K, etc. Push your body as you step out in faith. Put fear behind you and believe and trust that the Healer has restored you.

Testimony: I used to play basketball. Well, the last time I played was over fifteen years ago. So, when asked to play in a league by some of my former teammates, I freaked out. I was so worried about my back and had just gotten to the point of jogging in my workouts. Nonetheless, I sought my Helper, and He said to just do it (#nike). So, I began running sprints to get into basketball shape. I was so happy because my muscles actually worked and I could even walk afterward! But from those sprints, I then developed shin splints. I was not able to walk for two weeks before the first game. But I stuck it out, and when driving to the game, I used some essential oils and simply prayed. I chose to trust that my body was ready and it would not fail me. I stepped out in faith. Sure enough, I was able to participate in my game and run! Better yet, I didn't have any more shin splints or pain in my legs the following days! God is faithful, and I began to fall a little in love with this body He gave me.

5. Have fun

Stop worrying. Simply enjoy life! This will come as you continue to apply these principles. Our bodies retain stress and anxiety. But, we don't have to live this way. We can live in freedom and experience joy *now*! Here are some ideas: date nights with your husband, spend time with friends, go shopping, have a lady's night, plan vacations, dance with music blaring, go to concerts and sporting events, wrestle with your husband! Be playful with him like children! Enjoy your friendship with the man you love. You will be pleasantly surprised by how much joy this simple act alone will bring you (#wrestlingisfuninsomanyways #hinthint). Finally, invest in other people's lives.

Testimony: Shame had me isolating myself. I didn't feel like I had anything to offer or any light to bring because I hadn't yet received the blessing of children. But through this process, I quickly learned that I was believing another lie. As my faith strengthened and I went through each one of these chapters, I found a measure of freedom. Freedom equals joy. Joy is not defined or based on circumstances. It is in God, knowing who I am in Him, knowing what His Word says, and believing His promises for me. I'm beginning to no longer worry about tomorrow. I simply want to enjoy today! Experience joy now!

6. Speak life

This one is short and sweet. Speak life to your body. Bless it, and don't curse it. We addressed previously on speaking life and confessing His truth. So do it now. Literally, speak life and blessings over your physical body (#lifeordeath #youdecide).

SPIRITUAL PREPARATION

Enlarge the place of your tent, and let the curtains of your habitations be stretched out; spare not; lengthen your cords and strengthen your stakes. Isaiah 54:2, AMP

Let's get spiritual, spiritual! Let's get spiritual! Nah, it doesn't work the same way, does it? Through the steps of applying these principles to our everyday way of thinking and speaking, we should automatically be experiencing spiritual preparation of our temple. The reason why is because of the enlarging, stretching, and lengthening of our faith. Three more ways to spiritually prepare your temple are:

1. Accept His love

God loves you. He is for you. His love for you is as great as His love for the woman with five children. But let's be real. When everybody else is popping up pregnant around us, and people are producing babies who don't even want them, it is so very easy to feel forsaken. Trust me, I know, because "Behold, children are a heritage and gift from the Lord, the fruit of the womb a reward." (Psalm 127:3, AMP) We think, *Being able to conceive is a reward? Then what am I doing wrong? Does God even love me? He must love her more than He loves me* (#keepinitreal).

But friend, here's the deal: everybody struggles. If not infertility, then they are dealing with something else. We just may not see it. Jesus Himself tells us, "In the world, you have tribulation and trials and distress and frustration…" (John 16:33, AMP)

To truly accept the love of our Father is to stop comparing ourselves to others (#readthatagain). We don't know what people are going through. We *all* struggle with something. If we continue to compare, it leads to envy, jealousy, discontentment, and bitterness. We have to choose to accept God's love, especially in the midst of trials. We have to evaluate ourselves. Is our trust in circumstances or in His promises? Remember, His promises are in His Word, and His Word is His will, and His will is His heart for us. So, what does His Word say?

First of all, did you know that He is our Daddy? Abba means Papa/Daddy. And we are a "Daddy's girl." He gave us the desire for children in the first place. He purposely created us with a mother's heart. Our maternal instinct began when we were little girls. It is not just a coincidence. He created us to be a mother. He knew us in our mother's wombs (Psalms 139:13). He knows the number of hairs on our heads for cryin' out loud (Luke 12:7). Every single hair, He knows them all, including the ones clogging up the shower drain (#gross). He has our names inscribed on the palms of His hands (Isaiah 49:16). He bottles our tears. That's right; He saves our tears. Every tear we've shed over each negative pregnancy test, He knows (Psalms 56:8). We were bought with a price (1 Corinthians 6:20). We are so precious to Him that He sacrificed His only Son for our lives (John 3:16). He never leaves us or forsakes us (Hebrews 13:5). And finally, He desires we live life to its fullest, both physically and spiritually (John 10:10).

That sure sounds like love to me! But, in order to accept this love, we need to stop comparing ourselves to others and choose to believe what His Word tells us about His love (#moreonthiscomingsoon).

2. Love yourself

This goes way beyond just learning to love our bodies again. We must also learn to love who we are and who God initially created us to be. I will get to the reason behind that in a minute. For many years, I have looked at other women with their perfect little children and their perfect little house and their perfect little life. I wanted to *be* those women. I hated myself. I have felt unworthy; like something was wrong with me; like I wasn't good enough; like God had forgotten about me; like He didn't even love me (#canyourelate).

But then, I began to *believe* those feelings and accept them. They formed a cancer within me, and I began to change. I was no longer the bold, fun-loving, hopeful, vivacious woman that God created me to be. Instead, I became withdrawn, insecure, isolated, negative, and self-absorbed. Those lies, which is exactly what those emotions were, literally changed my personality. I hated my body, but I also hated who I had become (#amenanyone).

You've probably heard the saying, "you can't help others unless you first help yourself." Shoot, we've all been on an airplane and have seen that the oxygen mask goes on ourselves before the child. Well, throughout this entire process, God revealed to me this very profound and dynamic truth: we can't truly love others unless we first love ourselves.

Take a look at what Jesus said, "And you shall love the Lord your God with all your heart, with all your soul, with all your mind, and with all your strength.' This is the first commandment. And the second, like it, is this: 'You shall love your neighbor as yourself.' There is no other commandment greater than these." (Mark 12:30-31, NKJV)

First of all, we are to love God with all our heart, soul, mind, and strength. Secondly, when Jesus speaks of the next commandment, He uses the words "the second is like it," which clearly means it is as important as the first. Lastly, Jesus summed up all of the previous ten commandments with this one: "Love your neighbor as yourself." This not only means our actual neighbors, but anyone who comes into our lives. Simply put, love people as much as you love yourself.

When I realized I hated who I was because of my barrenness, I looked at these scriptures and realized that if I'm supposed to love others as I do myself, I'm not truly loving them if I can't even stand myself. I knew that I knew, that I knew that something had to change. How could I obey His greatest commandment? Just like we discussed in the previous section, I had to make a choice to accept His love for me and see myself as He sees me (#easiersaidthandone).

Why is this so important? Because Jesus said that all people would know that we are His disciples by the way we love one another, "I give you a new commandment: that you should love one another. Just as I have loved you, so you too should love one another. By this shall all [men] know that you are My disciples, if you love one another [if you keep on showing love among yourselves]." (John 13:34-35, AMP) Oh man! So, people will know that I follow Jesus if I love others and show love to others (#nopressure).

As you can probably guess, *not* loving myself was no longer an option; especially when I did further study and learned how much God cares about this topic, "Love one another with brotherly affection [as members of one family], giving precedence and showing honor to one another." (Romans 12:10, AMP) And, "Above all things have intense and unfailing love for one another, for love covers a multitude of sins [forgives and disregards the offenses of others]." (1 Peter 4:8, AMP)

Love goes beyond just simply (or not so simply) obeying our God in Heaven. Loving others results in unity with our fellow man, "Beloved, let us love one another, for love is (springs) from God; and he who loves [his fellowmen] is begotten (born) of God and is coming [progressively] to know and understand God [to perceive and recognize and get a better and clearer knowledge of Him]." (1 John 4:7, AMP)

So, there it is. We must love others out of the love we have for ourselves. This results in being obedient to Jesus' commandment. What does all of this equal to? Unity. Not just for us and our household, but with everyone with whom we come in contact; the whole church, the body of Christ. Every mandate and commandment in the Word of God is always, always, always for our good (Deuteronomy 6:24). But it is also for a greater good for the whole of mankind. Jesus knew what He was doing.

3. Forgive

When I think of the word forgive, I automatically think of Jesus on the cross. He prayed, "Father, forgive them, for they know not what they do." (Luke 23:24) This passage reveals Jesus' love loud and clear and still blows my mind every time I see it. Forgiveness is an action of love. It is not easy and can be the most difficult thing we'll ever do, but it must be done. Here's why:

> *And whenever you stand praying, if you have anything against anyone, forgive him and let it drop (leave it, let it go), in order that your Father Who is in heaven may also forgive you your [own] failings and shortcomings and let them drop. But if you do not forgive, neither will your Father in heaven forgive your failings and shortcomings.*
> *Mark 11:25-26, AMP*

#ouch: These were Jesus' own words. Why do we need to forgive others? Because Jesus said so. What does this have to do with spiritually preparing your temple to conceive? I have no clue (#justkidding)! In all honesty, I was hesitant to include forgiveness because it sounds like a condition or mandate that we must do in order to conceive. Nonetheless, everything the Teacher has revealed to me throughout this process has been about getting my joy back and bringing me to this place right here: strengthening of faith in God's Word. That is my goal for you, dear reader. And as you continue this process with me, you will find that reconciliation and unity instinctively become more important to you.

So how do we continue to get there? By forgiving others and forgiving ourselves, "Since by your obedience to the Truth through the Holy] Spirit you have purified your hearts for the sincere affection of the brethren, [see that you] love one another fervently from a pure heart." (1 Peter 1:22, AMP) We are to love one another from a pure heart with sincere affection. We are to love others without hypocrisy and without putting on an act. How do we do this? By forgiving them, by releasing their shortcomings, by letting go of their failures, and by dropping it.

The same goes for us. Because, most likely, we aren't going to blame someone else for not being able to conceive. I'm assuming that, like me, you blame yourself. You are bitter, and you hate yourself. But remember, if we are to love others as we do ourselves, we need to receive God's love and love ourselves again. A primary way to do this is by releasing shame, revulsion, and hate. Receive forgiveness, release your shortcomings, let go of your failure to conceive, and just drop it. It's not even your fault anyway.

Going Deeper:
- In what ways will you begin physically preparing your temple?
- In what ways have you changed during your season of barrenness?
- What do you think God loves most about you?
- Record what you love most about yourself.
- Who do you need to forgive? Record the process of forgiving this person in your journal (even if it is yourself).
- Scriptures to study: Jn. 14:16, 26; 1 Cor. 6:19, 20; Is. 54:2; Jn. 16:33; Ps. 139:13; Lk. 12:7; Is. 49:16; Ps. 56:8; Jn. 3:16; Heb. 13:5; Jn. 10:10; Mk. 12:30, 31; Jn. 13:34, 35; Rom. 12:10; 1 Pt. 4:8; 1 Jn. 4:7; Mk. 11:25, 26; 1 Pt. 1:22.

Chapter seven
WHEN AF STILL VISITS

#ANEXHORTATION

AF is AuntFlo (#yourperiod). By this time in your reading, I hope your faith is being strengthened and you are living out your joy. But you POAS'd (#peedonastick), and it was *still* negative. So now what? Well, right about now is the moment in this process where you need some encouragement. Because let's face it. There is no magic formula to conceive. You can follow all-of-the-above and still be barren and depressed. This chapter is what I like to call an exhortation, so consider me your very own motivational speaker. The following six steps are additional exhortations I experienced along the way and I hope they encourage and strengthen you as well.

KEEP BELIEVING. KEEP CONFESSING. KEEP SINGING. KEEP PREPARING. KEEP LOVING...

1. Keep waiting

When Aunt Flo still makes her big, ugly, unwanted appearance, keep waiting on the Lord. Now, this doesn't mean that you stand there looking at your watch, tapping your foot in annoyed impatience. Waiting, in the Biblical sense, means to hope for, expect, and trust. Take a look at the following verses to grasp what this truly means (#biblestudy101):

> *I waited patiently and expectantly for the Lord; and He inclined to me and heard my cry. Psalm 40:1, AMP*
>
> *Wait and hope for and expect the Lord; be brave and of good courage and let your heart be stout and enduring. Yes, wait for and hope for and expect the Lord. Psalm 27:14, AMP*
>
> *But those who wait for the Lord [who expect, look for, and hope in Him] shall change and renew their strength and power; they shall lift their wings and mount up [close to God] as eagles [mount up to the sun]; they shall run and not be weary, they shall walk and not faint or become tired. Isaiah 40:31, AMP*

In a nutshell, when we wait on the Lord, He hears us; does not put us to shame; does not disappoint us; helps and shields us; blesses us; renews our strength; renews our power; causes us to run and not be weary; walk and not become tired (#boom). My favorite promise, of course, is the one from Isaiah 40. This journey has been so tiring and weary. Look at the promises we receive when we continue to wait, though!

You may say, *But I've waited 3, 5, 8, 10 years now!* I hear ya, sister. In fact, I'm reminded of the story of Abraham and Sarah. If we look at how the New Testament describes Abraham in Hebrews, we see a picture of faith that seems to be all sunshine and roses, "And so it was that he [Abraham], having waited long and endured patiently, realized and obtained [in the birth of Isaac as a pledge of what was to come] what God had promised him." (Hebrews 6:15, AMP)

Hmm, really? I'm pretty sure that when I read the story of Abraham in the Old Testament, I don't see a man who endured patiently. I see a man and a woman who were so desperate for children, they took matters into their own hands, believing they needed to help God out in His promise (#soundsfamiliar). The result? A baby through Sarah's maid that created strife within the family, and later, strife between people groups. What I love most is that even though they made a mistake, God was still faithful to His promise to Abraham and Sarah. More than that, God still blessed Hagar and her baby. Shoot, He even sent an angel to speak to and encourage her (#Godsloveamazesme #nobabyisamistake)!

We see, then, that after Abraham and Sarah concocted their little scheme, it was still another thirteen years before Isaac, the son of promise, was born. Talk about waiting! Do you think Abraham and Sarah woke up every day with a smile on their faces and joy in their hearts knowing they were soon to be parents? Do you think Sarah loved and adored Ishmael as her own while she waited for her son of promise? Do you think, after suffering a menopausal hot flash, that Sarah spontaneously praised God for the baby to come? Umm, nope. Pretty sure Sarah experienced jealousy and envy, shame and embarrassment, hopelessness and unbelief, just like the rest of us. In fact, in Genesis 18, we hear about Sarah's disbelieving laughter in reference to God and a couple of angels, speaking about His promise to Abraham. She didn't believe it even when God Himself was in the next room! And yet, here is what the Word records of Sarah:

> *Because of faith also Sarah herself received physical power to conceive a child, even when she was long past the age for it, because she considered [God] Who had given her the promise to be reliable and trustworthy and true to His word. Hebrews 11:11, AMP*

Dear friend, waiting is not all puppy dog kisses and chocolate. It is *so* incredibly painful. As the Psalmist says, "I am weary with my crying; my throat is parched; my eyes fail with waiting [hopefully] for my God." (Psalm 69:3, AMP)

So, yes, we will still make mistakes like Abraham and Sarah and continue to be stretched in our faith and belief, but God will get us where He wants us as we go through this grueling process. We will be considered women of faith. Not because of our strength. Rather, because we didn't give up. We kept waiting, expecting, hoping, and trusting in His Word.

As Habakkuk put it, "Even though it delays, wait [patiently] for it, Because it will certainly come; it will not delay." (Habakkuk 2:3, AMP) I love how The Message translation says it even plainer, "If it seems slow in coming, wait. It's on its way. It will come right on time."

So, while we wait, let's wait on the Lord instead (#whathaveyougottolose). And if AF still decides to visit the following month, six months, or even a year from now? What do we do then?

KEEP BELIEVING. KEEP CONFESSING. KEEP SINGING. KEEP PREPARING. KEEP LOVING. KEEP WAITING…

2. Keep living

Live as though your prayer has been answered. Live as though you are The Joyful Mother of children *now*. Realize God wants to use you now in all your barren glory (#saywhat). How many times have you thought or said, *When I get pregnant, I'll do such and such?* Or, *When I have children, I'll do this and that?* If you're anything like me, then A. LOT. *So* many years were wasted on those two phrases.

I told you previously how much I hated my body; how I became this foreign, insecure woman, no longer recognizable; not believing God could use me for anything, all because I had not yet received my greatest heart's desire. But friend, throughout this process, I soon learned that I had believed yet another BIG. FAT. LIE.

Have you believed this same thing? Have you backed down from certain ministry opportunities because you felt you weren't worthy to help others? Maybe you felt something nagging you from the inside to help out in children's ministry, but you refused because you didn't have children. Do you currently put your life on hold until you get that positive pregnancy test? Have you stopped spending time with friends who are already enjoying motherhood because you feel so insignificant? Have you made excuses not to socialize with your neighbors because you're the only couple without kids (#youarenotalone)?

This lie is *so* subtle. Too subtle. It just kind of creeps in when you don't even realize it. It is like one of those hideous, painful pimples that begin just under the skin. We feel the pain and irritation but, by the time it comes to a head, it's marred our appearance before we could stop it (#disgustingmetaphoriknow).

However, I'm here to tell you that God still wants to use you. Yes, you! Big, ugly pimple and all! Remember, Sarah and Abraham even wavered and struggled with unbelief, but God is still using their story to this day as examples of faith. They were literally praised for their patience and faith in Hebrews, but when we look back in Genesis, we see their human imperfection. That's us! We are so imperfect and weak, but here is the good news: God loves us in our weaknesses.

This is confirmed all throughout Scripture. For example, we never learn what it is, but we learn that Paul had some sort of weakness that caused him great difficulty and affliction. He writes about the mysterious "thorn in his flesh" to the Corinthians:

And He said to me, "My grace is sufficient for you, for My strength is made perfect in weakness." Therefore most gladly I will rather boast in my infirmities, that the power of Christ may rest upon me. Therefore I take pleasure in infirmities, in reproaches, in needs, in persecutions, in distresses, for Christ's sake. For when I am weak, then I am strong. 2 Corinthians 12:9-10, NKJV

Now we see Paul quoting someone. Guess who he's quoting? Jesus! Jesus tells us that His strength is made perfect in our weakness. Unless we experience weakness or difficulty, how else would we know to rely on our Father to help us? That's why Paul said he takes pleasure in his distress because he is then "forced" to yield to an absolute trust upon God. Does that sound familiar? Yes ma'am! Let's look at it in The Living Bible:

Each time he said, "No. But I am with you; that is all you need. My power shows up best in weak people." Now I am glad to boast about how weak I am; I am glad to be a living demonstration of Christ's power, instead of showing off my own power and abilities. Since I know it is all for Christ's good, I am quite happy about 'the thorn,' and about insults and hardships, persecutions and difficulties; for when I am weak, then I am strong – the less I have, the more I depend on him. 2 Corinthians 12: 9-10, TLB

That is so good! "My power shows up best in weak people." My favorite! So once again, I reiterate. God still wants to use you. Ask Him to direct your steps and to be strong in His power where you are so utterly weak. Boast in His strength and keep living (#amen).

KEEP BELIEVING. KEEP CONFESSING. KEEP SINGING. KEEP PREPARING. KEEP LOVING. KEEP WAITING. KEEP LIVING…

3. Keep renewing

What, my library card? All joking aside, we know what the Word says regarding conception and pregnancy. We know The Truth. We've been confessing The Truth. But, because we're weak humans, with huge sneaky pimples of unbelief all over our faces, we have to address the issue of our mind, "…And be constantly renewed in the spirit of your mind [having a fresh mental and spiritual attitude]." (Ephesians 4:23, AMP)

I tell you, I can be feeling good, *so* good, with all those early pregnancy signs and symptoms. I can think, *This month is gonna be it!* So, I buy up some pregnancy tests and start pinning more items to my secret "Baby Windsor" Pinterest board. Then, days later, my hopes are completely crushed; I'm looking at another BFN (#bigfatnegative), bawling my eyes out, while the stupid AF cramps begin yet again.

If my mind is not being renewed constantly, daily, hourly, and sometimes even every second, I have tendencies to fall back into that horrible barren-woman-depression (#bwd). This is real. Shoot, I'm the one writing this book, giving you things to do to strengthen your faith, but all of these words mean nothing if I don't constantly renew my mind.

This is wisdom. It is a discipline; a necessary discipline that keeps our thoughts in the "sane department." So how is this done? By "…casting down arguments and every high thing that exalts itself against the knowledge of God, bringing every thought into captivity to the obedience of Christ." (2 Corinthians 10:5, NKJV)

Do you need to take captive any thoughts that go against God's Word? Take some time to think about it. It's okay if you've never been one to read the Bible on a daily basis. It's okay if you don't even own a Bible. Guess what? They have free Bible apps! But, I do encourage you to seek the Word and find out what it has to say about any thoughts floating around in your mind (#homework). In fact, I imagine worry is one of those thoughts. Let's find out what God's Word says about that:

> *Therefore I say to you, do not worry about your life, what you will eat or what you will drink; nor about your body, what you will put on. Is not life more than food and the body more than clothing? Look at the birds of the air, for they neither sow nor reap nor gather into barns; yet your heavenly Father feeds them. Are you not of more value than they? Which of you by worrying can add one cubit to his stature? So why do you worry about clothing? Consider the lilies of the field, how they grow: they neither toil nor spin; and yet I say to you that even Solomon in all his glory was not arrayed like one of these. Now if God so clothes the grass of the field, which today is, and tomorrow is thrown into the oven, will He not much more clothe you, O you of little faith? Therefore do not worry, saying, "What shall we eat?" or "What shall we drink?" or "What shall we wear?" For after all these things the Gentiles seek. For your heavenly Father knows that you need all these things. Matthew 6:25-32, NKJV*

I feel like all we are missing at the end of this passage is, "Love, Jesus." He is such a poet. He doesn't stop there, though. He goes on to say, "But seek first the kingdom of God and His righteousness, and all these things shall be added to you. Therefore do not worry about tomorrow, for tomorrow will worry about its own things. Sufficient for the day is its own trouble." (Matthew 6:33-34, NKJV) I love the way The Message breaks down verse 33, "Steep your life in God-reality, God-initiative, God-provisions. Don't worry about missing out. You'll find all your everyday human concerns will be met." Hence, instead of worrying, we seek God first. We steep our life in God's reality, God's initiative, and God's provisions.

And not only are all our concerns and daily needs met, but we also receive perfect and constant peace, "You will guard him and keep him in perfect and constant peace whose mind [both its inclination and its character] is stayed on You, because he commits himself to You, leans on You, and hopes confidently in You." (Isaiah 26:3, AMP) Perfect and constant peace. In Hebrew, this type of peace is expressed by *shalom*. Shalom implies health, happiness, well-being, peace, and nothing missing or broken. Beautiful, isn't it? This is what we get when our minds are renewed and kept on Jesus. But wait, there's more (#infomercialvoice)!

> *Don't fret or worry. Instead of worrying, pray. Let petitions and praises shape your worries into prayers, letting God know your concerns. Before you know it, a sense of God's wholeness, everything coming together for good, will come and settle you down. It's wonderful what happens when Christ displaces worry at the center of your life.*
> *Philippians 4:6-7, MSG*

Simultaneously, as we're renewing our minds, taking our thoughts captive, keeping our minds on Jesus, seeking Him first, we pray. As we talk to God and process out with Him what we are feeling, there's an exchange; and worry becomes peace (#shalom).

Whew! That was some heavy stuff! Take a selah moment and search your thoughts. Maybe it's time for some Bible study on your own to see what God's Word says about the struggles or "thorns" you are enduring. And since that was a lot of information, I'll close out this section with a simplified version of "Keep renewing":

- Constantly participate in the renewing of your mind
- Take captive the thoughts that don't agree with God's Word
- Stop worrying and seek God first
- Pray
- Experience peace

KEEP BELIEVING. KEEP CONFESSING. KEEP SINGING. KEEP PREPARING. KEEP LOVING. KEEP WAITING. KEEP LIVING. KEEP RENEWING...

4. Keep rejoicing

#AKArejoicewithothers: Didn't we already talk about rejoicing? Yes, we talked about singing and rejoicing in the Lord. This section, though, is about rejoicing with others; and even mourning with others.

A phrase my home church loves to say is "doing life together." Honestly, I used to think it was a little cheesy. But that was my pride talking. Now that I have been stripped of most of my pride (#infertilitywilldothattoya), I see I cannot *not* do life together. In fact, I actually *need* people (#thehorror)! Even now, this is hard for me to admit. People can be straight mean! Trust me; I know this as a personal fact. Remember? I was a divorcee at a young age. Because of the way my "friends" treated me in the church, I ended up leaving the church for two years. I practically walked away from God.

#rabbittrail: Please don't be like me and leave the church just because some of God's people are human. Check your heart first before allowing others to have that much power over you. If I would've been in the right place in my own relationship with Jesus, I never would have gotten so offended (#ouch). That's right. I said it. If you allow offense to direct your decisions, then you are not in the right place. It took me years to overcome that offense. Not that I didn't forgive them, but because of the way I allowed the offense to change me. Along with the insecurity and shame of being divorced and then barren, now came an inability to trust anyone. I was a hot mess (#Jesusloveshotmesses #rabbittrailcompleted).

Alright, if you're still reading, then I'd love to show you some truth from the Word to back up why we need each other on this grueling, long journey to motherhood. First of all, our main man, Jesus Christ, was almost never alone. During His ministry on earth, He was almost always found with people. In Matthew 14, we see an instance in which He wanted to be alone after receiving the news that John the Baptist was killed. He avoided a premature conflict with Herod and wanted to be sure that His death would be according to God's will, not Herod's.

What happened then? The multitude of people *still* followed Him. Did He turn them away and say, "no room at the inn"? Or call in sick? Did He isolate? Nope. The Bible says He was moved with compassion for them and healed their sick. Not only that, later, even as the disciples were telling Him to send the people away, Jesus refused. He then ended up performing a well-known miracle; the infamous five loaves of bread and two fish. He healed their sick and fed them all with the original intention of wanting to be alone. This is Jesus. At a time when He desired to be alone, instead, He performed miracles and met people's needs. We should be like Jesus.

You know those times where you want to isolate because you just got another BFN (#bigfatnegative)? Well, those are the times you need to perform miracles and meet people's needs. Or the time you make up excuses not to have lunch with that friend because you are having a bad week with the BWD (#barrenwomandepression)? Keep that lunch date because you need each other.

Also, in Acts, we see the early church being established and learn that fellowship was tantamount to their survival, "They were continually and faithfully devoting themselves to the instruction of the apostles, and to fellowship, to eating meals together and to prayers." (Acts 2:42, AMP) The Greek word for fellowship is *koinonia*, which is a unity brought about by the Holy Spirit. It cements the believers to Jesus and to each other. Some synonyms of koinonia are: sharing, unity, close association, partnership, a society, a communion, a fellowship, contributory help, and my favorite, a brotherhood (#orsisterhood). We were never meant to do life alone. We are one through Jesus Christ; one Unit, one Body, one Church. In fact, Paul writes this:

> *The way God designed our bodies is a model for understanding our lives together as a church: every part dependent on every other part, the parts we mention and the parts we don't, the parts we see and the parts we don't. If one part hurts, every other part is involved in the*

hurt, and in the healing. If one part flourishes, every other part enters into the exuberance. 1 Corinthians 12:25-26, MSG

So when my fellow sister is hurting, I am hurting too. When she grieves the loss of her recent miscarriage, I grieve too. When a sister, who just began trying for a baby, pops up pregnant after one month, what am I supposed to do (#pleasedontsayit)? Enter into her exuberance! Hey, nobody ever said this stuff was easy.

Here's another one for you, "Rejoice with those who rejoice [sharing others' joy], and weep with those who weep [sharing others' grief]." (Romans 12:15, AMP) And again, in The Message, "Laugh with your happy friends when they're happy; share tears when they're down."

Here we go again! This whole getting pregnant thing is supposed to be about me. *Me* getting pregnant. *Me* going through this process. *Me* becoming The Joyful Mother of children. However, by being obedient to the Word of God, when has it *ever* been just about me? Never. Because it isn't just about me. God's purposes always encompass the Body. It is always for the good of the Body, more so, for all of mankind. Your journey and the story evolving from it are not just about you (#moreonthiscominglater).

Rejoice with others, mourn with others, don't isolate, and bring others along with you on your journey. Trust me, they need you just as much as you need them.

KEEP BELIEVING. KEEP CONFESSING. KEEP SINGING. KEEP PREPARING. KEEP LOVING. KEEP WAITING. KEEP LIVING. KEEP RENEWING. KEEP REJOICING…

5. Keep stretching

No, this isn't about physical therapy or yoga. This is about that spiritual preparation of your temple again. Because I'm not gonna make any promises or guarantee anything, but, most likely, as you walk this walk and grow in your faith and spiritual maturity, God is going to ask you to do something that seems crazy (#saywhat).

#disclaimer: I'm not saying your life will look like quitting your job and staying home to write. That's my story. Please don't go out and quit your job and blame it on me. I'd rather not have a bunch of angry husbands sending me hate mail (#pleaseandthankyou).

In any event, in this natural progression of the stretching of your faith, you will notice your life becoming a never-ending adventure. As your faith strengthens, your actions will reflect it. And it doesn't always make sense to our human minds. Sometimes our actions can become quite radical and crazy. Here's a little "Sunday School" for you:

> *What good is it, dear brothers and sisters, if you say you have faith but don't show it by your actions? Can that kind of faith save anyone? Suppose you see a brother or sister who has no food or clothing, and you say, "Good-bye and have a good day; stay warm and eat well" – but then you don't give that person any food or clothing. What good does that do? So you see, faith by itself isn't enough. Unless it produces good deeds, it is dead and useless. Now someone may argue, "Some people have faith; others have good deeds." But I say, "How can you show me your faith if you don't have good deeds? I will show you my faith by my good deeds." You say you have faith, for you believe that there is one God. Good for you! Even the demons believe this, and they tremble in terror. How foolish! Can't you see that faith without good deeds is useless? Don't you remember that our ancestor Abraham was shown to be right with God by his actions when he offered his son Isaac on the altar? You see, his faith and his actions worked together. His actions made his faith complete. And so it happened just as the Scriptures say: "Abraham believed God, and God counted him as righteous because of his faith." He was even called the friend of God. So you see, we are shown to be right with God by what we do, not by faith alone. Rahab the prostitute is another example. She was shown to be right with God by her actions when she hid those messengers and sent them safely away by a different road. Just as the body is dead without breath, so also faith is dead without good works. James 2:14-26, NLT*

First off, this whole theme of "faith without works is dead" gets totally misinterpreted. "Works," or "good deeds," leads to thinking of serving others, feeding the hungry, clothing the poor, caring for the orphans and widows, and taking care of basic needs. This is so very important. However, James takes it further. He gives the example of Abraham when he offered Isaac, his son, on the altar. He gives the example of Rahab (#aprostitutebytheway) when she helped the messengers in Jericho scout out the city. I don't see how either of these examples are simply "good deeds." Seriously. Abraham getting ready to sacrifice his son for God wasn't meeting anyone's needs; it was just plain nuts. And when Rahab hid the scouts of Israel in her home, that was just simply unheard of! What is my point here?

Faith, without action, is meaningless (#boom).

We can believe all day long that we will conceive and bear children. We can even have faith and truly believe the Word. However, if we don't back up that faith with action, then it's dead (#ouch). I'm not saying go out and do something impossible, then label it faith. Like I said before, everyone's story and process will look different. But, I am saying to listen and be prepared. You will be tested in some capacity. You will be asked to perform some action of faith. It might possibly be the most difficult thing you have ever done. You will feel totally crazy and will question yourself on a daily basis. This will force you to have your mind renewed. It is a crazy, radical process that will require your constant stretching and growing. It will be your wildest adventure.

And oh, my friend, what an adventure! I am currently in the process of my faith action (#thisbook). I question my sanity on a daily basis in the same breath as thanking my Abba Father. It's the weirdest experience I've ever gone through, but I wouldn't trade it for anything in the world. It feels so, so good to walk by faith and not by sight (2 Corinthians 5:7). So, keep on stretching! Your biggest and best adventure awaits you! And I don't just mean motherhood!

KEEP BELIEVING. KEEP CONFESSING. KEEP SINGING. KEEP PREPARING. KEEP LOVING. KEEP WAITING. KEEP LIVING. KEEP RENEWING. KEEP REJOICING. KEEP STRETCHING…

6. Keep running

#vulnerabilityalert: Here I am. Nearing the last section of this chapter, and yep, you guessed it, still physically barren. If you've made it this far in your reading, then I hope you will continue. Every story has to have a happy ending, right? Well, I can promise you one is coming. So please continue, dear friend (#dontgiveuponmeyet).

Speaking of happy endings, have I mentioned that I love to read? I especially love to read historical romance (#sappynotsmutty). The reason why is that most of them often have a happy ending. I usually read for pleasure. Throughout this whole grueling process, however, I began to read to escape reality. Life is so much grander in the novels. The maiden is always rescued, the hero is always handsome, they always fall in love, get married, and – what happens last? The epilogue shares how quickly the beautiful couple becomes "with child." Oh, by the way, they live happily ever after. Frankly, for many years, their lives seemed a whole heck of a lot better than mine.

But, throughout my process, with all the stretching and growing, I've realized something: God is my Dream Maker. He is the Prince of my fairy tales. He creates the most beautiful settings. He designs the best action-packed plots. He offers adventure far better than any storybook. The reason why, dear friend, is because our Father in Heaven is our very own Master Author, "looking unto Jesus, the author and finisher of our faith…" (Hebrews 12:2, NKJV) He is the author and finisher of our faith. He began this story, and no matter how weary we become, He will complete it, "He who begun a good work in you will complete it until the day of Jesus Christ." (Philippians 1:6, NKJV) Now we know that He began the good work in us, and we know He will finish it. What do we do in the meantime, though? What do we do when things just straight get tough?

We run! No, we don't run away. We run with endurance:

> *Therefore we also, since we are surrounded by so great a cloud of witnesses, let us lay aside every weight, and the sin which so easily ensnares us, and let us run with endurance the race that is set before us.*
> *Hebrews 12:1-2, NKJV*

The Amplified says, "...stripping off every unnecessary weight and the sin which so easily and cleverly entangles us, let us run with endurance and active persistence the race that is set before us, [looking away from all that will distract us and] focusing our eyes on Jesus..." (Hebrews 12:1-2, AMP) Run with endurance and active persistence. There's that word again. Active. Sounds like action. Hmm, maybe I'm really on to something here!

Anyhow, what is the picture in your mind when you read "run with endurance"? Do you picture a sprinter or a hurdler? Of course not! You picture a long-distance runner (#thisisamarathonpeople). In fact, you might even be one of those runners. What do we know about marathon runners, then?

#visualize: it's a solo race; there's possibly a cheering section waiting for the runner at the finish line; other participants are either way ahead or way behind; the runner battles fatigue, extreme thirst, potential weather elements, sore joints and muscles, and loneliness; the runner also begins the race without seeing the finish line. By the time the runner reaches the finish line, she is sweaty, exhausted, bedraggled, sore, and victorious. Does she give up without seeing the finish line? No, she knows the finish line is there. However, it's going to take great endurance and persistence to arrive there. To the runner, the race is worth the effort.

Ours will be as well. Because, dear friend, the difference between the marathon and our race is, we are not alone. We have the Holy Spirit inside of us, giving us the strength to endure. Endurance is the fact or power of enduring an unpleasant or difficult process or situation without giving way; the capacity of something to last or to withstand. *This* is how we must continue to run our race; with endurance, with active persistence, with undivided attention and our eyes focused on Jesus, with no plan B, and with boldness:

> *Therefore let us [with privilege] approach the throne of grace [that is, the throne of God's gracious favor] with confidence and without fear, so that we may receive mercy [for our failures] and find [His amazing] grace to help in time of need [an appropriate blessing, coming just at the right moment].* Hebrews 4:16, AMP

And in The Message, "So let's walk right up to him and get what he is so ready to give. Take the mercy, accept the help." We are not running this race alone. We are also not running this race oblivious to the finish line. We know what He's promised us. So, when we get fatigued and sore and lonely, let us continue to keep running. As long as we don't quit or give up, we *will* get to our finish line.

So, when AF still decides to pay you a visit, what are you going to do?

KEEP BELIEVING. KEEP CONFESSING. KEEP SINGING. KEEP PREPARING. KEEP LOVING. KEEP WAITING. KEEP LIVING. KEEP RENEWING. KEEP REJOICING. KEEP STRETCHING. KEEP RUNNING.

GOING DEEPER:
- In what ways will you begin living as though you are already The Joyful Mother of children?
- Get quiet and make a list of all thoughts floating around in your mind. What does God's Word say about each one?
- Think of people in your life you can begin rejoicing or mourning with. Invite them on your journey as well.
- What action of faith do you feel God leading you to do?
- Scriptures to study: Ps. 40:1; Ps. 25:3; Ps. 27:14; Ps. 130:5-6; Is. 40:31; Heb. 6:15; Heb. 11:11; Ps. 69:3; Hab. 2:3; 2 Cor. 12:9-10; Eph. 4:23; 2 Cor. 10:3-5; Matt. 6:25-34; Is. 26:3; Phil. 4:6-7; Matt. 14; Acts 2:42; 1 Cor. 12:25-26; Rom. 12:15; James 2:14-26; Heb. 12:2; Phil. 1:6; Heb. 12:1-2; Heb. 4:16.

Chapter eight
THE WILDERNESS

#THEPROCESS

The Wilderness (#eek). That can't be good, right? Don't freak out. The reason for this chapter is simply because there is a process; a method to this madness, if you will. You know I'm writing because this is my faith action. I'm writing each chapter as I live it. I don't have a permanent outline written down from start to finish. The Holy Spirit daily gives me revelation in my quiet times as I walk out my own grueling, heartbreaking journey. In fact, if you saw my journal entries, you might be tempted to think I was seriously unbalanced.

With that said, there have been many, many days throughout this last number of years that I have literally refused to write. This is crazy to me. Authors don't write books like this; no one writes their testimony down before it even happens, do they? Then again, a virgin can't conceive, a man can't be raised from the dead, and a donkey can't speak, and yet, it happened. Anything is possible with God. That doesn't mean I still don't feel cray-cray. Nor that I don't still struggle.

#vulnerabilityalert: This chapter's outline came to me on October 24, 2015, but I am finally writing it on January 20, 2016. Since October, I had been stuck in the dreaded BWD (#barrenwomandepression). I've gone back and read my book multiple times and am now just coming out of it. That exhortation chapter really does help! Now I know why He wanted me to include it before this one.

In this chapter, I will reveal to you how I came out of the BWD. But I warn you; it's not pretty. This whole journey is not pretty. I am not at all sugarcoating anything, nor sitting here enduring this race with my sense of humor intact and a smile on my face. Umm, no. Being barren is horrific. It is the most difficult experience that I have ever gone through. It is one I would not wish on anyone. See if you can relate from my journal:

> *Every month I grieve for the children I never conceive. I get my hopes up and try to have faith, but then when AF comes, I mourn. Every holiday, I mourn. Every time one of my friends or family announces their pregnancy, I mourn. I'm never satisfied or content; constantly thirsting for the drink of water I'm not sure I'll ever have; starving with a hunger that's never sated; always wanting and dreaming; a huge gaping hole in my already broken heart. The broken heart that hardly has time to mend before the next cycle and the next broken heart. The Barren Woman is the saddest and loneliest woman you will ever meet. She is greatly misunderstood. She is not jealous or envious; she is broken and hopeless. She is fighting for her joy and sanity on a daily basis, fighting for her faith and fighting to convince herself that God still loves her, that God hears her prayers, that God created her with a mother's heart for a reason...*

This is my reality. Is it yours? You are not alone. However, throughout this next chapter, you may *feel* very alone. In fact, *Oh how He loves me* is what you might keep telling yourself over and over again as you hit this process in your journey. You might question everything: your purpose, your sanity, and God's love for you. But, at the same time, you might be praising Him and thanking Him and rejoicing. Weird, I know.

Now, don't be scared. The Process is a necessary part of your wilderness journey. It is part of the big fight. You can do this. You are ready for it. God has been preparing you, stretching you, and growing you for this season. I'm right there with ya sister! Truly. I am enduring a couple of these processes as I write. You might find yourself in one of them, as well:

1. Testing

At some point, you might feel like you are being tested in one area or another. It's like you *know* there's some test you are supposed to pass. Perhaps, you even thought you had failed a test that seemed to cycle over and over again. Scripture tells us to test all things carefully (1 Thessalonians 5:21); more specifically, from a preacher or teacher. God Himself tells us to test Him in the area of our tithe and giving:

> *"Bring all the tithes (the tenth) into the storehouse, so that there may be food in My house, and test Me now in this," says the Lord of hosts, "if I will not open for you the windows of heaven and pour out for you [so great] a blessing until there is no more room to receive it."*
> *Malachi 3:10, AMP*

Testing is indeed a Biblical principle. It is something we are encouraged to do in several different passages, which we will see as we go on. But first, did you know we are actually supposed to test *ourselves*? Paul encouraged the body to, "Test and evaluate yourselves to see whether you are in the faith and living your lives as [committed] believers…" (2 Corinthians 13:5, AMP) And the Psalmist said it like this, "Examine me, O LORD, and try me; Test my heart and my mind." (Psalm 26:2, AMP)

As you see, in our walk with the Lord, we are to ask Him to examine us and test our hearts. If we are to make testing ourselves a discipline and pattern in our lives, wouldn't it make sense that God would then test us in that very area? Also, if we don't test ourselves, do you believe God might test us instead (#hmm #gettindeep)? Anyhow, here is why we are tested:

- to reveal what's in our hearts (Deut. 8:2, 2 Chr. 29:17, 32:31, Jn. 6:6)
- to know our love (Deut. 13:3)

- to humble us (Deut. 8:2, 8:16)
- to test our obedience (Ex. 16:4, 20:20)
- to test our faith (Gen. 22:1, Jas. 1:3, 1 Pt. 4:12)
- and to refine us (Ps. 66:10, Ps. 105:19, Prov. 17:3, Is. 48:10, Jer. 9:7, Zech. 13:9)

#disclaimer: I am not in any way saying that God inflicted us with infertility to test us. Barrenness is *not* a testing of our faith, obedience, or refinement. That, my friend, is a lie and goes against the very nature of God. I repeat, He did *not* put barrenness on our bodies to test us.

However, as we seek God on our journey to become The Joyful Mother of children, we might notice that we are indeed being tested in the above areas in our spiritual lives. As a matter of fact, being tested in our faith is one of the most difficult tests we will probably ever go through. Abraham was tested in his faith when he was getting ready to kill his own son as a sacrifice. This was the very son God promised him. Do you think that was easy? Do you think that made sense? (#heckno) But, it was a test that he just so happened to pass successfully. Is God going to ask you to do something this radical? (#idontknow) Are you going to be tested in *something*? (#youbetcha)

2. Discipline

Not only are we tested, more than that, we are also disciplined. Am I purposely scaring you? Actually, no. Again, The Process can be ugly. Discipline can be ugly; and painful. But why is it done? Because of love:

> *...My child, don't underestimate the value of the discipline and training of the Lord God, or get depressed when he has to correct you. For the Lord's training of your life is the evidence of his faithful love. And when he draws you to himself, it proves you are his delightful child.*
> *Hebrews 12:5-6, TPT*

God is our Father. Therefore, our Abba loves us as His children. Do children need discipline? (#duh) Just in the same way, *we* need discipline as God's daughters. Until I fully realized the blessings of discipline,

I had not believed this because we don't see any blessings whatsoever when we are in this process. Afterward, though, we are so very thankful for His intervention and guidance. Here is why:

> *No discipline is enjoyable while it is happening – it's painful! But afterward there will be a peaceful harvest of right living for those who are trained in this way. Hebrews 12:11, NLT*

#sigh: A peaceful harvest. Doesn't that sound divine? But, let me be clear on something: discipline is *not* punishment. In a process such as this, it is imperative we remember that Jesus has already died on the cross for our sins. He *was* the punishment. God doesn't sit up there in Heaven waiting to strike us dead with a bolt of lightning if we mess up. Likewise, He is not punishing us with infertility or miscarriage. If that is your thinking, get rid of it (#throwitout)!

The whole purpose of going through the discipline process with the Lord is to teach us self-discipline (1 Corinthians 9:27, 1 Timothy 4:7). It is also so we can share in His holiness (Hebrews 12:10). God wants us to be holy, and He wants us to be self-disciplined, controlled, restrained, able to withstand temptation, and able to boldly endure hardship and come out as overcomers (#thatslove).

Honestly, on this journey and in this season as The Barren Woman, we come up with some pretty messed up mindsets. I know I've been guilty of several. But, I now look back and am thankful for His discipline, the loving way He corrected me and showed me how to change my thinking, and the way He removed me from comfortable relationships, situations, or jobs. That's discipline. And it is during these times we need to seek Him more than ever to find out what He is teaching us. Because, as a teacher myself, I am 100% positive the Great Teacher sees every moment as a teachable moment. He loves us so much that He's always going to be teaching us something in order to build our characters to become more like Him.

If you feel like you're being disciplined right now, rejoice! Because, dear friend, you *will* get there. You *will* reap a peaceful harvest.

3. Pruning

"All growth is rewarded with pruning." -Bill Johnson

In this wilderness journey, pruning is my least favorite part of The Process. Think about it. You trim back both dead and living branches. It kind of doesn't make sense, right? Like, why cut off the branches that are doing just fine?

I have rose bushes on the side of my house. They are beautiful and resilient. Right after we planted them, they shot up. They didn't shoot out in a full, pretty bush; but up, like a short, not-so-pretty tree. I knew after the winter I needed to prune them, but because we didn't have much of a winter this year, buds started showing up on these bushes earlier than usual. Guess what I had to do? Yep! I had to cut off perfectly healthy branches and buds to get them in the correct shape. Months later, my bushes are beautifully filling out like a normal bush. Here soon, I expect to see some gorgeous roses.

To get to this state of fruitfulness, I had to cut off healthy branches. They looked healthy from the outside, but on the inside, these branches were totally misshapen. They were growing up instead of out. If this continued, it would have been at risk of snapping off in the wind. So yeah, the reason I dislike this process so much is because God prunes what I think are perfectly healthy branches; branches that I wasn't ready to get rid of; branches that were bearing perfectly good fruit; fruit with which I was perfectly comfortable. However, the branches that I thought were bearing good fruit were actually hurting me and causing my insides to be misshapen (#dowegetityet).

Jesus says, "I am the true vine, and My Father is the vinedresser. Every branch in Me that does not bear fruit He takes away; and every branch that bears fruit He prunes, that it may bear more fruit." (John 15:1-2, NKJV) Therefore, every moment is not only a teachable moment; it is also a pruning moment. Living for the Lord is truly a constant adventure! One definitely never gets bored, that's for sure:

> *Abide in Me, and I in you. As the branch cannot bear fruit of itself, unless it abides in the vine, neither can you, unless you abide in Me.*

> *I am the vine, you are the branches. He who abides in Me, and I in him, bears much fruit; for without Me you can do nothing. John 14:4-5, NKJV*

Abide; remain; do not depart; continue to be present; be held and kept continually; remain as one with Him. *This* is how we are supposed to live our lives. We are to allow Him to be with us and within us, allowing ourselves to be held by Him continually. This is how we overcome and get through the pruning with our joy intact.

But *why* does He prune us? For our good; because He loves us; so we bear much fruit, and bring glory to Him. That's why we are on this earth to begin with; for His glory. As we make the decision to serve Him and do things His way, pruning will forever be a part of our lives. And it's okay if we're not at a place where we can be happy about this. Truly, it is.

We *will* get there, dear friend. Here's why: After we are pruned, we are promised a "new thing," "Do not remember the former things, Or ponder the things of the past. Listen carefully, I am about to do a new thing, Now it will spring forth…" (Isaiah 43:18, AMP) So get excited, sister! Just as my rose bush flourished and became healthier, so will you! Just as it produced big, beautiful blooms, so will you!

4. The breaking point

After you go through these phases of testing, discipline, and pruning, you reach a place called the breaking point. This place might be attained years into this process (#likeme), or it may be sooner. For several years, I was stuck in the testing and discipline phases, but the pruning hasn't lasted as long. The reason why is that I have been abiding in Him through it all. Therefore, the testing period of my heart has lessened. With that said, this section is going to be filled with so much content that I encourage you to go slowly and fully take it in (#deepbreaths).

What is the breaking point? It is a place you reach on this journey where you get straight fed up. It's the crossroads you reach after you have tried it all; after you have exhausted every ounce of energy and attempt; and I finally have. Let's see if you can relate. Here is my journal entry from March 22, 2016:

> *I am so exhausted. Exhausted from my expectations. Exhausted from others' expectations of what my life should look like. So exhausted from the hoping and dreaming and the high expectations; the grief and the mourning and brokenness. So tired of trying and working and charting and timing...*

#sigh #vulnerabilityalert: As you already know, my husband and I tried for years just to "let it happen." In my fear, without knowing, I was too afraid to get checked out physically. We thought I wasn't conceiving because I was so stressed out with my full-time teaching position. I began reading books and building my knowledge of what the Word said. We then began lining up the dates and using the ovulation predictor kits, but still no results. It was after this that I quit my job to stay home. I was stress-free, but still no BFP (#bigfatpositive).

I thought that something must be wrong with my faith or something was wrong with our bodies. So, I finally made sure to get our physicals and adjusted accordingly. I began to chart and take temps, research natural fertility supplements, etc. I worked through some of the fear and got a full physical evaluation. It turns out, everything was functioning properly. We were both perfectly able to conceive.

As you can probably guess, I began to seriously question God. I thought that since our bodies were capable, there must be some reason why God was preventing us from having children. We started praying, confessing, and attempting to build our faith with what the Word said.

Then, we made sure to explore some fertility treatments. But, these stressed us out more than anything else we had ever done. Still, nothing happened. We got angry, and bitter, and depressed, and it was all we thought about and all we talked about, and all our marriage revolved around until we couldn't even enjoy a date night because we used it to escape and/or to vent our frustrations. Whew! See what I mean?

We. Have. Exhausted. It. All.

What did we do? We prayed. We re-evaluated (#breakingpointsummeduprightthere). We thought, *Hmm, what are we missing here? We're doing all the "right" things. The other areas of our lives are prosper-*

ous, except this one area. What are we doing wrong? Through prayer and re-evaluation, we began to focus on Him and not ourselves; at least, I did. My husband was in a different place, and that's okay. The Holy Spirit was working on him differently than me. If you are frustrated and feel like you are not getting support from your hubby, that's normal and is okay for now. Leave him be (#easiersaidthandone).

Back to focusing on God – I kept thinking, *What does He want from us? What are we missing?* You see, the breaking point is a place where you have become so utterly sick and tired, fed up, and exhausted of striving with God (#andagainstGod). That is what my husband and I had been doing all along. And dear sister, that's what you might be doing, too. I'm not saying that everything else previous to this chapter is moot. The opposite is true. In fact, this is all part of the "grand plan" to get us to this point right here (#anewthing).

5. A new thing

Now, don't get your hopes up. This new thing is not a baby (#notyetanyways). To recap, after we are tested, disciplined, pruned and pruned again, and pruned some more, we arrive at the breaking point. There are no guarantees it'll be after steps one, two, and three, however, I guarantee that you *will* get there.

While you're being pruned, a new thing will begin to bud in your spirit. As you abide in Jesus and continue to seek Him and know Him more, He will show you glimpses of what He has for you. Once you reach the breaking point and begin asking the tougher questions, these new things will become even more evident. Here is why:

> "DEEP TRIALS WILL CAUSE DEEP CHARACTER FLAWS TO COME TO THE SURFACE."
> -ROBERT MORRIS

I love this quote, but seriously. This is the new thing? Character flaws? In case you didn't already know, we are in a trial. In fact, we are in a tribulation, which is a really long, especially difficult trial. As I've mentioned previously, this is not a punishment from God, nor is it even caused by God. However, I believe He does some of His most miraculous work in the midst of tribulations for this reason: character, "...we also glory in tribulations, knowing that tribulation produces perseverance; and perseverance, character; and character, hope." (Romans 5:3-4, NKJV)

We all have a purpose and assignment here on earth. Outside of desiring to be a mom, we were created for something more. However, *I* always felt like my main purpose in this life was to be a wife and a mother. So that's where my focus continued to be, as you already know (#obviously). Yes, I am a wife. I am also a mother to my stepson. As my womb continued to be unfulfilled, though, I eventually realized that there must be something more I am meant to do; something eternal; something that can only be achieved through the power and grace of the Holy Spirit; a seed He planted within me when I was a child; the beginning pages of the book He's already written for my life; my specific assignment; in more glamorous terms, my destiny. You have one, too, dear friend. And I'm sorry to burst your bubble, but the only way you will arrive at your destiny and fulfill your assignment is if you have the character to sustain it (#ouch).

God is building our characters. One of the ways we get there is through tribulation and perseverance. Not only that, we are encouraged to *glory* in this tribulation. Glory equals rejoice. Yep. Here is where you will praise and thank God for your season of barrenness. You may not be there yet, but you will be (#trustme).

#disclaimer: I am fully convinced that it is God's will to give children to anyone who wants them. It is not His will for us to go multiple years without conceiving. With that said, character building through tribulation seems to be one of those supernatural laws of the universe. It just happens. It is one way in which our merciful Father turns around what was meant for evil into good.

In the next few paragraphs, you will see how the Holy Spirit revealed these new things to me. They all occurred simultaneously, surprisingly (#thatshowyouknowitsGod). But, during my striving and questioning over the years, I began questioning God's love for me. To be truly honest,

I have questioned His love for me my entire adulthood. I knew this was not okay. I became absolutely sick of this unbelief. How could I have faith or even believe for a baby if I didn't truly believe that God loved me? Some seasons I knew God loved me. Some seasons I questioned Him. In fact, every month, oh say, around the middle of the month, I would question His love for me. I was fed up with the wavering. I knew I desperately needed help with this character flaw. But, how was I to change this deep-rooted way of thinking? Where did I start?

At the same time I acknowledged this character flaw, I began experiencing an irrational, inexcusable fear. I became terrified that something deeper was going on with me. This didn't make sense. I thought I had already managed this fear back when I got all the testing done. My thoughts became completely morbid. Not only that, I was having dreams that I was sick with a terminal illness, or that my husband and stepson were going to die. Like I said, morbid. I figured out pretty quickly I was being tormented by that evil, ugly guy named Satan. How was I to change this? How was I to do battle against this irrational fear when I was wavering in my faith of His love for me?

Finally, during this season, I kept getting this impression that I needed to fast. I didn't know why. I didn't understand the correlation between fasting and fear and questioning God's love for me. In fact, I didn't even know a whole lot about fasting, period. But I knew it was Biblical and was practiced by the New Testament church. I knew it was something I wanted to do. I needed to begin fasting regularly as I grew closer to the Lord. I knew that, in the past when I participated in our church-wide fasts, I was blessed. I just didn't understand why He wanted me to fast *now* (#funfact: The original outline of this book was the result of a fast).

As I mulled over the fast for a few weeks, I came to study it because it was the most concrete new thing He had given me. So, it was the simplest place to start. Here is what I learned from The Principle of the Fast[1]:

- We receive a reward from the Father (Matthew 6:16-18).

---

1   Morris, Robert, Gateway Church, The Principle of the Fast, January 6, 2007, www.gatewaypeople.com

- Fasting weakens our body/temple through this discipline. Therefore, He can be our strength (1 Corinthians 9:27).
- Fasting strengthens our soul (the mind, will, and emotions) to rely on Him (James 4:7).

Shortly after I listened to this message, I had my hallelujah moment (#lightbulb). Here are parts of my journal entry:

For The Barren Woman, who has gone years without feeling loved, it takes a fast to retrain and strengthen the soul; to break habits of wrong thinking; to learn that God desires her to be a mother more than she does. The fast acts as a detox of the mind, body, and emotions. It must be done in order to have faith/belief. Wow! I've had fasting on my mind knowing that it was to be studied and used somehow in my book. I just had no clue that it was to be used as a cleanse and detox. But it's true. It's what I need. God, You have revealed my wrong and toxic thoughts. The only way to change these thoughts at the root is to detox and cleanse my mind. Fasting is the only way to accomplish that. I desperately need a detox of the mind. Something needs to change within my thinking. I cannot have great faith and authority while still having doubts about Your love for me. I'm tired of feeling like I'm crazy because I jump around from my soul (mind, will, emotions) to my spirit and back again. I desire consistency and clarity to hear You speak to me. I'm tired of my undisciplined mind having control, and my up and down emotions guiding me. I need this self-discipline, and I need my willpower to be strengthened in order to go all out in my faith.

After writing all of that down, you would think I'd begin the fast, right? Umm, no. I still didn't know *why* I was fasting. Yes, I needed the mind detox to eliminate the questioning of God's love for me but, what about that mysterious, morbid fear? Shouldn't I tackle that first? I just didn't have peace that fasting was solely meant for removing the toxic thoughts. I'm stubborn, and I'm easily distracted. I needed concrete logic to support my decision (#itsthenerdinme).

A few more weeks went by as I sought the Lord and studied fasting. I also studied up on that mysterious fear I had been experiencing. Because He knows me and loves me, He allowed me this extra time. One day, after a morning of this study, I had another hallelujah moment. This one deserves a drum roll (#dumdumdum).

Fear.

Fear is the toxic root. Fear is the reason why I didn't feel like God loved me. Fear is the reason I avoided doctors for over ten years. Fear is why I had been stuck in this seemingly endless cycle of soul to spirit and back again. Fear had been my BFF my entire life up to that point. So much so that I didn't know what life was like without it. I could so clearly see what I couldn't see before. As fear escalated, I could finally see and completely purge this deeply rooted character flaw, this character flaw that had paralyzed me and prevented me from walking in obedience to the Lord. It could have even hindered me from reaching my destiny and achieving my assignment!

What, then, did I do? Began my fast! I put my book and any other kind of ministry commitments on hold. I knew, that I knew, that I knew, that I needed to get this taken care of once and for all. God is so good and loving. He even provided the time to plan my fasting menu and even gave me a book study to assist in my healing (#ilovetoread). Thus began my mind and body detox through what I call the fast; thus began my new revelation of His love.

#disclaimer: Don't misunderstand me. This is not a "step" to get pregnant, nor is it something that I am encouraging you to do. I am simply explaining the new thing revealed to me after my pruning; the character flaw brought to light and set free. *I* had to fast and get that full detox of the mind. Because, you see, in order to move forward in this process, we need a new revelation of God's love.

Because I had such deep-seated fear, I wasn't able to fully experience His love. As I studied fear, however, I soon learned that anywhere I am afraid is an area where I don't know the love of God. Because "There is no fear in love; but perfect love casts out fear, because fear involves torment. But he who fears has not been made perfect in love." (1 John 4:18, NKJV) If I am afraid in a specific area, it is because I have not allowed God's love to *perfect* me in that area (#nowthatsquotable).

If you struggle with the same tormenting question of God's love for you, I encourage you to allow the pruning and abiding in Him to reveal this new thing. What character flaw may be preventing you from perfectly knowing God's love; preventing you from reaching your destiny; not just your desire to be a mother, but preventing your eternal assignment here on earth?

Is it unforgiveness, perfectionism, anger, rebellion, your coping mechanisms, self-pity, insecurity, fear, selfishness, unbelief, past trauma? Search your heart and seek God. Continue to allow those character flaws to make their ugly appearance. Yes, you might feel conviction (that's what the Holy Spirit does), and even have some things to repent of, but you will be set free and closer to your destiny (#convictionisnotcondemnation).

After my fast, it was like falling in love for the first time. I didn't want to be around anyone else but my Lover, reading His love notes to me and singing cheesy love ballads in return (#ilovepsalms).

In closing, tribulation builds our characters and brings us closer to sharing God's glory. This is why we get to rejoice in this season of barrenness. Because, as we reach this new place, we can tangibly experience His love and His presence.

As we learn, grow, and weed out deeply rooted issues, which we never knew we had, let us study and dig deeper into this new love. Let us search the Word and find all we can about His love for us. Then, as we rejoice and glory in our barren wombs, we will finally discover who we were meant to be; our identity, not as The Barren Woman, not as a mother, but as a daughter of the Creator of the universe. And that will become enough for us. In fact, it will become *more* than enough. So much so that we will be willing to sacrifice anything that is competing for our affections.

GOING DEEPER:

- In your spiritual life, think of a test that keeps cycling. What do you think God wants you to overcome? What steps will you take to do so?
- Think of a time when you were disciplined by the Lord. What was the fruit of His discipline?
- Are you at the breaking point? Why or why not?
- What new things/character flaws are being revealed to you? How is God leading you to overcome them?
- Describe how you've been striving with/against God.
- Participate in a fast. Record your experience.
- Scriptures to study: 1 Thess. 5:21; Mal. 3:10; 2 Cor. 13:5; Ps. 26:2; Lam. 3:40; Deut.8:2; 2 Chron. 29:17, 32:31; Jn. 6:6; Deut. 13:3; Deut. 8:2, 16; Ex. 16:4, 20:20; Gen. 22:1; Jas. 1:3; 1 Pt. 4:12; Ps. 66:10; Ps. 105:19; Prov. 17:3; Is. 48:10; Jer. 9:7; Zech. 13:9; Prov. 13:24; Heb. 12:5-6; Rev. 3:19; Heb. 12:10-11; 1 Cor. 9:27; 1 Tim. 4:7; Jn. 15:1-5; Is. 43:18; Rom. 5:3-4; Gen. 50:20; Rom. 8:28; 1 Jn. 4:18.

Chapter Nine

THE PROCESS OF SURRENDER

At the conclusion of The Process, we come to a fork, a choice: strive or surrender. This is a choice that only you can make. It takes determination, intentionality, and that new revelation of God's love, which you hopefully discovered after reading the previous sections and taking time to go through them (#hinthint). Both options are not so pleasant. For me, however, the direction I chose was an easy one to make after receiving the new revelation of God's love (#thatskey).

One of the positive new things I learned was that I had reached a place where I wanted to be in His presence *more* than I wanted a baby. I wanted His will for me so much more than my own will, my own agenda, or even my own heart's desires. Do I still believe that God's will is for everyone to have a baby who wants one? Yes, I do. Why? Because His Word is truth. Yet, because I was having so much fun falling in love with Jesus all over again, what I wanted didn't matter as much anymore. I was beginning to be okay with being the exception to the rule. I trusted Him, and with such deep conviction, knew that no matter what, I would serve Him and fulfill what He's called me to do. If He could use me for His purposes more as The Barren Woman than the Joyful Mother of children, so be it. I was perfectly okay with that.

However, after about five days, give or take, the euphoria wore off. The initial joy was short-lived. Because, dear friend, from this choice of surrender came another process (#noooo #characterdevelopment). Yes, ma'am. The Process of Surrender.

You see, it's not as if my desire to have a baby diminished. If anything, it grew. Trust me; I have prayed many, many times for God to take this desire away (#sillyprayer). Yet, it is still within me, like a fire in my soul, burning and raging and aching throughout my entire body. I didn't want anything competing with this newfound love, yet I still wanted to hold onto this lifelong dream. Back and forth. Hot and cold. Strive and surrender.

So, in my journal writing one day, God gave me the process of surrendering this desire once and for all. Scary huh? Umm, yeah. I was petrified. You think the thoughts, *But I was meant to be a mom. But it's all I've ever wanted. What am I supposed to do now? Can I really lay this down? God, first take the desire away, and then I'll surrender it to you. You're asking me to surrender a dream that's been within my heart since I was a toddler? What kind of love is this? Can't I just enjoy your love without you asking me to do something this hard? I just had to deal with all those character flaws, and now this, too? I don't think I can do it, Abba. God, please! I don't want to give up this dream! What if I really am barren for the rest of my life? I don't think I can do this! Please, daddy, please!*

But, because I was so secure in His love for me and knew He had my best interests at heart, I decided to go through with giving Him this dream. He is a good God. He is a good Daddy. I knew, if I did surrender this desire, He would either restore it or replace it. So, I made the choice to do something I had never done before in all my years of adulting: I chose to surrender.

1. Choose to surrender

God is sovereign. He is the Boss. He is the King. For me to admit this was the first step in The Process of Surrender. He is almighty, unchanging, unwavering, all-knowing, worthy of all my praise, and worthy of my life. In order to fully surrender, we must acknowledge that He is sovereign.

What does this look like? For me, it came through my journal writing. I wrote out the words of submitting to His sovereignty, and I wrote down exactly what I was surrendering: my desire to conceive with my husband; my desire to have my husband's child; my desire to be pregnant; my desire to give my stepson a baby brother or sister. I confessed every single desire associated. It could look different for you. You could kneel by the side of your bed, go to the front of the church for prayer, or lay prostrate on the floor, face to the ground (#beentheredonethat). Whatever it takes.

2. Die to yourself

Eek. This sounds painful, doesn't it (#yep). However, it goes along with choosing to surrender and submitting to God's sovereignty. As hard as it sounds, it must be done. Even Jesus said, "If any of you wants to be my follower, you must give up your own way, take up your cross daily, and follow me." (Luke 9:23, NLT)

The cross is an instrument of death; thereby, it symbolizes our willingness to give our lives sacrificially. That's what "die to self" means; taking up our cross and choosing to die to our wants and desires. When we make this sacrifice, we speak God's love language, for we know sacrifice is one way in which He receives love. Because this was the very way He evidenced His love through His Son, "For God so loved the world that he gave his one and only Son, that whoever believes in him shall not perish but have eternal life." (John 3:16, NIV)

What better way to surrender to our Abba God than by taking up our cross and dying to ourselves, sacrificing the very desires that we have carried within us since we were little girls. Is it easy? Heck, no. Will this be your most difficult step? Quite possibly.

3. Repent

Step three is another doozie. Who likes to hear the word "repent"? Unfortunately, it can conjure up thoughts of fire and brimstone and holy rolling preachers from back in the day. They would chuck condemnation all over you from the pulpit. This is *not* that repentance. Rather, as you surrender and die to yourself, true repentance genuinely occurs. What is true repentance? It is simply a turning away of the heart and mind off oneself to God.

In the midst of enduring this process, I couldn't stop bawling my eyes out and slobbering all over the place (#uglycryupinhere). I instinctively began repenting and asking forgiveness for making my desire to conceive more important than my desire to be close to my Father, asking forgiveness for trying to be in control, for pouting and wallowing in self-pity when my period would come around, for – you name it.

This repentance flowed from the brokenness I was experiencing within my heart, "You do not desire a sacrifice, or I would offer one. You do not want a burnt offering. The sacrifice you desire is a broken spirit. You will not reject a broken and repentant heart, O God." (Psalm 51:16-17, NLT)

From surrender; to dying to oneself; to sacrifice of a broken and repentant heart. How pleased He is by this! Dear friend, He is so pleased with you right now. I love to picture Jesus sitting on His throne with a big cheesy grin across His face.

4. Mourn and grieve

What a perfect entrance into the next step. After repentance comes the time to mourn and grieve. Not in self-condemnation, but in the cleansing release of our beautiful surrender. My journal entry from March 24, 2016, says it all:

Here, other couples are celebrating new life, and we are experiencing the death of a dream. I'm grieving, and as I die to myself, my soul is grieving and in pain. I'm scared. I've always had hope and knew that eventually, I'd have a baby. It was always an eventuality and a possibility. Now I'm not too sure. Holy Spirit, how do I kill this dream? How do I surrender this expectation and desire without losing hope? Without doing so in defeat and hopelessness? I have to be prepared that I may never have children; I may never know the joy and miracle of life growing inside of me, or the intimacy that comes from creating a child with my soulmate. It just would've been so nice to have a baby together and to answer the desire of Jr.'s heart as well. Our little family feels so incomplete. Empty. A void. I hurt so bad. It feels like a piece of me is being ripped from my body, like an abortion of a piece of my soul...

As you mourn and grieve, you need to be honest with God without holding back. He already knows what is in your heart, so you can let it all out. Give yourself some time. It will probably last a few days (#orweeks #ormonths).

5. Sacrifice of praise

You can see my turmoil, fears, and concerns in the above journal entry as I mourned and grieved. But, what came next took me totally by surprise. I was studying the story of Mary of Bethany (Mark 14). This is the Mary, of the "Mary and Martha" fame (Luke 10:38-42), and she was also Lazarus' sister. You know the one? "Lazarus, come forth!" Lazarus was raised from the dead, and if you've ever seen a passion play, this scene from John 11 is almost always reenacted.

In this particular account, Mary took her alabaster flask of expensive oil and anointed Jesus for His burial. Did she know she was anointing Him for burial? Probably not. She was probably using her expensive and precious oil simply to show her extravagant devotion to Jesus, an act of worship, a sacrifice of praise (Psalm 116:17; Hebrews 13:15-16). After all, He did bring her brother back from the dead.

We don't quite know, but she was probably either single or a widow and was sacrificing her dowry and her livelihood in that oil, worth a year's wages. I like to imagine she was softly crying as she lovingly sacrificed her future. I imagine her hands moving reverently over Jesus' head and face and smoothing back His hair, I imagine her releasing her hair from her messy bun and using it to rub in the oil on His feet while her tears fell unabashedly from her eyes to wipe the oil away, and I imagine Jesus with a satisfied smile on His face as He shushed the disgruntled disciple who thought she was wasting her money.

What took me by surprise is how completely and utterly okay I was with surrendering after studying this story more deeply. It was an act of extravagant devotion done to a worthy man who just happened to be the

Savior of her soul, of *my* soul. This was not something He was making me do or something I *had* to do, but something I was *honored* to do.

His pleasure is shown in what He said, "I assure you and most solemnly say to you, wherever the good news [regarding salvation] is proclaimed throughout the world, what she has done will be told in memory of her." (Mark 14:9, AMP) Mary's act of extravagant devotion, her sacrifice, has been told right along with the good news of the gospel. How significant is that (#mindblown #worldrocked)?

So, I got down on my knees and cried and poured out my surrender and praise and thanksgiving like I was Mary herself. In my journal entry from March 25, 2016, see if you can tell the difference:

My dream surrendered to You, simply in worship, in reverence of who You are. Because I love You more than I want to conceive a baby with my husband. I want Your dream and Your will more than mine. I give it all to You, Abba. I cheerfully release it and give it all to You because I love You more. Oh, how You love me. And how I love and adore You. And when I begin speaking to broken and hurting women, Mary's story will be told as a memorial, as You requested those so many years ago because You want all of us, including our deepest dreams and desires. Not as a demand but as worship. You want us to give it to You because we love You. This shows You just how much we love You. Because You are jealous, You want all of me – every crevice, every need, every dream, every hurt, every laugh, every joy. I am Yours. I anoint Your head and Your feet with my oil – my dream of conceiving. I pour every drop of this precious oil onto Your body. Every last bit of this desire, it's Yours. How You love me, Abba. You love that I am a worshiper, a woman after Your heart. I worship You in the deepest way I know how, and I release and give You all of my dreams and desires. Just as the tears stream down my face, so is the oil streaming down Yours as I anoint You with my surrender...

6. Surrender again

Now that we have learned what true surrender is, it's time to do it again. I know, I know, but now surrender your dream as a sacrifice of praise. This will probably need to happen daily, or hourly, by the minute, or by the second. (#sorrynotsorry #itssoworthit #trustme).

7. Mourn and grieve again

Allow yourself more grieving and mourning. This is normal, I assure you (#itsaprocess).

8. Embrace your weakness

Finally, let's move forward! This desire you have to conceive and be a mother may still be very prevalent. So, how do you handle this desire while in the process of surrendering it?

By embracing your weakness.

Clearly, our current weakness is our barren womb (#ouch). We are living a surrendered life, but we are still barren. We still hunger and thirst for that baby. Every day we have to die to ourselves and surrender our dreams all over again. But, here is where the relief comes into the picture. Because now, the Holy Spirit comes and takes all the pressure.

Previously, in the "Keep waiting" section, we discussed "boasting in our weakness." At first, when the Holy Spirit took me back to this same principle, I was surprised. Not really, though, because, ironically enough, throughout this process of surrender, I began to feel more secure with myself (#theloveofJesuswilldothat); so much so that I began studying "weakness."

I actually couldn't stop rejoicing over my barren womb since the very thing I used to despise had brought me to this intimacy with the Father. There was nothing like it. And I decided to embrace it fully. Let's look again at what Paul quoted:

> *That's why I take pleasure in my weaknesses, and in the insults, hardships, persecutions, and troubles that I suffer for Christ. For when I am weak, then I am strong. 2 Corinthians 2:10, NLT*

I now truly know what Paul was talking about. Taking pleasure and embracing our weaknesses comes in the course of living a surrendered life. Whereas we used to convince ourselves to be thankful, to boast in our weaknesses, it now flows from our hearts since we have become so secure in His love. I mean, I was *so* secure in my weaknesses that I actually made a list of every weakness I have! And I thanked God for each one.

You see, the things I dislike about myself or struggle with are the very things that provide the opportunity for God to "Daddy" me. When I acknowledge my weaknesses, that I need Him, He finally gets the opportunity to show me His love. My weaknesses are *why* I need the Good Shepherd to lead me. I am a sheep, a dumb, silly sheep. I would walk right into the path of a hungry wolf if I didn't embrace my weaknesses and let Him be strong for me (#dontbeasillysheep #beawisesheep).

9. Be satisfied

#vulnerabilityalert: I will continue to be real here. I know I was super excited and positive in the previous section. Truthfully, though, it wears off (#thisiswhyitsaprocess). The reality is, you will see another pregnancy announcement on your social media account. Worse yet, Mother's Day rolls around while Aunt Flo is just beginning to visit (#ouch).

How do we get through these tough days? How do we cope? After we have surrendered, died to self, and continued to embrace our weaknesses again and again, how do we find joy? How can we learn to be okay with our barrenness?

By choosing to be satisfied (#hangwithmehere).

I know, I know. You're probably thinking, *Huh? We're just supposed to be okay with our barrenness? This is the exciting end of the story?* No ma'am. Like I've said over and over, I am still, if not more so now, fully convinced that anyone who wants a baby can have one. Why? Because the Word is truth. I continue to measure anything and everything by it. Remember, your story might look completely different from mine, or maybe not. In obedience through the process, I am just writing it all down (#dontshootthemessenger).

Anyhow, if you are still up for the journey, let's move on, shall we? Let's look at this scripture again:

There are three things that are never satisfied – no, four that never say, 'Enough!':
the grave,
the barren womb,
the thirsty desert,
the blazing fire." Proverbs 30:15-16, NLT

Yet, I have good news for you! Your barren womb *can* be satisfied. But not like you think. As I have gone through The Process of Surrender and made the choice to surrender daily, I found myself journaling this statement: *Only You can satisfy me.* I began to study the word "satisfy." I thought I was going to get some big revelation. Instead, I received one verse, one scripture that has revolutionized my entire prayer life. It is, "For He satisfies the longing soul, and fills the hungry soul with goodness" (Psalm 107:9, AMP)

Does your soul long to conceive and become a mother? Does it ache with longing? Are you always thirsty? Always hungry for that dream to come true? Then this is the verse for you, "For he satisfies the thirsty and fills the hungry with good things." (Psalm 107:9, NLT) That's a promise, friend! *He* satisfies our longing soul; *He* quenches our thirst; *He* fills our hunger with good things!

However, we must let Him (#truth).

We use the same principle when letting Him be our strength when we are weak. We choose to allow Him to be our satisfaction; we learn to replace our longing with Him; we ask Him to fill our every need, every crevice of longing, with His love; we ask Him to be our joy, our strength, our fulfillment, and our happiness; we ask Him to make our deepest heart's desire to be simply in His presence and know Him more; we ask Him to fill our empty womb; we ask Him to complete the void, and we ask Him to be more than enough for us. He will do it. Try it and see and be satisfied.

10. Learn to be content

Finally, the last step in The Process of Surrender (#bigsighofrelief)! Trust me, I'm ready to move forward, too. Although I say that now, a few weeks from now, I'll be feeling all cray-cray again as we head into the topics of the next few chapters (#staytuned).

The Amplified Bible defines being content as satisfied to the point of not being disturbed or uneasy. So, learning to be content goes along with being satisfied. Once again, it should flow naturally (#orsupernaturally). Although, it's still not easy. Why? Because being content does not actually *come* naturally, we have to learn it. So, how do we do that?

By enduring times of tribulation and trial (#myopinion #takeitorleaveit).

I truly believe contentment is the key to abundant life here on earth, not just in this area but in every area. That's a topic for another day, however. Paul writes, "...for I have learned in whatever state I am, to be content..." (Philippians 4:11, NKJV). He learned how to be content, and so can we, just by being barren and following The Process of Surrender.

You will know you have entered true surrender if you get to the point of not being disturbed. That's not to say you won't have tough days, but tough days should no longer lead to the BWD (#barrenwomandepression) that you had previously. Instead, you should be able to bounce back more quickly and maintain hope. In fact, dear friends, maintaining hope is how we are technically fighting the big fight of faith.

When we go through tribulations, we are fighting while waiting with contentment. We are actively battling our minds and working through our deeply seated character flaws. But here is the good news! Tribulation produces perseverance. What does perseverance produce? Character. And, what does character produce? (#drumrollplease)

Hope!

Hope is a necessity on this journey to become The Joyful Mother of children. For a heart of hope is the healthy, fertile soil in which our desires are fulfilled, "Hope deferred makes the heart sick, But when desire is fulfilled, it is a tree of life." (Proverbs 13:12, AMP)

I know, I know. You're probably totally confused because we just surrendered, right? We made the choice to be content in our situations as they are, so why on earth is this inner hope bubbling to the surface, threatening to overflow?

Umm, yeah. I was wondering the same thing. After I got through this last step in The Process of Surrender, I was ready and willing to be content with my husband, my stepson, and my fur-babies. Seriously. I was ready, and I knew I would be okay. I would find happiness for the rest of my life.

However, God still hadn't removed the desire. In all honesty, the desire became even greater, more all-consuming. But it *felt* different. Instead of the desire accompanying thoughts of fear and despair, I felt hope, and excitement, and possibility, and peace. Why? Because, dear friend, I no longer have a sick heart! As difficult as all these processes have been, the hopelessness and fear were completely gone (#praiseJesus #areyourejoicingyet)! All that is left is healthy, fertile soil, primed and ready for that tree of life:

> *How joyful are those who fear the* LORD *– all who follow his ways! You will enjoy the fruit of your labor. How joyful and prosperous you will be!* **Your wife will be like a fruitful grapevine, flourishing within your home. Your children will be like vigorous young olive trees as they sit around your table.** *That is the* LORD's *blessing for those who fear him. (emphasis added) Psalm 128:1-4, NLT*

We are fruitful vines. We "will bear children as a vine bears grapes, our household lush as a vineyard." (Psalm 128:3, MSG) Big sigh. Doesn't that sound divine?

What is the point of all of this? Well, obviously, surrendering does not equal giving up. In fact, the opposite is true, *"Great faith doesn't come out of great effort, but out of great surrender." (Bill Johnson)* So, where do we go from here? You guessed it! Onward to great faith!

Going Deeper:

- Journal through each step in the Process of Surrender. Take your time and don't hold back.
- Scriptures to study: Lk. 9:23; Jn. 3:16; Ps. 51:16-17; Mk. 14; Ps. 116:17; Heb. 13:15-16; 2 Cor. 2:10; Prov. 30:15-16; Ps. 107:9; Phil. 4:11; Prov. 13:12; Ps. 128:1-4.

Chapter ten
The Faith Chapter

#RabbitTrailAlert:

So yeah, as you know, I am writing this book while I go through these processes or shortly after I receive my aha moments, hallelujah moments, and revelations. So technically, I've already been through this chapter I am about to write. In fact, I am way past it. I'd like to apologize in advance, if at any time I sound flippant or insensitive. As I write, I am simply assuming that, like me, you've come out of The Wilderness with guns a-blazing.

I realize that some of you might still be going through the processes. That's okay. That's why it was called The Process. It takes time. Thankfully, the beauty of a book is if you're not ready to keep reading, you can put it down. Because in order to truly grasp these next few chapters, you will have needed to come through The Process with your own bubbling hope and faith. Unfortunately, you can't ride on the coattails of mine. Does that make sense?

Please remember, this is *my* journey. There is no perfect "how-to" when conceiving a baby. All that I am doing is simply journaling and documenting my journal in book format; at least, that is what I'm attempting to do. Don't forget that every chapter has been written previously in my ripped-up, worn-out, tear-stained spiral notebooks. Please remember that I am not an educated writer, Bible scholar, theologian, or even a pastor. I am simply a woman who has a story to tell. I encourage each one of you to do the same. As you walk out this season of barrenness, journal and find out for yourself what God is speaking to you. And if you're not ready to move forward, then don't.

When I first received this outline almost three years ago now, what I call The Faith Chapter didn't even exist. The original outline went straight from Prepare Your Temple to Tell Your Story, which happens to be coming up. Well, if you go back and read from the beginning of the book, it sounds like I had it all together, right? I had the much-needed faith and belief to speak Life and confess and expect my miracle (#orsoithought).

However, unbeknownst to me, I had some serious character development to process through (#understatement). As you might realize by now, I am so incredibly thankful for my character development. I've been so tempted to go back and make changes to the previous chapters based on my newly found wisdom. But, surprise, surprise! The Holy Spirit doesn't want me to. For some reason, He wants me to be vulnerable and continue to show you how I have evolved and strengthened in my faith.

You see, in all appearances, it looks like I've come full circle. In fact, I was praying (#akawhining) to God about that very thing just a few months ago, wondering what the heck I just went through. Seriously. What was the point? Especially if it has just taken me back to where I was at the beginning of this book. But, as I said, everything feels so different. *I* feel so different. Instead of just knowing things in my head, His truth has become something wholly and completely believed in my heart. Hope has taken root. Deeply. Irrevocably. Nothing can change my course. I will never be the same again (#bornagainagain).

#backtothetopic: So, the entirety of God's Word is truth, right? As you know, I began with this seed of truth. However, it needed to be discovered, uprooted, re-planted, watered, fertilized, and nurtured. How did God accomplish this? By taking me through all of the previous chapters leading up to this one: The Faith Chapter. What is this supernaturally modified seed that is ready to grow and bloom?

Well, dear friends, I call it the mustard seed of faith. Weird, right? It's especially weird if you're not familiar with references to the mustard seed in the gospels, but that's okay. I will do my best to explain. But first, let's talk about faith. I believe the Holy Spirit has given me six discoveries to share with you. Let's get started, shall we?

1. You already have faith

Let's jump right in and establish this almost incomprehensible truth; this truth, which I only began to understand as I researched this chapter. Simply stated, you already have all the faith you will ever need for your miracle.

Here's why, "God has dealt to each one a measure of faith." (Romans 12:3, NKJV). Every one of us has been given a measure of faith. We already have faith, just like we have been given the gift of grace (Ephesians 2:8). Faith is a gift we received when we accepted His grace and became followers of Jesus, "To those who have received and possess [by God's will] a precious faith of the same kind as ours, by the righteousness of our God and Savior, Jesus Christ…" (2 Peter 1:1, AMP) So yeah, that means we have the same gift of faith as Jesus' disciples; a gift freely given to us just like our salvation.

Is this news to you like it was to me? Any hallelujah or aha moments out there? I was absolutely floored when I received this revelation. It completely rewired my thinking. For years, I have beaten myself up because I believed the untruth that *I* didn't have enough faith to please God (Hebrews 11:6). When in actuality, I have carried all the faith I will ever need simply from making the choice to follow Him (#mindblown)!

What is the problem, then? Why don't we see miracles? And more specifically, why don't we see that positive pregnancy test? Hang tight; I'll get there in a bit. First, let me clear up another misconception.

2. You have Jesus-faith

I have learned that I have all the faith I'll ever need. I. Me. I'm still making it about myself, right? *My* measure of faith. Given to *me*. But is that what we say about His grace? Does it become *my* grace? Umm, no.

It is given to us, but it is a free gift from Jesus. The same goes for faith. He is the gift Giver; therefore, it is *His* faith we are receiving:

> *I have been crucified with Christ; it is no longer I who live, but Christ lives in me; and the life which I now live in the flesh I live **by faith** in the Son of God, who loved me and gave Himself for me. (emphasis added) Galatians 2:20, NKJV*

I like to study the different translations to get the fuller meaning behind a scripture. Let's look at this same verse in Young's Literal Translation (YLT). It's not normally the one I go to, but you'll see why in just a sec, "...in the faith I live of the Son of God, who did love me and did give himself for me." In the NKJV, it says, "I live *by* faith in the Son of God," but in the YLT, it says, "in the faith I live *of* the Son of God."

Yes, I'm getting nerdy on you. What do two different prepositions have to do with anything? Everything! You see, I live in the faith *of* the Son of God. I live in the faith of Jesus. I operate in the faith of Jesus. I have Jesus-faith on the inside of me. It has never been, nor will it ever, be my own faith. I have been given the faith of Jesus Christ Himself. Besides Jesus on earth, here's an actual example of this Jesus-faith in operation. This is the account after a man was healed who had been lame since his mother's womb:

> *Now as the lame man who was healed held on to Peter and John, all the people ran together to them in the porch which is called Solomon's, greatly amazed. So when Peter saw it, he responded to the people: "Men of Israel, why do you marvel at this? Or why look so intently at us, as though by our own power or godliness we had made this man walk? The God of Abraham, Isaac, and Jacob, the God of our fathers, glorified His Servant Jesus, whom you delivered up and denied in the presence of Pilate, when he was determined to let Him go. But you denied the Holy One and the Just, and asked for a murderer to be granted to you, and killed the Prince of life, whom God raised from the dead, of which we are witnesses. And His name, through faith in His name, has made this man strong, whom you see and know.*

Yes, the faith which comes through Him has given him this perfect soundness *in the presence of you all." (emphasis added)*
Acts 3:11-16, NKJV

So, did Peter heal that man? Did he have to work really hard and pray for God to increase His faith? Did he have to strive and then berate himself because he didn't have enough faith? Of course not! It was Jesus' faith that gave that man perfect soundness and health. Peter simply yoked with Jesus and believed (#easypeasy).

But, back to this mustard seed thing. What does a mustard seed have to do with anything? Well, a not-so-wise prayer that my husband and I used to pray years ago was, "Lord, increase our faith." Because, of course, we had put the pressure on ourselves and thought our faith needed to grow in order to get where we wanted to be in our walks with God. In our spiritual immaturity, we didn't know that we already had all the faith we ever needed.

Thankfully, our patient God, in His mercy, saw to our hearts and continued to bless us throughout the years with new revelation and intimacy with Him. However, when it came to this issue of conceiving and getting pregnant, we always thought our faith needed to be increased or added to in some way. I don't feel so bad now knowing that the apostles asked Jesus for the same thing:

> *And the apostles said to the Lord, "Increase our faith." So the Lord said, "If you have faith as a mustard seed, you can say to this mulberry tree, 'Be pulled up by the roots and be planted in the sea,' and it would obey you." Luke 17:5-6, NKJV*

So, in reply, Jesus says, "If you have faith as a mustard seed..." Have you seen a mustard seed before? If not, look it up. It is so very teeny tiny. Truly, it's itsy bitsy. I currently use an image of a mustard seed as my cell phone's background. It reminds me throughout the day that something this tiny is all I need; and more than that, this mustard seed faith is already within me because it was given to me by Jesus Himself; and even more than that, this mustard seed faith is my catalyst to yoke with Jesus-faith and fully operate in His power.

3. Faith is rest

Here's why things feel different this time around; another reason why I have hope and peace and possibility; a reason why I cannot honestly say I've come full circle (#drumrollplease). Because I no longer carry the burden; this lie I have partnered with for so long; this lie that I'm supposed to have faith out of my own strength. Dear friend, this faith that I have now, this Jesus-faith, is so very easy and light. For now, I truly understand what Jesus is saying:

> *Come to Me, all you who labor and are heavy laden, and I will give you rest. Take My yoke upon you and learn from Me, for I am gentle and lowly in heart, and you will find rest for your souls. For My yoke is easy and My burden is light. Matthew 11:28, NKJV*

When we yoke with Jesus, our faith to conceive can be easy, and light, and restful, and peaceful, because we also…

4. Judge God faithful

> *By faith Sarah herself also received strength to conceive seed, and she bore a child when she was past the age, because she judged Him faithful who had promised. Hebrews 11:11, NKJV*

Now, I know we have talked about Abraham and Sarah a lot, but we are still not finished with them. We know that Sarah's first reaction to hearing that she would conceive and bear a son was nothing like the above scripture. We also know that she and Abraham took matters into their own hands because they were tired of waiting.

Then what do I mean by judging God faithful? Well, here's a little test: If I were to tell you with absolute conviction and confidence, based on God's Word, that you were going to conceive and have a baby, what would be your first reaction? Rolling your eyes; a big sigh with *I wish* under your breath; a *yeah right*; *been there, done that, already tried, and failed*; disbelief; wariness; fear to get your hopes up? If you experience any similar reactions or thoughts, then you have judged God *un*faithful. Deep down in your heart of hearts, you don't believe He means what He says (#ouch #truthhurts).

Now, before you close the book and toss it in the trash, please know that I am not condemning you. I only speak from experience, from one scarred soul to another. Blame it on being too cerebral; too many years being barren; too many false alarms. I had finally come to terms with the fact that I *just didn't believe God's Word* about me. I judged Him faithful to others, but not to me. This had to change, and thankfully, it has.

Soon after The Process of Surrender, I realized I contain all the faith I will ever need to please God. Not only that, but I also made the choice to believe that He is a rewarder, "But without faith it is impossible to [walk with God and] please Him, for whoever comes [near] to God must [necessarily] believe that God exists and that He rewards those who [earnestly and diligently] seek Him." (Hebrews 11:6, AMP)

Have I been earnestly and diligently seeking Him? Yes! Did He reward me? Heck, yes! No, not with the positive pregnancy test (#yet), but with a closeness and intimacy I would never have received otherwise. And oh, what a reward! I've tasted and seen that He is good (Psalm 34:8). Better has one day been in His courts than thousands elsewhere (Psalm 84:10). I would rather have free access to His presence than a BFP (#bigfatpositive) any day! He has rewarded me with His presence! He is a rewarder! He is faithful! He keeps His promises! We can rest in this because we judge Him faithful.

So, how do *you* judge God? Judge means you form an opinion or conclusion based on the evidence presented regarding something, a choice, a verdict. What opinion have you formed about God? What conclusion have you decided? What is your verdict? The Amplified Bible says about Sarah, "because she considered Him who had given her the promise to be reliable and true [to His word]." (Hebrews 11:11) What have you considered? If what you see when you search your heart doesn't line up with the truth, then I have good news for you. Because...

5. Faith can be strengthened

I know, I know. I just said that we have all the faith we will ever need. However, in talking to His disciples, Jesus said, "O you of little faith" (Matthew 8:26). So, this tells me that we can have little faith and/or great faith, possibly even at the same time (#morecomingsoon). Also, faith comes through hearing, believing, and confessing (Romans 10:17); faith is tested through trials and/or tribulation (James 1:2-4), and faith can be strengthened through surrender (Romans 4:20).

So, what we *should* have from our beautiful surrender is great faith. But let's cut to the chase. If all we need is a mustard seed of faith yoked with Jesus, then what is still hindering the reality of that big fat positive?

6. Unbelief

#dundundun: Unbelief may be self-explanatory, but here is a working definition for us: active doubt in one's mind. We may know the truth in our head, but we don't truly and wholly believe it. Simply stated, unbelief is a roadblock to your BFP (#bigfatpositive). Likewise, it can be a hindrance if you desire to experience signs, wonders, and miracles. This quote by Creflo Dollar explains it best, *"The problem is not the absence of faith, but the presence of unbelief."* Wait a second! Another contradiction? We go from great faith to little faith to great faith again, and now to unbelief?

#rabbittrail: Because the Word seems to contain so many so-called contradictions, we can't truly get life from the scriptures without a relationship with the Spirit. If we read the Word solely with our intellect, little will make sense. However, if we read the Word while in relationship with Jesus, it will come alive, and He will shepherd and guide us into revelation and truth.

Just as we can have great faith and little faith at the same time, we can also have belief and unbelief at the same time (#boom). Check out this example. After a time of solitude, Jesus came down the mountain and learned that His disciples could not help a tormented little boy by casting out a demon. The boy's father was pretty desperate and asked Jesus:

> *"But if You can do anything, take pity on us and help us!" Jesus said to him, "[You say to Me,] 'If You can?' All things are possible for the one who believes and trusts [in Me]!" Immediately the father of the boy cried out [with a desperate, piercing cry], saying, "I do believe; help [me overcome] my unbelief." Mark 9: 22-24, AMP*

I do believe; help me overcome my unbelief! This has been my heart's cry in a nutshell. What happened next? Jesus cast out that demon with no issues because He used His own faith and belief. However, let's look at what the disciples asked Him afterward:

> *"...Why could we not drive it out?" He answered, "Because of your little faith [your lack of trust and confidence in the power of God]; for I assure you and most solemnly say to you, if you have [living] faith the size of a mustard seed, you will say to this mountain, 'Move from here to there,' and [if it is God's will] it will move; and nothing will be impossible for you." Matthew 17:19-20, AMP*

Psst! There's that mustard seed thing again (#hinthint). Remember how unbelief can be a hindrance to miracles? Well, here is what happened when Jesus took a road trip to visit his hometown:

> *Jesus left there and came to His hometown [Nazareth]; and His disciples followed Him. When the Sabbath came, He began to teach in the synagogue; and many who listened to Him were astonished, saying, "Where did this man get these things [this knowledge and spiritual insight]? What is this wisdom [this confident understanding of the Scripture] that has been given to Him, and such miracles as these performed by His hands? Is this not the carpenter, the son of Mary, and the brother of James and Joses and Judas and Simon? Are His sisters not here with us?" And they were [deeply] offended by Him [and their disapproval blinded them to the fact that He was anointed by God as the Messiah]. Jesus said to them, "A prophet is not without honor (respect) except in his hometown and among his relatives and in his own household." And He could not do a miracle there at all [because*

of their unbelief] except that He laid His hands on a few sick people and healed them. He wondered at their unbelief. Mark 6:1-6, AMP

He could not do a miracle there at all because of their unbelief (#burn). Did unbelief within the minds of the people hinder Jesus from doing miracles? Yes. Do you think that we, too, can hinder a miracle from occurring in our own life because of unbelief? Do you think we have hindered our positive pregnancy test because of our unbelief (#crickets)? I know, I know. We are not intentionally doing so, truly. We are not setting out to be doubtful and unbelieving. When walking with God, the last thing we choose to do is not believe. Shoot, it takes belief even to accept Jesus and to become a new creation. So, why would we purposely partner with unbelief?

#disclaimer: I realize I'm walking a very thin line regarding this topic. These are only a few examples of unbelief. There are many examples in the Bible where signs, wonders, and miracles occurred without the need for belief. Shoot, Lazarus probably couldn't confess his belief when he was lying in the grave dead as a doornail. And take Jesus, when He calmed the storm or multiplied the fish and loaves, He didn't require anyone's belief. What is my point? Well, when you spend time and study the gospels, you should be able to see that a pattern of belief by the individuals receiving the miracle was usually the norm (#seeforyourself). If unbelief is not where we intended to go, though, how have we gotten there?

Through the entrance in our souls.

#mrswindsorinthehouse: We are a body, soul, and spirit. The body is our physical body, shell, or temple. The soul contains our mind, will, and emotions. The mind is our logic, reasoning, and intellect. The will is our intentions and motives that derive from the heart, which is the center of our being. The emotions are our feelings that respond to our natural senses. The spirit is what becomes born again when we accept Jesus. This is our true identity, where we have received everything Jesus did for us on the cross.

The reason we can have belief and unbelief at the same time is that our spirit truly believes, but our soul does not; our spirit has great faith, while our soul has little faith; our spirit has been transformed, but our soul is still in process. It is a tug-of-war, which is why it's impossible to have rest with unbelief. It is this very unrest that makes us feel all crazy in the head.

It goes back to this question, what do we choose to believe? What is the intention of our hearts? To believe God's Word and His promises, or to believe what we see in the natural? It is all about the battle of the mind. What are we thinking on? What are we considering? Consider means to reflect on and to contemplate. When we consider the impossibility of conceiving more than the truth of God's promises, what happens? When we become an expert on all things infertility, what comes out of our mouths? When we contemplate and think about the ticking of our biological clock or what the test results show, what do we speak? How do we feel? Fear, worry, and anxiety, right (#beenthereoverit)? This is the entrance to unbelief. This is also called being double-minded:

> *...for the one who doubts is like a billowing surge of the sea that is blown about and tossed by the wind.* **For such a person ought not to think or expect that he will receive anything [at all] from the Lord, being a double-minded man, unstable and restless in all his ways [in everything he thinks, feels, or decides].** (emphasis added) James 1:6-8, AMP

I don't know about you, but I am sick and tired of being double-minded; of wavering; of being restless; of believing and not believing. So, here is the big question we have all been waiting for. How do we get rid of this unbelief? (#yeshow)

By feeding our souls, by meditating day and night, and by stewarding.

First of all, feeding our souls isn't a new concept. Remember my reference to feeding on the Word like chocolate? Well, here we are again. We feed on the Word because it feeds our souls (#akarenewingthemind). We feed on the Word because this is how we intimately get to know God. We feed on the Word because the Word is Jesus. We feed on the Word because as we give attention to it, the truth will begin to flow out from our spirits and into our souls. This begins to transform our unbelief into belief.

Secondly, we meditate day and night. Biblical meditation; whereby the application of this practice, the impossible begins to become possible. What is Biblical meditation? The Hebrew definition for meditation is to reflect, to ponder, to mutter, to contemplate something as one repeats the words, eliminating outside distractions. So, to break it down, this looks like: feeding on the Word, then allowing certain scriptures to be memorized, chewing on it all day and all night. It could be writing it on a notecard, memorizing it, singing it, praying it, dissecting it, or going to bed with it on your mind. You might even dream about it and wake up with it on your heart:

> *But his delight is in the law of the* L*ord*, *And on His law [His precepts and teachings] he [habitually] meditates day and night. And he will be like a tree firmly planted [and fed] by streams of water, Which yields its fruit in its season; Its leaf does not wither; And in whatever he does, he prospers [and comes to maturity]. Psalm 1:2-3, AMP*

#bigsighofpleasure: Now tell me, doesn't that sound amazing? Being like a tree firmly planted; no wavering; no back and forth; no double-mindedness; no great faith vs. little faith; no belief vs. unbelief; just a tree, firmly planted, prospering in all I do!

How does this happen? Well, when the seed of God's Word gets planted within our hearts, a seed is sown. First, we feed on the Word from our thoughts, our minds, our intellect, and our logic. Then, to nourish and water the seed, we meditate. This causes it to burrow within our hearts; establish deep roots; replace incorrect thinking; to eventually bear fruit, and transform our minds. The seed grows even while we are sleeping (Mark 4:27)!

So, we get a double-whammy here, a two-fold benefit when we meditate. Not only are we no longer stuck in the natural, wavering back and forth with double mindedness, rather, we are also prospering in all we do (#moreproof):

This Book of the Law shall not depart from your mouth, but you shall read [and meditate on] it day and night, so that you may be careful to do [everything] in accordance with all that is written in it; for then you will make your way prosperous, and then you will be successful.
Joshua 1:8, AMP

Interesting, huh? Perhaps the key to successful living is through meditating on His Word. Could it also be the key to a successful conception and pregnancy? (#somethingtothinkabout) The last way to oust unbelief deserves its own chapter. Keep reading, if you dare (#evillaugh #notreallythough).

Going Deeper:

- What was your first reaction after learning that you already have all the Jesus-faith you will ever need for your miracle?
- Find a picture of a mustard seed. Meditate on Luke 17:5-6 and record your thoughts.
- Do you feel at rest in your faith? Why or why not?
- How do you judge God?
- Has unbelief hindered you from receiving the promises of God? From receiving your BFP (big fat positive)?
- On your journey, in what ways have you been double-minded?
- Do you see open doors in your soul where you have welcomed unbelief?
- If you're not already, begin feeding and meditating on the Word of God
- Scriptures to Study: Rom. 12:3; 2 Pt. 1:1; Gal. 2:20; Acts 3:11-16; Mt. 11:28; Heb. 11:6, 11; Ps. 34:8; Ps. 84:10; Mt. 8:26; Rom. 10:17; Jas. 1:2-4; Rom. 4:20; Mk. 9:22-24; Mt. 17:19-20; Mk. 6:1-6; Jas. 1:6-8; Ps. 1:2-3; Josh. 1:8.

Chapter eleven
The Promised Land

#STEWARDINGYOURBELIEF

You may be reading this book straight through; however, it's been a much longer process for me. But. Oh. My. Goodness. I have been waiting *so* long to get to this section! Why, you ask (#drumrollplease)? Ta-da! I have made it to The Promised Land!

> *Every commandment that I am commanding you today you shall be careful to do, so that you may live and multiply, and go in and possess the land which the LORD swore [to give] to your fathers. And you shall remember [always] all the ways which the LORD your God has led you these forty years in the wilderness, so that He might humble you and test you, to know what was in your heart (mind), whether you would keep His commandments or not. He humbled you and allowed you to be hungry and fed you with manna, [a substance] which you did not know, nor did your fathers know, so that He might make you understand [by personal experience] that man does not live by bread alone, but man lives by every word that proceeds out of the mouth of the LORD. Your clothing did not wear out on you, nor did your feet swell these forty years. Therefore, know in your heart (be fully cognizant) that the LORD your God disciplines and instructs you just as a man disciplines and instructs his son. Therefore, you shall keep*

> *the commandments of the* L<small>ORD</small> *your God, to walk [that is, to live each and every day] in His ways and fear [and worship] Him [with awe-filled reverence and profound respect]. For the* L<small>ORD</small> *your God is bringing you into a good land, a land of brooks of water, of fountains and springs, flowing forth in valleys and hills; a land of wheat and barley, and vines and fig trees and pomegranates, a land of olive oil and honey; a land where you will eat bread without shortage, in which you will lack nothing; a land whose stones are iron, and out of whose hills you can dig copper. When you have eaten and are satisfied, then you shall bless the* L<small>ORD</small> *your God for the good land which He has given you. Deuteronomy 8:1-10, AMP*

Mmm. I love those scriptures so much! They give me so much hope! However, I realize you may not be as hopeful and excited as I am (#yet). I mean, I get it. Isn't the Promised Land full of olive oil and honey and everything good? So, where is our positive pregnancy test? Why are we being tasked out with more things to do instead of feasting and drinking and resting? We shall get there, dear friends. But first, let's get out our Bibles and begin reading in Joshua. We will quickly see that, even though the Israelites crossed over to the Promised Land, they still had things to take care of. That is what this chapter is all about.

Who remembers what "stewarding" means? Stewarding means managing, protecting, or taking care of something that doesn't belong to you. We just learned that belief is a choice. We are only able to make the choice of belief with the grace of the Holy Spirit. We now know it is not something we can do with our natural ability, mind, or logic. When we try to force it, we become double-minded. Belief comes from our spirit. And anything that doesn't come naturally, i.e., doesn't belong to us, we have the responsibility to steward (#thatsgood).

Before I list some more steps, please remember that I process as a list maker, or what you might call a "linear learner" (#typeApersonality). I comprehend things better when they are listed in a formula. You might have a different way, which is why it's important to journal through any tribulation or process you are going through. With all of that said, I believe there are five ways to steward your belief:

1. Circumcise

I know, right? So weird. Why are we talking about circumcising? I'll get there. First, let me be real straight with you; this is a little blunt; here goes...

Unbelief is actually a sin. Unbelief is the sin of disobedience.

In fact, if we continue in unbelief, we will not be able to enter the Promised Land. We will be stuck in The Wilderness going through The Process over and over again. It may be a yucky thought, but it's the truth.

> *So we see that they were not able to enter [into His rest – the promised land] because of unbelief and an unwillingness to trust in God.*
> *Hebrews 3:19, AMP*

This verse is talking about the generation of Israelites that Moses led out of Egypt; the same ones who walked on dry ground through the Red Sea; the same ones who were fed manna that miraculously fell from Heaven. Some scholars believe the distance from Egypt to the land they were to possess was really only eleven days. Eleven days! And they wandered for forty years instead! I don't know about you, but I am tired of wandering. Like the Israelites, some people wander their whole lives and never make it out of The Wilderness; they *die* in The Wilderness (#eek).

Nope, not me. I don't want to be in The Wilderness any longer, just like I don't want to waver in my belief. I know too much; I contain too much truth, too much knowledge of God's character within me to doubt any longer, and I have no excuse for it, "Jesus said to them, 'If you were blind [to spiritual things], you would have no sin [and would not be blamed for your unbelief]; but since you claim to have [spiritual] sight, [you have no excuse so] your sin and guilt remain.'" (John 9:4, AMP)

Ouch. No excuse. If we were ignorant to His promises in the Bible, then we would have no sin in this area. But, because we do know them, our sin and guilt remain. What do we do, then?

We circumcise.

If you read in Joshua like I told you to (#teachervoice), then you will notice that God commanded Joshua to circumcise the Israelites *again* (Joshua 5:2). The reason for this is because all the previously circumcised men of war had died in The Wilderness. This next generation, then, had never been circumcised. They needed their own covenant with God. They could no longer ride on the coattails of their ancestors. It was time to make a commitment to do things differently. Their circumcision was a physical, symbolic act of that.

We, too, must commit to doing things differently. We must make our own choice. We must repent and cut away the former things, press forward, obey, and *choose to believe*. How do we steward our belief? Circumcise, dear friend. Repent, obey, and commit (#soundsfun #yeahright).

2. Put them all outside

Here is a story about a man named Jairus (Mark 5). Jairus was a synagogue official who had a deathly ill daughter. He was distraught, fell at Jesus' feet, and begged Him to come lay hands on his daughter so she would be healed. Jesus agreed and followed him. But a large crowd also followed and surrounded Him. Jesus was, at this time, interrupted and took the time to heal and acknowledge a woman with a blood issue. While this was going on, people from Jairus' house came and said his daughter had died and there would be no use bothering Jesus after all. Jesus overheard and said, "Do not be afraid; only keep on believing [in Me and my power]." (Mark 5:36, AMP) Then, He allowed no one to go with Him, except for Peter, James, and John. Here is what happened next:

> *They came to the house of the synagogue official; and He looked [with understanding] at the uproar and commotion, and people loudly weeping and wailing [in mourning]. When He had gone in, He said to them, "Why make a commotion and weep? The child has not died, but is sleeping." They began laughing [scornfully] at Him [because they knew the child was dead]. But He made them all go outside, and took along the child's father and mother and His own [three] companions, and entered the room where the child was. Mark 5:38-40, AMP*

Friends, when stewarding our belief, there are times when we need to make some people just go outside (#preach). Who? Anyone that will hinder our belief, any doubters or haters; it could even be family, friends, or our doubt-filled churches! The Message is a bit blunter:

> *He permitted no one to go in with him except Peter, James, and John. They entered the leader's house and pushed their way through the gossips looking for a story and neighbors bringing in casseroles. Jesus was abrupt: "Why all this busybody grief and gossip? This child isn't dead; she's sleeping." Provoked to sarcasm, they told him he didn't know what he was talking about. Mark 5:37-40, MSG*

#ouch: No wonder Jesus kicked them all outside! We know we have people currently in our lives who are gossiping and grieving because we haven't yet conceived. They mean well, truly they do, but their doubt and pity and "have-you-ever-thought about-adopting?" comments do nothing for our faith and belief (#ihavenothingagainstadoption).

So, kick them out. Put them all outside. Not in a rude way, but let's put up boundaries; let's guard our hearts. If we surround ourselves with doubters, we will probably continue to struggle with unbelief. If we surround ourselves with a few faith-filled companions, however, then our belief will prevail (#amen).

P.S. The little girl comes back to life.

Another way we "put them all outside" is to silence unbelief. One example of this is when Joshua was talking to the people before the walls of Jericho came down, "…You shall not shout [the battle cry] nor let your voice be heard nor let a word come out of your mouth, until the day I tell you to shout. Then you shall shout!" (Joshua 6:10, AMP) Joshua remembered how in the wilderness, grumbling and complaining delayed the people. He changed things up and commanded them to stay silent until it was time to shout for the victory. Seriously. He made the people stay silent for six whole days! Could you imagine not being able to speak at all? That's how determined he was to silence unbelief. And so shall we.

What does this look like? Well, we may need to silence what our husband is speaking, or what we have been speaking (#dontshootthemessenger). We may need to silence what we are watching or listening to, or take time away from social media or the news or that blog we like to follow. We need to pray about it for ourselves and see what the Holy Spirit wants us to silence, or who He wants us to put outside. And the motive of our hearts must still remain pure. We are not kicking people out because they disagree with us; we are silencing unbelief. Sometimes that requires us to do things differently than we have ever done before (#somethingtothinkabout).

3. Only believe

As soon as Jesus heard the word that was spoken, He said to the ruler of the synagogue, "Do not be afraid; only believe." Mark 5:36, NKJV

Easier said than done, right? Aren't we stewarding our belief so we can get to this point? How can we go from wavering in our belief to only believing?

By shutting up our souls.

King David is one of my favorite Bible heroes. Truth be told, I even have a little crush on the dude (#donttellmyhusband). I love his authenticity, his boldness, his tenderness. Oh, I just described my husband; go figure. Anyhow, King David learned how to shut up his soul, "...I don't concern myself with matters too great or too awesome for me to grasp. Instead, I have calmed and quieted myself, like a weaned child who no longer cries for its mother's milk. Yes, like a weaned child is my soul within me." (Psalm 131:1-2, NLT)

Again, our soul is our mind, will, and emotions; the emotions react off of our five senses. Therefore, in order to steward our belief, we must ignore our five senses; ignore what we see; ignore what we hear, ignore what we feel; never rely on what we feel or reason in the mind; leave our emotions and logic out of it. Completely. Shutting up our souls like a weaned child means that we no longer pitch a fit so as to be heard. Instead, our soul becomes controlled, quiet, and calm, not relying on anything but God's truth (#easiersaidthandone).

Just yesterday, I had to tell myself to shut up. Okay, I didn't just say it, I *screamed* it while I was driving on a curvy road with tears rolling down my face and snot dripping from my nose. I definitely do not recommend that, but I recommend saying shut up to your feelings. I was acting way too emotional from Aunt Flo's recent visit, and yes, it was partially hormones, but I also knew that it was my soul. I even began to reason things in my mind that were cray-cray, and once I went there, I yelled at my soul to be quiet. Guess what happened? It worked. No more crazy thoughts. Yes, the tears were still running down my face, but my roller coaster emotions no longer had control over me. I shut up my soul, meditated on God's truth, and went on to have a great day.

The next way to "only believe" is to: K.I.S.S. I love acronyms. And, no, it doesn't mean exactly what you think.

K-keep

I-it

S-simple

S-sister

Okay, so maybe it does, but I did change it up just a tad (#riiight). What do I mean by K.I.S.S.? Keep it simple. Simply believe and simply become like a child.

As believers, we strive to learn and grow in knowledge which can be a good thing. But then, we can get to a place of knowing too much intellectually and, therefore, neglect to let the knowledge come alive within our hearts. Again, our hearts are where we choose to believe what we know in our heads:

> *At that time the disciples came to Jesus and asked, "Who is greatest in the kingdom of heaven?" He called a little child and set him before them, and said, "I assure you and most solemnly say to you, unless you repent [that is, change your inner self – your old way of thinking, live changed lives] and become like children [trusting, humble, and forgiving], you will never enter the kingdom of heaven. Therefore, whoever humbles himself like this child is greatest in the kingdom of heaven." Matthew 18:1-4, AMP*

We must trust. We must live humbly as a child, not all bloated of superior knowledge, intellect, or theology. We must become children who simply and humbly believe. This is the secret ingredient to K.I.S.S.ing.

The precious son of my heart will believe anything I tell him. Why? Because he trusts me. Upon receiving this revelation to "only believe," I observed him and marveled at how much of a skeptic I had become. Seriously. I truly did have to repent and make an intentional effort to believe everything I read in the Bible. I think this is what Jesus was trying to teach; the simple gospel, the simple truth.

You know I like to research and study, which is all well and good when writing a book or teaching others, but honestly means zilch when trying to please my Father. If He wasn't ever impressed with the Pharisees, how will He ever be impressed with my intellectual knowledge?

#warning: I'm probably going to step on some toes here because this also goes for our fertility expertise. I don't know about you, but I seem to be an expert on all things fertility. I know everything; from the miraculous journey the little sperm and egg have to make, to the likelihood of percentages, to the stages of hormones throughout the month, to which supplement or medication increases sperm quality, to the exact consistency of fertile cervical mucus, to which position is best for gravity. I even know without looking at *any* calendar when I have ovulated and have an increase in progesterone. And no, not by sticking my finger up there to feel my cervix. Seriously people. If you take a step back and think about it, this stuff is just plain gross (#truethat). But I am an expert, I know it all, and most likely you do too.

Please realize I am not dissing the many women, who like myself, have become experts. In fact, just as the fertility clinics have their methods that have worked for them, so do we. Plus, we must be advocates for our own health care. But, is all this expertise really helping us? Or does it just contribute to unbelief and discouragement?

I'm reminded of Rachel in the Bible. Rachel was adored by her husband, yet she was miserable because she was barren. She was so loved by her husband that he chose to live with her and sleep with her rather than Leah. However, Rachel blamed Jacob for her barrenness. In fact, we can all relate to her heart's cry, "Give me children, or else I die!" (Genesis 30:1, NKJV #sayitwithafistshake). So, what did Rachel do? Actually, something similar to Sarah, believe it or not. She gave Jacob her lady's maid so she could have children through her. The maid conceived two sons, but evidently, that was not enough for Rachel. One day, she barters with her sister-wife, Leah, and offers her a night with Jacob in exchange for the mandrakes her son was out collecting. Guess what mandrakes were supposedly used for? Fertility!

So, here is a Biblical example of a woman who became an expert on all things fertility. Did it do her any good? No. In fact, Leah went on to have two more sons and a daughter! Then, finally, after who knows how many years, "...God remembered Rachel, and God listened to her and opened her womb." (Genesis 30:22, NKJV) Along came Joseph. It makes me wonder if she finally reached a place of surrender and chose to "only believe".

I finally surrendered only after I stopped all methods of trying to conceive (with the exception of the act, of course #duediligence). But again, this is a story of my journey, and I am not encouraging anyone to make this same decision. However, I am encouraging you to stop being an expert. Instead, take all of the knowledge and wisdom found in the Word, apply it to your mind to knock down strongholds, and "only believe." You will begin to see something happen. When you make choices like this and go all out to become like a child, you will be challenged to back it up with actions that require faith. Surprised? Honestly, I actually found myself *wanting* to do something!

So, I spoke with my husband, and we decided to do something we had never done. We decided, as a family, to pray and believe every night that God would give us a baby. Now I know this doesn't sound like much, but trust me, when you have a little boy in the house who wants to be a big brother so badly that he cries after baby showers, then this is a huge step. It is also a risk. Here we are, bringing a vulnerable child in on our faith to conceive. It was so scary, and my heart pounded out of my chest probably the first two weeks doing this. I knew, though, it was the right thing to do. Because, for the first time ever in my journey as The Barren Woman, I no longer felt isolated and alone. As I listened to the prayers of this sweet boy every night, prayers he truly believed, I got to witness exactly what childlike faith looks and sounds like. My belief was strengthened.

What happens when two or more are gathered together in prayer? He is there in the midst of them (Matthew 18:20). I began to feel the presence of God right there in the midst of our little family unit, and my belief was strengthened even more. Yes, it was a risk, but taking risks is just part of becoming like a child. I was more than willing to do it. K.I.S.S. and try it out for yourself!

4. Hope against hope

We briefly talked about hope in a previous chapter; how hope should have been developed in us because it is produced through tribulation, perseverance, and character building. We should have hope like never before because of His salvation, but also because we hope in His truth. Hope is not only the fertile ground for the mustard seed, or where we become fruitful vines, but it is also the *movement*. The wind. Can we see the wind? No, but we feel it; we know it is there. We simply cannot believe without hope, period, "For we were saved in this hope, but hope that is seen is not hope; for why does one still hope for what he sees?" (Romans 8:24, NKJV). Hope is hoping for the unseen. Abraham was known for this kind of hope when Paul wrote about him,

> *In hope against hope Abraham believed that he would become a father of many nations, as he had been promised [by God]: "So [numberless]* SHALL YOUR DESCENDANTS BE." *(Romans 4:18, AMP)*

In hope against hope, we can believe. What does this mean? Well, contrary to ordinary human expectations or natural hope from the five senses, we can, with *supernatural* hope, believe God will fulfill His promises. The Bible is *full* of promises. In fact, the only way we can really have this kind of hope is to hang on to a promise. In order to get a promise, we must know what the promises are. This is our responsibility; to delve into His Word. This is how we overcome trials and tribulation in all areas (#readyourBiblepeople):

> *Without becoming weak in faith he considered his own body, now as good as dead [for producing children] since he was about a hundred years old, and [he considered] the deadness of Sarah's womb. But he did not doubt or waver in unbelief concerning the promise of God, but he grew strong and empowered by faith, giving glory to God, being fully convinced that God had the power to do what He had promised.*
> Romans 4:19-21, AMP

Talk about hope! One hundred years old, and Abraham grew strong and empowered by faith! I love this same passage in The Message:

> *Abraham didn't focus on his own impotence and say, "It's hopeless. This hundred-year-old body could never father a child." Nor did he survey Sarah's decades of infertility and give up. He didn't tiptoe around God's promise asking cautiously skeptical questions. He plunged into the promise and came up strong, ready for God, sure that God would make good on what he had said.*

Let's take this even further, "In alert expectancy such as this, we're never left feeling shortchanged. Quite the contrary – we can't round up enough containers to hold everything God generously pours into our lives through the Holy Spirit!" (Romans 5:5, MSG) Hope equals alert expectancy; hope equals overflowing confidence. "But if we hope for what we do not see, we eagerly wait for it with perseverance." (Romans 8:25, NKJV) Hope equals eagerly waiting; hope equals perseverance. What does this look like? I mean, we can learn about Abraham's hope all day long, but how do we actually apply it? Honestly, I'm still figuring that out (#notthereyet).

#vulnerabilityalert: I don't know how to get my hopes up in alert expectancy while keeping everything surrendered. Trust me, dear friends, we are on this journey together. As you read this, I will already have gone through it. However, as I'm writing this, I don't know how its application will unfold.

I took a break and did some studying (i.e., spent time with the Lord in the Word). What was the first thing He asked me? He wanted me to start up my "Windsor Baby" Pinterest board again (#ugh). So, I obeyed even though I knew it was going to hurt, and sure enough, I began pinning and hoping and planning and all the old fears tried to come back. Thankfully, I knew to silence unbelief and shut up my soul, and through my snot and tears and longing, I was able to remember the truth.

Honestly, I have never felt the pull to waver from belief to unbelief so clearly. In the past, wavering was done in immaturity. This time, however, felt in slow motion as I observed my soul trying to partner with hopelessness and unbelief. I clearly knew what was happening, which made this experience all the more surreal.

So then, to apply the hope exemplified by Abraham, we might have a different action. Obviously, it makes sense that He will allow us to get our hopes up again and give us permission to begin hoping and planning. However, we need to be prepared for the enemy who will tempt us with unbelief and fear. But, be sure to celebrate the victories! If you succumb, don't beat yourself up; just get your soul in check and hop back on the horse of hope and belief.

#whew: I know that was a lot of information. To recap, hope is the fertile soil and the movement. We cannot move forward without it. Believe me, I just tried, and it didn't work (#takemywordforit). Hope against hope is eagerly waiting with alert expectancy and overflowing confidence.

In fact, I'm reminded of a little kid at Christmas, eagerly waiting for weeks, fighting sleep on Christmas Eve, busting out of his room, charging down the hall to the gifts from Santa waiting underneath the tree. He knew it was coming. He was anticipating the gifts and knew they would be there. Dear friend, let us not be afraid to hope like this. Our Daddy is so much bigger and better than Santa Claus. He can be trusted. It is truly okay to get our hopes up. I know it is scary; I know it hasn't gone well in years prior.

Things have drastically changed, though. Today is a new day! We don't look behind. We keep pressing forward. We don't just hope through our natural senses and remember what our bodies have or have not done. We hope supernaturally in our Father who *can* be trusted and always keeps His promises.

5. Be strengthened in faith

Let's talk about Abraham and Sarah (#again). I cannot get enough of this example. It fascinates me so much. I mean, seriously. Can you imagine a ninety-year-old having a baby? That's how old Sarah was, and Abraham was one hundred! Not only that, but they were barren for many, many years before their son of promise was born. Check out what is said about them the longer they waited, though:

> *He did not waver at the promise of God through unbelief, but was strengthened in faith, giving glory to God, and being fully convinced that what He had promised He was also able to perform. Romans 4:20-21, NKJV*

Abraham didn't waver. He was strengthened in faith! The writer of Hebrews says about Sarah that by faith, she also received strength to conceive seed. Wait, isn't this the opposite? The longer they went and the older they got, wouldn't they give up and become hopeless? Not Abraham and Sarah, they grew stronger and even more convinced that God would keep His promise.

#rabbittrail: Dear reader, this is my prayer. This is why I continue to obey and write this book. No matter how many times I want to give up, I press on and keep journaling and writing so that my sisters will be strengthened in faith. This is possible; I know it is. I am living proof. I have been barren for over a decade, and I have more belief and active faith than I have ever had before (#thankyouJesus #endrabbittrail).

Now, back to Abraham and Sarah. How did they go about being strengthened in faith?

By giving glory to God. Believe it or not, giving glory to God is more than just worshiping and praising Him. Glory means giving honor and esteem. Yes, this can be done through singing and playing instruments, but it goes a lot deeper than that. I believe this kind of giving glory to God is having a healthy dose of the fear of the Lord.

What is the fear of the Lord? It is being terrified to be away from Him or out of His presence, being in awe of Him more than anyone else in the universe (#myopinion). Personally, this kind of fear developed instinctively. I couldn't put a name to it, but this longing and desire not to be separated from my Father for any reason became hugely important to me. Throughout this journey, my greatest reward has been this special intimacy with God. I have had thoughts of not being sure that I wanted to conceive anymore because I didn't want to lose this closeness with my Abba. When I sin, I am quick to repent. When I succumb to the old habits of my soul and cannot feel His peace surrounding me anymore, I will literally grieve, like snot and tears crying. I absolutely hate feeling like I am far away from Him! This is the fear of the Lord; this is giving glory to God; this is *friendship* with God.

Abraham was a friend of God (James 2:23). God desires to be a friend of ours as well. When we reach this level of intimacy, we cannot help but be strengthened in every way. So, switch things up! Seek friendship with God, seek Him like never before, dive into His Word, spend more time with Him than usual, and sit at His feet. Be quiet and listen to what He wants to reveal. He desires it. His Word promises us that as we draw near to Him, He will draw near to us (James 4:8). He already made the first move; the next move is on us. Isn't this what Abraham did? He learned to fear the Lord. He kept God's promise close to his heart. Because his fear for God was so great, he had no choice but to obey and believe; otherwise, he would have been separated from God in the sin of unbelief.

The second way Abraham was strengthened in faith was by being fully convinced that God *can* and *would* perform His promise. In his friendship with God and genuine fear of Him, Abraham developed an unshakeable resolve, an intentional, firm, unwavering decision to anchor his faith in the truth of God's promise.

Abraham took God's covenants and promises very seriously. In the Greek language, we see the word for promise is *epangelia*, which is what the promise from God is, and at the same time, assuring what is promised *will* be done. Thus, it is both the announcement and the intention; the commitment and the service rendered; a pledge and then an action to follow through.

#rabbittrail: Two days ago was Christmas. I have OCD (#obsessivechristmasdisorder). I have a tree in every room, as well as the numerous mini trees all over the house. Christmas music is on year-round, I record every sappy Christmas movie on TV that I can, and I have always desired to announce my pregnancy at Christmas. I used to fantasize about it. I had it all planned out. Instead, over the years, I've watched friends and family announce pregnancies at Christmas time while I smile and cheer them on (#oratleasttryto).

We just went through another Christmas without a baby or a positive pregnancy test. Two friends announced pregnancies, and two others gave birth to Christmas babies. I congratulated them, but it was rough. I do so look forward to the holiday season, and I love planning for it, but once the day arrives, this heaviness just overwhelms me. Christmas day is quiet for us, not at all like I imagined my life would be.

I am familiar with this decision Abraham made, this intentional, firm resolve. If we don't have hope, what do we have? If we cannot believe God when He makes a promise, then what are we even doing? Knowing that this heaviness hits every year no matter how much I prepare, this year, I made the decision to be fully convinced. As my mind went rampant with deceptive thoughts, I began to ignore them. When emotions kept me crying, I instead told my soul to shut up and spoke through my lips, "I trust You, Abba." I may have had to say it over and over and over again, day and night, but I resolved to fully trust.

Dear sister, God is *so* able. He truly is able to perform that which He has promised. We can know it with every cell of our being. Like Abraham, we *can* become fully convinced (#trustGod #stewardyourbelief).

Going Deeper:

- Do you need to repent for the sin of unbelief? Take the time to do so and journal your process.
- Can you think of who/what you need to put outside? Who/what do you need to silence?
- The next time your soul begins to pitch a fit, shut it up and journal your experience.
- What action steps will you take to KISS and "only believe"?
- In what way will you begin to hope against hope?
- In what way will you begin to seek friendship with God?
- Journal about your resolution to be fully convinced.
- Scriptures to study: Deut. 8:1-10; Heb. 3:19; Jn. 9:4; Jos. 5:2; Mk. 5:38-40; Jos. 6:10; Mk. 5:36; Ps. 131:1-2; Mt. 18:1-4; Gen. 30:1, 22; Mt. 18:20; Rom. 8:24-25; Rom. 4:18-21; Rom. 5:5; Jas. 2:23; Jas. 4:8.

Chapter twelve
FIGHT FOR YOUR TESTIMONY

Here we are, still in the Promised Land, although we're not seeing any olive oil and honey and BFPs (#bigfatpositives). In fact, it feels like we're continually battling and going to war. But maybe, just maybe, you begin to feel strengthened, alive with hope, and more confident and determined than ever before. Just maybe, you begin to have courage and boldness to step out and believe without barriers; without hindrances; without unbelief; without doubt; just pure, undaunted childlike faith (#maybe #ihopeso).

I like to call this "warrior princess status." That is who you are now, a warrior princess. You have been promoted (#luckyyou). Through The Wilderness, we learned who we truly are. We learned our value, how loved we are, and how *so worth it* this journey is; this journey not only to become The Joyful Mother of children, but more importantly, to become a friend of God. From precious daughters of our Abba to valiant warriors in the Lord's army (#hooah). What do we do with this new status, then?

We fight.

We fight for the future of our family. We fight for the unborn children that God already knows by name. We fight for our testimony. Is this Biblical? Yes. Are we being attacked every day in the battle of our minds? Yes. Are Satan's minions looking for any and all ways to infiltrate and steal our joy? Yes. In fact, we will continue to war and fight for the rest of our lives on earth as long as we continue to serve God. This is called the fight of faith. We will war and fight especially hard when we have been given a promise and begin standing on that promise believing it will produce fruit (#literally).

When we pray and believe for certain promises to be fulfilled, there are times God will tell us to stand still and watch Him move. I have had this kind of answer to prayer occur throughout most of my life. It may not seem obvious to you, but after a decade-plus of barrenness, I have realized that my conception and pregnancy will *not* be one of those times. Instead, this is a circumstance where my role drastically changes. I believe God wants me to *become* the answer; to believe the promises, partner, co-labor, and yoke with Him for the answer. He wants me to fight. He wants *us* to fight. And so, we fight out of obedience to Him.

In the beginning of the book of Joshua, when God was raising up Joshua to replace Moses, He commanded him to be strong and courageous. He also assured him, "Every place that the sole of your foot will tread upon I have given you..." (Joshua 1:3, NKJV) God had promised this land to the Israelites for years. It was already theirs. The promise, however, also came with the responsibility of weeding out the current inhabitants. This meant lots of fighting, some with giants no less. The same goes for us. Just as God promised the land to the Israelites, He has promised to make us The Joyful Mother of children. Just as Israel had to fight to enter fully into the Promised Land, so do we in order to receive, inhabit, and possess God's promise to us. This is called taking ground (#hopethatmakessense)

Should we be scared, leery of what lies ahead? No, because the work is already done. He has already given us the land. He has already given us our positive pregnancy test. He already knows the number of hairs on our unborn baby's head. More so, He goes with us. We are privileged with the promise "...I will be with you. I will not leave you nor forsake you." (Joshua 1:5, NKJV)

If the Lord commands us to be strong while battling in the Promised Land, then being strong and courageous is within our reach. However, in order to fight for our testimony, we will need a healthy dose of strength and courage. If you do not already have it, hopefully, you will soon (#fingerscrossed). This is heavy stuff, dear friend, so hang on tight and take your time reading and meditating.

POSSESS THE LAND

> *Every commandment that I am commanding you today you shall be careful to do, so that you may live and multiply, and go in and possess the land which the LORD swore [to give] to your fathers. Deuteronomy 8:1, AMP*

In Hebrew, the word for possess is *yarash*, meaning to inherit, seize, and occupy. This is what we get to do when it comes to believing for that BFP and new title as The Joyful Mother of children. It is our inheritance, and it is time to seize and occupy it (#hooah).

Did you happen to see in the above scripture how multiplication is an outcome of obedience? That's for us! In fact, the same promises the Israelites received are the same ones that we get to believe for. Here is why, "…And you Gentiles, who were branches from a wild olive tree, have been grafted in. So now you also receive the blessing God has promised Abraham and his children…" (Romans 11:17, NLT)

Abraham and his children are the Israelites. This means we get to partake of the same Old Testament promises because we have been grafted into God's family through Jesus' sacrifice (#howcoolisthat). However, the best news is that we don't have to be perfect and obey the law in order to receive. Jesus fulfilled the Old Covenant and gave us the New Covenant through His blood. This means that we can expect to stand on these promises and believe they *will* come to pass as we yoke with Jesus (#moreonthiscomingsoon).

Here is how to Possess the Land:

1. Remember the promise

First of all, we see how God continually reminded Joshua not to be fearful or dismayed, that He would deliver Joshua's enemies into his hands. This is what the Holy Spirit is saying to us. We need not fear when we get to this place of bold faith. He is with us. He goes before us. And He will not let us be put to shame. We can trust Him. However, we must remember what He has promised. In Deuteronomy, we can see the blessings of obedience for the Israelites once they possessed The Promised Land. In The Amplified Bible, the title of this section is even called "The Promises of God":

> *He will love you and bless you and multiply you; He will also bless the fruit of your womb… You shall be blessed above all peoples; there will be no male or female barren (childless, infertile) among you or among your cattle. Deuteronomy 7: 13-14, AMP*

Not including this verse, I saw six other times where the womb is to be multiplied and blessed in the entire chapter of Deuteronomy. Clearly, multiplication was to be expected in the Promised Land (#getexcited). So, when I finally realized I was through The Wilderness, I looked back and recalled what God had promised: *multiply you, no male or female barren,* and *the Lord will grant you plenty of goods in the fruit of your body* (Deuteronomy 28:4). And, out of the depths of my heart came this confident, gut-level trust. Talk about boldness! I *owned* those promises! They were now mine to seize and possess! From within the deepest parts of my being flowed this gushing fountain of confident, undaunted authority.

2. Take authority

Dear friend, this is *the* key section for breakthrough. This is where the beauty happens! I can feel it in my bones. So, please make sure you are reading with an open mind and at a time when you are not distracted. In fact, let me pray for you before moving on:

Abba Father,
I lift up the amazing woman who is reading this book. I pray that You would take away all distractions, all preconceived notions,

and renew her mind with a clean slate. I pray that Your truth would be confirmed within her spirit and that a fire would begin to burn with the revelation of who she truly is in You and what You actually paid for.
In Jesus' name,
Amen.

Now, here's the thing; we are fighting for our testimony. We are fighting for our positive pregnancy test, healthy pregnancy/delivery, and healthy newborn baby to snuggle in our arms. So yes, there are some things for which we fight. However, the big aha is that there are also some things that we already contain, not because we prayed for it, but because Jesus already bought it for us. We still fight, though not in the way we might at first think. What do I mean by that? Well, dear friend, we need to honestly and truly understand what Jesus did for us on the cross. I thought I understood, but oh, how wrong I was.

#checkitout: He paid for our white-as-snow clean slate every day. No matter how many times we mess up or sin, He has already paid to have it erased. He bought every sickness we will ever have; He took it upon His body and paid for it in full with the stripes on His back. Every emotional result of sin, sorrow, shame, guilt, remorse are all paid for; every physical result of sin, sickness, pain, and premature death, He bought it *all*. Then, what happened after He died that day on the cross? He didn't just rise again. No, He also spent three days in Sheol stripping away the keys of authority from Satan (#sheolequalsthegrave). Jesus took *all* authority away from Satan; all power stripped, gone. Then, He went on to defeat death by being raised from the dead. On top of that, when He ascended into Heaven, His Spirit came to dwell in our hearts. Now, Jesus sits at the right hand of God (#micdrop).

What does this mean for us? I am getting there, but first, I am laying the foundation and giving background knowledge as to why we are *legally* allowed to take authority. So, get excited! This is good stuff.

What, then, is authority? Authority actually comes from the Greek word *exousia*, meaning power, the authority or right to act and delegate authority. Let's look at what Jesus said about authority, "...All authority (all power of absolute rule) in heaven and on earth has been given to Me." (Matthew 28:18, AMP) When did Jesus say this? After He had risen from the grave. Who did He say it to? His disciples, just before He gave the Great Commission. Why did He tell them about His authority before sending them off? So they could go make disciples and wage war against the enemy who now had no power (#booyah):

> *Listen carefully: I have given you authority [that you now possess] to tread on serpents and scorpions, and [the ability to exercise authority] over all the power of the enemy (Satan); and nothing will [in any way] harm you. Luke 10:19, AMP*

Wow, that is so good! Jesus gave His authority to His disciples. That means He has given us His authority as well, like a gift. He bought it for us. Therefore, we do not have to strive for authority; we simply believe it and receive it (#thatsfighting).

Among others, Paul clearly understood this fact and encouraged his fellow believers of the same:

> *And [I pray] that the eyes of your heart [the very center and core of your being] may be enlightened [flooded with light by the Holy Spirit], so that you will know and cherish the hope [the divine guarantee, the confident expectation] to which He has called you, the riches of His glorious inheritance in the saints (God's people), and [so that you will begin to know] what the immeasurable and unlimited and surpassing greatness of His [active, spiritual] power is in us who believe. These are in accordance with the working of His mighty strength which He produced in Christ when He raised Him from the dead and seated Him at His own right hand in the heavenly places, far above all rule and authority and power and dominion [whether angelic or human], and [far above] every name that is named [above every title that can be conferred], not only in this age and world but also in the one to come. And He put all things [in every realm] in subjection under Christ's feet, and appointed Him as [supreme and authoritative]*

> *head over all things in the church, which is His body, the fullness of Him who fills and completes all things in all [believers]. Ephesians 1:18-23, AMP*

My goodness, I still have to read this passage over and over again to grasp everything Paul is saying. His power is *active, immeasurable,* and *unlimited.* Not only is Jesus far above all power and authority, but so is His name. Another gift for us is the use of His name. He is far above every name that is named and every title, which means He is far above the title of The Barren Woman. Also, God has put all things in every realm under His feet and appointed Jesus as head over the church. That's us! We are the church. We are the fullness of Him who fills and completes all things through His power and authority. How amazing is that?

How about some more? (#yesplease) "And He raised us up together with Him [when we believed], and seated us with Him in the heavenly places, [because we are] in Christ Jesus." (Ephesians 2:6, AMP) Dear friend, we are in Jesus, and He is in us. When we choose to believe in Him and confess Him as our Savior, He raises us up to be seated with Him in Heaven (#aha #lightbulb). This is it! This is the reason we can take authority and believe for our positive pregnancy test. This is why we can receive supernatural health from what He did for us on the cross (#drumrollplease).

We are not of this world! We are seated in Heaven with Jesus!

We are citizens under His kingdom rule, not this evil and diseased and barren earth. How do I know this? "For He has rescued us and has drawn us to Himself from the dominion of darkness, and has transferred us to the kingdom of His beloved Son." (Colossians 1:13, AMP)

Where and what is His kingdom? Are we talking about Heaven here? Nope! We are talking about the here and now because His Spirit dwells within us.

The Pharisees, the know-it-alls of the Old Testament covenant, had similar questions:

> *Now having been asked by the Pharisees when the kingdom of God would come, He replied, "The kingdom of God is not coming with*

signs to be observed or with a visible display; nor will people say, 'Look! Here it is!' or, 'There it is!' **For the kingdom of God is among you [because of My presence].**" *(emphasis added) Luke 17:20-21, AMP*

The Kingdom of Heaven is at hand, right here, right now. This world and all its evil decay ain't got nothin' on us! But wait, there's more! We are under Heaven's rule, and we currently live on the earth; you might say we are dual citizens. Even so, Jesus has already overcome it! (John 16:33)

You may be thinking, *But, I thought we live in a fallen world!* How many times have I heard that? How many times have I said it myself? It's crazy, isn't it? We accept everything so readily as "normal" in this world just because it's the result of sin or because we want answers to why bad things happen to good people; so then, we make up our own theologies to comfort ourselves and others (#ouch #guiltyascharged). I know, I know. The Bible tells us that Satan is the god of this world (2 Corinthians 4:4). Yes, we know that evil, death, disease, and tragedy all entered this world through sin. And yes, in this world we have tribulation and distress and trials, but the Bible also tells us that this is the very way we enter into God's kingdom (#saywhat), "It is through many tribulations and hardships that we must enter the kingdom of God." (Acts 14:22, AMP)

We have already established that a tribulation is a really long trial. The Greek word is *thlipsis* means pressure, crushing, squashing, squeezing, and is used when describing grapes in an olive press. If tribulation is simply pressure, then what do you suppose we are to do with that pressure? And, yeah, okay, it's more like a distressful, heavy, I-feel-like-I'm-gonna-die sort of pressure, but do we just give up and get smashed? Or do we fight through it? Maybe that is why Paul said, "I **press** on toward the goal…" (Philippians 3:14, NKJV emphasis added) What is my point? Well, how often do we not enter God's kingdom when under adversity? How often do we just accept sickness, disease, and barrenness? How often do we neglect the reality of our citizenship in Heaven and the legal rights that go with it? What if the very area in which we are dealing with adversity is the same area in which He wants us to have authority (#selah #readthatagain)?

Here is the truth: No matter if we are surrounded by sickness and disease, tribulation or suffering, we can still have perfect health, perfect peace, and abundant joy because we are abiding in Christ and belong to His victorious kingdom. In fact, we have *so* much authority that we have the power to bring Heaven's kingdom to earth:

> *I will give you the keys (authority) of the kingdom of heaven; and whatever you bind [forbid, declare to be improper and unlawful] on earth will have [already] been bound in heaven, and whatever you loose [permit, declare lawful] on earth will have [already] been loosed in heaven. Matthew 16:19, AMP*

The Lord's Prayer is beginning to make a bit more sense, then "... Our Father who is in heaven, Hallowed be Your name. Your kingdom come, Your will be done on earth as it is in heaven. Give us this day our daily bread." (Matthew 6:9-11, AMP) I included verse 11 so that you could see how this prayer is to be said *daily*. We can pray that His kingdom will come and His will be done on earth as it is in Heaven *every day*! How does this get accomplished? Through His body, that's us!

Because we belong in Heaven's kingdom, we can take authority for the gifts He has already given us through the promises in His Word. For example, He promises the forgiveness of our sin, so when we mess up, we know we don't have to allow shame or guilt to overwhelm us. He promises that by His stripes, we are healed; so, we don't have to accept the nasty flu bug dominoing through our neighborhood. He promises that He makes The Barren Woman a Joyful Mother of children, so we don't have to accept being barren any longer. He promises He will satisfy us with a long life, so we don't have to accept the fear of dying prematurely. He promises to send His angels to guard and protect us, so we don't have to worry about getting in a wreck during rush hour (#sogood #getmypointyet).

We also have the legal power and authority to forbid whatever is forbidden in Heaven. There is no disease in Heaven; therefore, we do not accept any disease in our household. There is nothing barren and desolate in Heaven; therefore, we do not accept barrenness. Everything about God's kingdom is fruitful, lush, and multiplied; therefore, we are fruitful, and we multiply in every area of our lives. We reject barrenness in our bodies because He tells us to be fruitful and multiply. It is our *legal right*, not because we deserve it or because we work for it, but because of His finished work on the cross and through the resurrection. This is where we get our authority.

I know it is somewhat difficult to wrap your mind around. Don't try to figure it out logically or even theologically. Everything God has given us is received through faith. Using our authority will not come to us naturally. We have to take authority and press through *in* that authority. We have to know that we possess it and that we have to fight *from* it (#hooah).

If all of these light bulbs weren't enough to get you lit up, then let's try another one. Let's talk about that cross again. Let's find out what it did to our barren womb.

The cross. The old rugged cross. I'm not going to go into depth about the actual history of the cross (#thankGod), but I do want to go into depth about what Jesus' death on the cross actually did for us. Remembering that it is not solely about what happened on the cross, it is also what Jesus did in Sheol before God resurrected Him from the grave. It is about His *completed* work on the cross. Everything about the cross, His storming the gates of hell, and His resurrection, is intertwined. So, in a nutshell, these are some truths the finished work of the cross made available to us:

- We are no longer slaves to sin, and our old nature was nailed to the cross (Romans 6:6)
- We are dead to sin and alive to righteousness (1 Peter 2:24)
- Jesus triumphed over all demonic forces of evil operating against us (Colossians 2:15)

- He reconciled all believers as one Body (Ephesians 2:16)
- He redeemed us from the curse of the Law by becoming a curse for us (Galatians 3:13)
- He bore our sins, sicknesses, weaknesses, distresses, sorrows, pains, punishment, guilt, iniquities, oppression, and griefs in His body (Isaiah 53, AMPC; 1 Peter 2:24)

Pretty amazing, isn't it? On the cross, Jesus bore our sins in His body. He became our sin; therefore, He also became the *effects* of our sin. What do I mean by this? Well, this works two ways: A) When we mess up, for example, when we don't believe what His Word says, that's unbelief, right? We now know this is sin. How do we then feel? Personally, I feel wretched, guilty, heavy, or oppressed. I look above, however, and see that in Isaiah 53, He took on this emotional effect for me. He became them, so to speak. Before I even repent, then, I do not have to accept feeling this way (#stickwithmehere). B) The effect of sin from Adam and Eve is this fallen world, rampant with disease, sickness, premature death, barrenness, miscarriage, tragedy, etc. Basically, anything opposite of the kingdom is an effect of sin. Jesus took these effects of sin on His broken body and removed them from us completely. Therefore, He removed barrenness from The Barren Woman (#boom).

Let's look at a few examples of this in the Bible. We can see how God took the effects of sin away from Hannah. Here is a recap: Elkanah, her husband, had two wives, Hannah and Peninnah. Like Rachel, Hannah was barren. Peninnah, however, would just look at her husband and pop up pregnant. Elkanah favored Hannah, though, and loved her more. He would give her double portions of the sacrifice even though she did not have children. Not only was Peninnah fruitful, she also bullied Hannah and made her miserable, weep, and refuse to eat (#soundsfamiliar):

*Then Elkanah her husband said to her, "Hannah, why do you weep? Why do you not eat? And why is your **heart grieved?** Am I not better to you than ten sons?" So Hannah arose after they had finished eating and drinking in Shiloh. Now Eli the priest was sitting on the seat by*

> *the doorpost of the tabernacle of the* LORD. *And she was in* **bitterness** *of soul, and prayed to the* LORD *and wept in* **anguish**. *(emphasis added)* 1 Samuel 1:8-10, NKJV

While she was praying, she made a vow. If God gave her a son, she would return him back to the temple when he was weaned. The priest thought she was drunk, which reveals how badly she was probably weeping; there might have even been some thrashing about, pounding of the floor, and wailing going on (#uglycry #beentheredonethat). Hannah defends herself by saying:

> *No, my lord, I am a woman of* **sorrowful spirit**. *I have drunk neither wine nor intoxicating drink, but have poured out my soul before the* LORD. *Do not consider your maidservant a wicked woman, for out of the abundance of my* **complaint** *and* **grief** *I have spoken until now. (emphasis added)* 1 Samuel 1:15-16, NKJV

Obviously, the words I emboldened are the emotional effects of The Barren Woman – these effects Jesus bore for us on the cross. In conclusion, Hannah conceives, names her son Samuel (meaning "heard by God"), and after he is weaned, dedicates him to service at the temple. Samuel grew up to become the prophet who anointed both King Saul and King David. And not only that, Hannah went on to conceive three more sons and two daughters! Talk about redemption. God redeemed her! That's His heart! That's His character! Dear friends, that is the same God we serve today. On that cross, Jesus bore our barrenness, our griefs, our sorrows, our bitterness, our anguish, and our reproach.

Speaking of reproach, the Greek word for reproach is *oneidizo*, which means mocking, ridiculing, scolding, insulting, and from Hannah's story, provoking. Jesus also suffered this while on the cross. Have you suffered reproach for being barren like Hannah? I have. It has been accomplished very slyly, but the job was still done. Being reproached wounds the heart. If it has not been done by others, it has been done by our own thoughts or by the enemy (#truethat). The good news is that Jesus took it away!

Let's look at what Rachel said when she conceived and bore Joseph, "Then God remembered Rachel, and God listened to her and opened her womb. And she conceived and bore a son, and said, 'God has taken away my reproach.'" (Genesis 30:22-23, NKJV) Another account of reproach being taken away is of Elisabeth, John the Baptist's mother. Elisabeth was barren and in her old age when an angel told her husband they would conceive a son, the very son who was the forerunner of Jesus. Here was her reaction while she was pregnant, "Thus the Lord has dealt with me, in the days when He looked on me, to take away my reproach among people." (Luke 1:25, NKJV)

Dear sister, we do not have to wait until we conceive for God to take away our reproach. Why? Because He has already taken it away! When Jesus' body was buried in the ground, so was our reproach (#hallelujah). On the cross and through His finished work, Jesus bore our sin and effects of sin; He bore our barrenness and effects of barrenness; He bore our reproach.

If we do some further study in the Bible, we will see that every barren couple who wanted children conceived and bore a child. In fact, all three "Mothers of Faith" were barren. Sarah, Rebekah, Rachel; all three of them conceived after God's intervention, yet they each had their own journey from The Barren Woman to The Joyful Mother of children; each made mistakes along the way, and each finally allowed God to complete His work in them. What would have happened if they had given up and didn't stand on the promise God gave them?

Or look at Hannah. Her son had a pretty big role in God's plan. He anointed King David, and Jesus just so happens to come from his lineage. What would have happened had Hannah not cried out that day in the temple and fought for her testimony? What about Sarah? What if Sarah didn't finally reach that place of judging God faithful? How about Mary and Elisabeth? What if they were persistent in their unbelief and never truly believed that with God, all things are possible?

In conclusion, we can all agree that the Bible shows fruitfulness as a blessing. As a matter of fact, it is one of the blessings promised to the

Israelites if they would keep God's commandments. If fruitfulness is a blessing, then what is barrenness? If the fruit of the womb is a reward (Psalm 127:3-5), then what does it mean if your womb is empty? If a man is blessed whose quiver is full of children, then what is a man who doesn't have children?

Cursed (#ouch).

Nobody really wants to admit it, but we can agree that barrenness *still* feels like a curse in today's day and age. I have some more good news for us, though. On the cross, Jesus became the curse for us, "Christ purchased our freedom and redeemed us from the curse of the Law and its condemnation by becoming a curse for us – for it is written, 'Cursed is everyone who hangs [crucified] on a tree (cross).' (Galatians 3:13, AMP) This means that spiritually and physically, we are no longer cursed. If we believe for physical and emotional healing from sickness and disease by the finished work of the cross, then we can believe for a baby by the same work. After all, barrenness is usually just another form of sickness in the reproductive organs.

#bigsigh: Dear friend, I honestly tried to prepare you for this heavy stuff. It is pretty radical. Then again, the Gospel has always been radical. Don't just take my word for it, though. Get in the Bible and study. Ask the Holy Spirit to reveal His wisdom to you. He will do so if you ask Him (James 1:5).

3. Stand your ground

Here we are, remembering the promises, walking in our authority, testing it out bit by bit, here and there. See what I mean by being promoted to "warrior princess" status? Because as you walk in your authority, you will also need to continue to stand your ground. You cannot do so without remembering what God has promised through the finished work of the cross. And, you need to be fully convinced that you have a right to believe for anything the Word promises for the simple fact that it is absolute truth and Jesus bought it for you (#amen). I am sorry, girls, but there is no more room for wavering or doubting while possessing the land. It *can* be done.

On the day I wrote this, I was feeling so fatigued and loopy from allergens floating around out there. Usually, when I am physically feeling rotten, the enemy has always taken the opening to get defeat into my thought process. However, I refused to go there. As I was out shopping and just not feeling like things were going smoothly, I continued to reject any self-pity or doubt. Trust me; this is huge. Normally when I am out and about, I see moms with babies everywhere. If I am feeling tired, my thoughts tend to go straight towards hopelessness. This day, though, I rejected those thoughts, cast my cares, and allowed the Holy Spirit to be strong for me. This is standing my ground (#inanutshell).

Yes, it's that simple, although your circumstances might be a tad different. It could be another big fat negative (#BFN), or a visit from Aunt Flo, or a bad report from the doctor. Whatever it is, stand your ground. Smith Wigglesworth described this best, *"I'm not moved by what I see. I'm not moved by what I feel. I'm moved only by what I believe."* But what about when we are just having "one of those days"? The following passage describes how to stand our ground:

> *...be strong in the Lord [draw your strength from Him and be empowered through your union with Him] and in the power of His [boundless] might. Put on the full armor of God [for His precepts are like the splendid armor of a heavily-armed soldier], so that you may be able to [successfully] stand up against all the schemes and the strategies and the deceits of the devil. For our struggle is not against flesh and blood [contending only with physical opponents], but against the rulers, against the powers, against the world forces of this [present] darkness, against the spiritual forces of wickedness in the heavenly (supernatural) places. Therefore, put on the complete armor of God, so that you will be able to [successfully] resist and stand your ground in the evil day [of danger], and having done everything [that the crisis demands], to stand firm [in your place, fully prepared, immovable, victorious]. Ephesians 6:10-13, AMP*

My goodness, that is good stuff! I seriously love the Word. If that doesn't get you fired up, I don't know what will! First of all, we must be strong in the Lord. Remember how we learned that we are seated with Jesus, and He is in us? Well, this is where that wisdom comes in handy. Paul said to be strong in the Lord and His power. We do this by not taking ownership of the negativity. How we are feeling, what we see, what we think, our natural circumstances, etc., we cast onto Him. We reject the thought or emotion, letting that rejection propel us into the strength of the Holy Spirit who is right there inside us. And, if we are feeling weak in soul or physical body, we simply tell Him. Don't be afraid to communicate with Him. When we are feeling weak, remember that He loves our weaknesses because He gets to be a Daddy and strengthen us with His power.

Secondly, the Amplified Bible describes putting on the armor of God as putting on His precepts. What are His precepts? His Word! His statutes, mandates, and commandments. Having the Word built up in our souls is the only way we can successfully stand against the strategies of the enemy. So then, this would be a good time to go back and revisit the scriptures of the previous sections.

Lastly, after we have done everything we can do, we need to stand firm in our place, fully prepared, immovable, and victorious. Dear sister, you are already prepared. Do not be moved. Do not be shaken. You are victorious! Stand your ground and refuse to allow anything less than truth into your thought lives and perceptions!

BECOME WHAT IS SPOKEN

#disclaimer: Honestly, God has taken me somewhere so completely unexpected that as I begin writing this section, it has become a little daunting. This is because He is having me write about a subject that I am still in the process of learning. Usually, He has me write about a subject *after* I have learned it, but this one is completely foreign to me. So, I'll do my best and trust that the Holy Spirit will come through like always (#wheniamweakHeisstrong).

The next way to fight for your testimony is to become what is spoken. In this section, we will learn to prophesy, declare, and decree. Here we go:

1. Prophesy

Before I attempt to explain this to you, let me start off with a backstory (#yesplease). One morning, during my worship time, the Holy Spirit gave me a picture that I will remember for the rest of my life. I was sitting in Jesus' lap, and He was holding me like you cradle a baby. He was running His hands through my hair, pushing it out of my eyes and caressing my face, and laying His hands on different parts of my body. He was speaking over and over again, "beautiful," "fruitful," "multiply," "joyful mother." Then, He would start back over and lay His hands on my womb and speak again. This went on and on until I was so overcome with peace and love that I could scarcely move. I was heavy with it (#inagoodwayofcourse).

I needed more than the experience, though. I wanted to find out what that picture meant. I needed my "what" and my "why" answered. It took me a few hours to process this experience. When I finally received revelation, it blew me away. You see, God's Word, the Bible, is not just made up of radical and wild historical stories for our instruction; it is not just a book of prophecy; it is not just an account of Jesus' life; it is not just a book where the words come alive, and we are transformed; it is *so much more than that.*

As Jesus was speaking those words over me with a lover's caress, I had the most poignant aha moment yet! Friend, the Bible and its promises are like a love letter, to me, to you, to us, from Jesus (#happysigh). To go even deeper than that, I believe that every promise in the Bible is Jesus Himself prophesying directly to us. Why is this significant? Let me explain.

First, to prophesy means to speak forth, declaring the will of God. Where do we find the will of God? His Word. What do we know about His Word? The entirety of it is truth. Who is the Spirit of truth? Jesus. It only makes sense that as He loves us, He prophesies His truth as a caress and a love letter to us as His beloved daughters and His dear friends (#andwarriorprincesses).

Second, prophecy is a gift of the Spirit and still very much a part of today's body of Christ, although not as much a part as it should be

(#iwontgotheretoday). If you're confused about the gifts of the Spirit, then I encourage you to do some study (see 1 Corinthians 12:7-11). He gives every believer these gifts to minister to the body. In fact, good ol' Paul encouraged every believer to pursue, love, and desire spiritual gifts, especially prophecy (1 Corinthians 14:1). This is most likely because prophecy brings edification, exhortation, and comfort to the body of Christ (1 Corinthians 14:3); also, Jesus Himself is the Spirit of prophecy (Revelation 19:20). So, to become more and more like Him, we must also prophesy.

Therefore, when the Word says He makes The Barren Woman a Joyful Mother of children (Psalm 113:9), He has prophesied. When we read, we are like a fruitful vine, and our children are like olive plants around our table (Psalm 128:3), He has prophesied. When He confidently speaks that none shall be barren or miscarry (Exodus 23:26), He prophesied. So then, dear friends, we must also prophesy. I know, I know. We need our "how" answered, and probably our "what" too. Like, what is the difference between speaking life (#akaconfession) and prophesying? (#gladyouasked)

I see the difference between confession and prophecy like this: confession operates through a choice of the will based on head knowledge; prophecy operates through the power of the Holy Spirit based on heart knowledge (#myopinion).

We learned in an earlier chapter, Speak Life, that confession is simply agreeing out loud with God's promises, but confession, if not partnered with the Holy Spirit through faith, can turn into a humanistic, ritualistic, unfruitful process, especially if you don't yet know your true identity or you are speaking out of your own strength. I learned this from experience. I thought all I had to do was agree with the Word. I even made up "I statements" that my husband and I spoke every day over our bodies. It was the same thing every day, and it got very ritualistic, dry, and exhausting. Plus, it didn't help that I didn't truly believe what I was confessing until after I went through the process of The Wilderness. However, as I learned my true identity as a friend of God and honestly believed it in my heart, my confession supernaturally morphed into prophecy because my words became empowered by the Holy Spirit (#readthatagain).

As I have continued to pursue and draw near to Jesus, I have been asking for the manifestation of His presence in the form of His spiritual gifts. Thus, I began prophesying. Seriously. Like speaking to random women at the gym. I had never even met them before, and I would immediately know pertinent information about them. Yeah, I know. Weird, right?

Remember, at the time of writing this section, I am still in the process of learning about all of this. So, when I began speaking to these random women, I didn't even know that what I was doing was actually prophecy. My husband kept saying that I was growing in the gift of prophecy, and I kept disagreeing with him. I didn't realize that words of knowledge were classified in the same category (#ihatewhenhesright). Going out there to "shock and awe" people by how much I know, especially about them, was not at all my intention. I was not proclaiming in a loud, booming voice, "Thus saith the Lord!" as I spoke to these women. My intention was to show the love of Jesus by simply being an open and willing vessel. I would ask the Holy Spirit the question, "What do you have for her this morning?".

Several times, He would reveal to me that I needed to pray for a family member, friend, or child. At other times, He would have me tell a woman that He thinks she is an amazing grandmother. To another, He wanted her to know He likes to listen to her sing. I had no clue that these were forms of prophecy until my brilliant husband brought it to my attention and wouldn't quit.

So anyway, there it is. We cannot prophesy without knowing who we are in Jesus (#myopinion), we cannot prophesy without faith, we cannot prophesy without being willing and available to carry His gift, and we cannot prophesy without pursuing love. Why? Because pursuing love and desiring spiritual gifts is synonymous. We cannot successfully have one without the other. Yes, it is true that people can operate in spiritual gifts without love, but as Paul said, if that is the case, then we are nothing (1 Corinthians 13:2). With love, however, we are everything. Our confession now has supernatural power behind it. It is no longer a ritual, but a Holy Spirit empowered prophecy (#boom #getexcited). So, what does this have to do with getting pregnant? And, how do we become what is spoken? When we…

2. Declare

Now we know the Bible contains hundreds of fulfilled prophecies. Even today, prophecies are being fulfilled. Some prophecies will not be fulfilled until Jesus' second coming (#studyitforyourself). What else do we know about prophecy? Well, it doesn't take much to see that before a prophecy can be fulfilled, it must first be spoken (#duh).

This is not just about speaking random scriptures over our lives, hoping and praying that they will come true. No, it is realizing that those scriptures we are speaking come directly from God's mouth to ours, "I have put My words in your mouth…" (Isaiah 51:16, AMP)

His Word and His prophecies never return void; they perform and produce fruit. We must have an immovable belief in this fact, "So will My word be which goes out of My mouth; It will not return to Me void (useless, without result), Without accomplishing what I desire, And without succeeding in the matter for which I sent it." (Isaiah 55:11, AMP) Surely, we can rest on this truth that, as long as we are speaking His Word, our words will bear fruit. This is called prophetic declaration.

Let's look again at the word confess. In Greek, it has the implication of a binding, public declaration. If we look at the dictionary definition, we see that declare is to make known formally, officially, explicitly, or to state emphatically. So, as we are prophetically declaring the truth of His promises, we are simultaneously making known and stating emphatically something to which we have a legal right. This is not because we have earned it. Rather, it is because Jesus already bought it. Nor because we deserve it. Rather, it is because we are His beloved daughters. Neither are we entitled to it. Rather, this is only because we have received His inheritance.

Prophetic declaration is powerful, so powerful that the earth was formed by it. The phrase "God said" occurs ten times in the first chapter of the book of Genesis. God literally declared the world into existence. More than that, the entire Old Testament prophetically declares the coming Messiah. Jesus, Himself, modeled prophetic declaration throughout His whole ministry on earth:

- Jesus declared that not everyone who says "Lord" will enter the kingdom of heaven (Matthew 7:21)
- Jesus declared that the Gentiles will sit down and feast with Abraham, Isaac, and Jacob in Heaven (Matthew 8:11)
- Jesus declared that whoever confesses Him before men, He will confess before His Father in Heaven (Matthew 10:32)
- Jesus declared His death and resurrection (Mark 9:31)
- Jesus declared the New Covenant (Mark 14:24)

As you can see, I didn't even get to Luke or John, or even through the full chapters of Matthew and Mark. These examples barely skim the surface of prophetic declarations spoken by Jesus.

#rabbittrail: I asked my brilliant husband to give me some more examples. He began rattling off so many I began to feel a little overwhelmed. I know this is deep. I know it seems as if I am speaking a foreign language, and that was never my intent. When I made the choice to obey and write this book, I had every intention of being real and just lil' ol' me. I have said it over and over again, I am no scholar or theologian. My wisdom and knowledge come straight from my experience in the presence of God. I told you at the beginning of this section that I felt ill-prepared to write about this topic. I don't want to lose you and be the reason for bored, glassy eyes. So please stick with me. I promise it will all make sense eventually.

Now for the question we have all been waiting for! How do we put this into action? How do we become what is spoken? By the power of the...

3. Decree

This is the action (#huh). We decree ourselves into the promise. We release what is inside of us and who we truly are through the power of the decree (#hearmeout).

What does decree even mean? Well, in Hebrew, there are two kinds of decrees. The first one is *ath*, meaning a law. This is similar to the dictionary definition of an official order issued by a legal authority. Just like in the previous section, "Take authority," we learned that those of us in covenant with God have the authority to *take* authority. So, a decree is an official order hammered down by us! Here are some synonyms for official order that might make more sense: edict, command, mandate.

#disclaimer: Please remember, I am not teaching some magic formula to get pregnant. Honestly, I don't even know if it works. Remember? I am writing all of this in faith. Technically, I have been decreeing since the Holy Spirit gave me the title for this book, but I didn't even know it until seriously right now. I didn't force the decree; I was simply being led by the Spirit, and He brought me here. As I keep saying, we each will have our own journey as we commit to follow Him and make several choices explained in this book. We each will have our own testimony. Remember, this is the process of mine.

So, before I go any further, let's tie all of this new-found knowledge together (#yesplease). Here is becoming what is spoken in a nutshell:

- We receive God's promises He has so lovingly prophesied over His children; which are found in His Word; the truth
- With our voices, we verbally and prophetically declare His truth and will
- This results in an active decree, law, official order, and command because of our legal authority in what Jesus accomplished for us through the finished work of the cross

Prophecy (truth/promise) + Declaration (the voice) = Decree (the action/law)

#deepbreaths #thatsalot: Here are a few examples from Jesus:

> *Now early in the morning, as Jesus was coming back to the city, He was hungry. Seeing a lone fig tree at the roadside, He went to it and found nothing but leaves on it; and He said to it,* **"Never again will fruit come from you."** *And at once the fig tree withered. (emphasis added) Matthew 21:18-19, AMP*

Jesus decreed that the fig tree would never again bear fruit. Basically, He cursed it through the power of the decree. Look what happened next:

> *When the disciples saw it, they were astonished and asked, "How is it that the fig tree has withered away all at once?" Jesus replied to them, "I assure you and most solemnly say to you,* **if you have faith [personal trust and confidence in Me] and do not doubt or allow yourself to be drawn in two directions, you will not only do what was done to the fig tree, but even if you say to this mountain, 'Be taken up and thrown into the sea,' it will happen [if God wills it]. And whatever you ask for in prayer, believing, you will receive."** *(emphasis added) Matthew 21:20-22, AMP*

The disciples didn't yet know it, but Jesus was prophesying over them throughout the rest of this passage. Not only to them, but to us over 2,000 years later. How cool is that? Another example I have for you is about a man who truly understood Jesus' authority. Not only that, he understood the power of the decree:

> *As Jesus went into Capernaum, a centurion came up to Him, begging Him [for help], and saying, "Lord, my servant is lying at home paralyzed, with intense and terrible, tormenting pain." Jesus said to him, "I will come and heal him." But the centurion replied to Him,* **"Lord, I am not worthy to have You come under my roof, but only say the word, and my servant will be healed. For I also am a man subject to authority [of a higher rank], with soldiers subject to me; and I say to one, 'Go!' and he goes, and to another, 'Come!' and he comes, and to my slave, 'Do this!' and he does it."** *(emphasis added) Matthew 8:5-9, AMP*

Cool, huh? The centurion just explained decreeing far better than I ever could! He has got to be one of my most favorite Bible characters. Firstly, because he is a soldier, and I have a soft spot for soldiers (#armywife), and secondly, because he just plain gets it. Let's keep reading:

> *When Jesus heard this, He was amazed and said to those who were following Him, "I tell you truthfully, I have not found such great faith [as this] with anyone in Israel. I say to you that many [Gentiles] will come from east and west, and will sit down [to feast at the table, and enjoy God's promises] with Abraham, Isaac, and Jacob in the kingdom of heaven [because they accepted Me as Savior], while the sons and heirs of the kingdom [the descendants of Abraham who will not recognize Me as Messiah] will be thrown out into the outer darkness; in that place [which is farthest removed from the kingdom] there will be weeping [in sorrow and pain] and grinding of teeth [in distress and anger]." **Then Jesus said to the centurion, "Go; it will be done for you as you have believed." And the servant was restored to health at that very hour.** (emphasis added) Matthew 8:10-13, AMP*

Not only does Jesus marvel at finding a man who understood His authority and the power of His decree, but this man was also a Gentile (an outsider). This man had no problem recognizing Jesus as Messiah, and because of this, Jesus then prophesied that the Gospel would reach the Gentiles and they would enter eternity, as well. All from a man who simply understood the decree (#woohoo)!

Dear friend, I want to be like that. I think we make the Gospel too difficult sometimes, although I know it doesn't help when people like me write books like this where it gets all detailed and complicated (#sorrynotsorry). Anyway, here is another example:

> *"Teacher, I brought You my son, possessed with a spirit which makes him unable to speak; and whenever it seizes him [intending to do harm], it throws him down, and he foams [at the mouth], and grinds his teeth and becomes stiff. I told Your disciples to drive it out, and*

they could not do it." He replied, "O unbelieving (faithless) generation, how long shall I be with you? How long shall I put up with you? Bring him to Me!" They brought the boy to Him. When the [demonic] spirit saw Him, immediately it threw the boy into a convulsion, and falling to the ground he began rolling around and foaming at the mouth. Jesus asked his father, "How long has this been happening to him?" And he answered, "Since childhood. The demon has often thrown him both into fire and into water, intending to kill him. But if You can do anything, take pity on us and help us!"
Mark 5: 16-22, AMP

If you can do anything. Eek. Them's fightin' words to Jesus. In the next part of the passage, we will see how Jesus made the father declare his belief. We will also hear Jesus prophesy that all things are possible to those who believe:

*Jesus said to him, "[You say to Me,] 'If You can?' All things are possible for the one who believes and trusts [in Me]!" Immediately the father of the boy cried out [with a desperate, piercing cry], saying, "I do believe; help [me overcome] my unbelief." When Jesus saw that a crowd was rapidly gathering [around them], He rebuked the unclean spirit, saying to it, **"You deaf and mute spirit, I command you, come out of him and never enter him again!"** After screaming out and throwing him into a terrible convulsion, it came out. The boy looked so much like a corpse [so still and pale] that many [of the spectators] said, "He is dead!" But Jesus took him by the hand and raised him; and he stood up. (emphasis added) Mark 5:23-26, AMP*

We saw how Jesus cursed the fig tree through the decree, healed a man's servant by the power of decree, and how He kicked out a demon and forbade it to enter into the boy again through decree. Wowsers. It kind of makes you want to study all of Jesus' miracles, doesn't it? Let's take a look at one more:

One of the criminals who had been hanged [on a cross beside Him] kept hurling abuse at Him, saying, "Are You not the Christ? Save

> *Yourself and us [from death]!" But the other one rebuked him, saying, "Do you not even fear God, since you are under the same sentence of condemnation? We are suffering justly, because we are getting what we deserve for what we have done; but this Man has done nothing wrong." And he was saying,* ***"Jesus, [please] remember me when You come into Your kingdom!" Jesus said to him, "I assure you and most solemnly say to you, today you will be with Me in Paradise."*** *(emphasis added) Luke 23:39-43 AMP*

All this criminal did was believe in his heart, acknowledge Jesus and His kingship, and Jesus then prophetically decreed that this man would be in Paradise with Him. Isn't that awesome? (#yesyesyes)

And you know something else? There is a pretty consistent trend with Jesus' miracles and decrees. The person to whom the miracle was given *had* to speak. That person not only had to speak, but they had to declare *something*. Even the woman with the issue of blood, after she touched Jesus' garment, had to own up to her act of faith (Mark 5:28-34). She believed it in her mind and heart, but Jesus wanted to hear something come out of her mouth. Pretty interesting, isn't it?

What does this mean for The Barren Woman, then? How do we put this into practical prophetic action? For me, I started with the declaration. I simply began singing. This was easy for me because I'm a singer and I love music. I wasn't singing my favorite worship songs, though; I was singing acapella, the words erupting straight from the Word built up in my heart. The primary phrase I began with was, "I am _____" (insert: joyful mother, fruitful vine, etc.). I followed this with "I receive it. I believe it." I just sang this over and over again anytime I found myself alone. I would go to bed with it in my heart and wake up with it on my lips. I began to keep the radio turned off and instead sang my declaration. At church, I ignored the words being sung all around me and instead sang my declaration. In fact, my favorite music to listen to right now is piano worship so that I can sing my own song! Is it the same tune and words each time? Actually, no. Each day is a new spontaneous tune and spontaneous lyric. I don't have to think about the words as they come forth; they just arise from the truth deep within my spirit (#thatsgoodstuff).

It's the same thing when it comes to journaling or prayer. I might write down declarations, but these also spontaneously arise from the Word rooted in my heart. I don't get the same thing each day. And it doesn't feel forced. It flows naturally (#supernaturally). Remember, though, no rituals! No long lists of confessions! Just write it or speak it or sing it all day long and meditate on it in the night.

As for the decree, I will be honest with you. This one took me a little longer to apply. You see, I had no problem declaring who I was. However, I did forget an equally important piece; that is, I forgot to actually take authority and issue the command to my body and its condition. I needed to command my body to line up with the Word to command barrenness and whatever sickness or disease is causing it to leave in the name of Jesus; to remind both my husband's and my bodies what Jesus provided for us through the finished work of the cross. But again, this is not to be done ritualistically. It needs to be led by the Holy Spirit. Decree when you're concerned or feel your thoughts trying to go in opposite directions. It also must not be forced. I do not have to convince myself of the truth. I actually *believe* the truth. I *believe* what I'm declaring. And I *believe* what I'm decreeing.

When you get to this place, you will know. You will know because a peace and confidence that you have never had before are there. You will know because your desire for God will not be in competition with your desire for a baby. You will know because your decree always, always evolves into praise, thankfulness, and authentic worship to our Father.

To wrap this section up, let's discuss the second Hebrew meaning for decree, which is *chaqaq*. This is the verb form meaning to cut in, inscribe, or engrave. This is significant because as we prophetically declare through our lips, the decree becomes a law, a written and inscribed law within the spiritual realm. This form of decree is equivalent to the permanency of our name being written, inscribed, and engraved on the palm of Jesus' hands (#likeatattoo Isaiah 49:16).

So, which name do you want etched on His palm, dear sister? As for me, I am no longer The Barren Woman but The Joyful Mother of children. I am no longer cursed but blessed. I am no longer infertile but fertile. I am no longer barren but abundantly fruitful (#happysigh). As this decree goes forth into the spiritual realm as a written and inscribed law, so too will my body eventually respond, and my name will change to become what is spoken and reflect His truth (#boom).

Yes, this name change is Biblical. Remember Abraham? God prophetically declared to Abraham multiple times while his name was still Abram (Exalted Father). But, it wasn't until He changed his name to Abraham (Father of a Multitude) that things *really* started happening.

John gives the account of when Jesus prophetically declared that Peter's name would be changed from Simon to Peter (John 1:42). Peter means "rock" in Greek. And yeah, this was way before Peter acted in cowardice the night Jesus was arrested. Knowing that Peter would still deny Him, Jesus prophetically decreed over Peter why He changed his name, "And I say to you that you are Peter, and on this rock I will build My church; and the gates of Hades (death) will not overpower it [by preventing the resurrection of the Christ]." (Matthew 16:18, AMP) Peter went on to preach and teach that we are "living stones," that is, we are being built into God's spiritual temple as His holy priests. Jesus' prophetic decree literally changed Peter's whole identity and mission on this earth, just as it did with Abraham, and just as it is doing with us.

Dear friend, I have found my identity. It is no longer as The Barren Woman. I am too pregnant with joy and peace and all things hopeful and expectant to consider myself barren any longer. Though it tarries, I know it will just be a matter of time before I physically become what is spoken (#Heisfaithful). Until then, "Hello, my name is The Joyful Mother of children."

SAY "AMEN"

Here we are; remembering the promise, taking our authority, standing our ground, prophesying, declaring. and decreeing. We are no longer identified by who we are not but by who we are prophetically becoming. It sounds like some serious warfare going on.

The third and final way to Possess the Land is unique. It is more subtle, but it is a powerful, defensive weapon in this fight for our testimony; more of a resolved conclusion that the fight is almost over. This is the grand finale, so to speak, the last chapter in our favorite book, the closure in a letter. This is the part of the prayer where we say "Amen" (#speakingofwhich).

One meaning of the word "Amen" is "Yes, so be it." Today, it's usually said in agreement to prayer or in response so as to make whatever was spoken our own. However, Jesus spoke it as "Truly, truly" or "This is truth," basically, "Pay attention people! This is fact!" Check this out:

> *For Jesus Christ, the Son of God, does not waver between "Yes" and "No." He is the one whom Silas, Timothy, and I preached to you, and as God's ultimate "Yes," he always does what he says.* ***For all of God's promises have been fulfilled in Christ with a resounding "Yes!" And through Christ, our "Amen" (which means 'Yes') ascends to God for his glory.*** *(emphasis added) 2 Corinthians 1:19-20, NLT*

If we have asked God for a baby, then His answer is already a big fat YES! (#BFY) We know it's His will because it's in His Word. So, through Jesus and His finished work of the cross, we have our Yes. Our job is to simply say, "Amen!" (#sobeit).

Going Deeper:

- Journal about a time when you stood still and watched God move on your behalf.
- We are grafted in and receive the Abrahamic blessings. What other promises would you like to possess?
- Meditate and record your thoughts, ahas, and revelations from Possess the Land. Because it was so much content, take your time with this.
- Activate "become what is spoken" by prophetically declaring and decreeing the Word planted in your heart.
- Scriptures to study: Jos 1:3,5; Deut. 8:1; Deut. 7:13-14; Rom. 11:17; Mt. 28:18; Lk. 10:19; Eph. 1:18-23; Eph. 2:6; Col. 1:13; Lk. 17:2-21; Jn. 16:33; 2 Cor. 4:4; Acts 14:22; Phil. 3:14; Rom. 8; Rom. 5:17; Deut. 28:13; Acts 1:8; Mt. 16:19; Mt. 6:9-11; 1 Pt. 2:24; Col. 2:15; Eph. 2:16; Gal. 3:13; Is. 53; 1 Sam. 1:8-16; Gen. 30:22-23; Lk. 1:25; Ps. 127:3-5; Jas. 1:5; Eph. 6:10-13; 1 Cor. 12:7-11; 1 Cor. 14:1,3; Rev. 19:20; Ps. 113:9; Ps. 128:3; Ex. 23:26; 1 Cor. 13:2; Is. 59:21; Is. 51:16; Is. 55:11; Mt. 7:21; Mt. 8:11; Mt. 10:32; Mk. 9:31; Mk. 14:24; Mt. 21:18-19; Mt. 21:20-22; Mt. 8:5-13; Mk. 5:16-26; Lk. 23:39-43; Is. 49:16; Gen. 17,18; Jn. 1:42; Mt. 16:18; 2 Cor. 1:19-20.

Chapter thirteen
LABOR INTO REST

#VULNERABILITYALERT:

I have been struggling. No, not with the BWD (#barrenwomandepression), but with a feeling of extreme heaviness. I am super tired and fatigued, not looking forward to the day ahead, and just wanting to sleep. Okay, so maybe it does sound more like the infamous depression (#rollingmyeyes). But anyway, I have felt heavy in my heart more than anything else, like I have been carrying around an enormous weight on my chest. So, this morning, after a bout of spontaneous worship, I decided to journal for a bit and wrote down what God was saying. He told me a few things the prior day that had unsettled me.

#sidenote: Yes, it is possible for the things of God to be unsettling. It can be an invitation for intimacy and discovery that we only get through seeking Him. You see, He told me to write all I can and then drop weight (#what). Umm, yeah. At first, I took this literally because it's not like I'm in the best shape of my life, but I am strong and healthy. As you can imagine, hearing God tell you to drop weight when you're technically not considered overweight, umm yeah, it kind of messed with my head. It was one of those times when I didn't know if it was His voice or my own. Just a few moments ago, though, I finally discerned that He was telling me to drop weight *metaphorically* (#wellduh). I needed to get rid of this spirit of heaviness. Now, why didn't He just tell me that in the first place? He just likes to keep things exciting, I guess (#Jesuslovesmetaphors).

Anyhow, this mandate to drop weight birthed this very chapter. In fact, this chapter hadn't even been included in any previous outline; it always hovered just out of reach. I've touched on bits and pieces of this idea here and there throughout this process, but I've never had enough clarity to make a distinct chapter. Until now. After some soul searching and some scripture surfing, the Holy Spirit reminded me of this passage:

Come to me, all of you who are weary and carry heavy burdens, and I will give you rest. Take my yoke upon you. Let me teach you, because I am humble and gentle at heart, and you will find rest for your souls. For my yoke is easy to bear, and the burden I give you is light. Matthew 11:28-30, NLT

#soundsfamiliar: Yes, we visited these verses in The Faith Chapter. When I studied them in a deeper context, however, I learned that Jesus is actually extending an invitation for freedom in exchange for the burden of Jewish legalism. In other words, legalism is heavy and burdensome, but Jesus is light and rest (#amen). Take a look at this same passage in The Message:

Are you tired? Worn out? Burned out on religion? Come to me. Get away with me and you'll recover your life. I'll show you how to take a real rest. Walk with me and work with me – watch how I do it. Learn the unforced rhythms of grace. I won't lay anything heavy or ill-fitting on you. Keep company with me and you'll learn to live freely and lightly. Matthew 11:28-30, MSG

What does any of this have to do with the nagging spirit of heaviness? Well, I'll be honest with you. I thought I had finished the book (#seriously). I wrote what I thought was the final chapter and thought it was complete, with the exception of an inner nudge to include a section called "eat" (#weirdiknow #itwillmakesenselater). At the same time, however, it still felt like *something* was missing. Obviously, the BFP was nowhere in sight. It was deeper than that, though, like the task wasn't complete. I was filled with worry, unrest, lack of peace, and heaviness, but I continued my pursuit and finally found some answers through this passage. So, here it is. My hallelujah moment, my aha, my lightbulb...

The spirit of heaviness equals religion (#aha).

After further seeking the Lord, He revealed to me that I had temporarily fallen from grace (Galatians 5:4). Now, that doesn't mean I entered into sin or that I had rejected the things of God. It simply meant that once again, I picked up the law of works, meaning I still felt I had to *do* something in order to receive my positive pregnancy test. I still felt I had to earn it or work for it. That, my friend, is religion (#doingequalsworks #worksequalslaw #lawequalsheaviness #heavinessequalsreligion).

I know the truth, right? I know all I have to do is say "Amen" to what Jesus already bought and paid for on the cross; that I am righteous and forgiven; that I am healed; that He has prophesied over me through the promises in His Word; that I can receive these promises for myself and decree them into existence. But what I didn't fully realize is that receiving them requires absolutely nothing of me; no working; no doing; no earning; nada; zilch; I receive them as a gift. Then, I rest.

On the cross, when Jesus said, "It is finished," He literally meant, "It is finished." It is over. It is complete. Jesus Himself is up there in Heaven sitting at the right hand of the Father; chillin' out, maxin' and relaxin' all cool, reclinin' in a chair with His feet on a stool (#90skid #freshprinceparody #yesIcameupwiththatonthefly).

Seriously, though. The work is over. And, not only is it finished for Jesus, but it is finished for those who believe. Check out this passage titled "The Believer's Rest":

> *Therefore, while the promise of entering His rest still remains and is freely offered today, let us fear, in case any one of you may seem to come short of reaching it or think he has come too late. For indeed we have had the good news [of salvation] preached to us, just as the Israelites also [when the good news of the promised land came to them]; but the message they heard did not benefit them, because it was not united with faith [in God] by those who heard. For we who believe [that is, we who personally trust and confidently rely on God] enter that*

rest [so we have His inner peace now because we are confident in our salvation, and assured of His power], just as He has said, "As I swore [an oath] in My wrath, They shall not enter My rest," [this He said] although His works were completed from the foundation of the world [waiting for all who would believe]. For somewhere [in Scripture] He has said this about the seventh day: "And God rested on the seventh day from all His works"; and again in this, "They shall not enter My rest." Therefore, since the promise remains for some to enter His rest, and those who formerly had the good news preached to them failed to [grasp it and did not] enter because of [their unbelief evidenced by] disobedience, He again sets a definite day, [a new] "Today," [providing another opportunity to enter that rest by] saying through David after so long a time, just as has been said before [in the words already quoted], "Today if you hear His voice, Do not harden your hearts." [This mention of a rest was not a reference to their entering into Canaan.] For if Joshua had given them rest, God would not speak about another day [of opportunity] after that. **So there remains a [full and complete] Sabbath rest for the people of God.** *For the one who has once entered His rest has also rested from [the weariness and pain of] his [human] labors, just as God rested from [those labors uniquely] His own. Hebrews 4:1-10, AMP*

#sosogood: Because that was so stinking long, let me break down a few important truths:

- The writer is explaining how the Israelites were not able to enter the Promised Land of rest because of their unbelief
- The writer explains how God's works were actually completed from the foundation of the world, which is why He rested on the seventh day
- The writer describes another opportunity to enter into that rest for the people of God
- This rest is found through being confident in our salvation and assured of His power
- The writer tells us that God is at rest

I came to finally see that because God is at rest, our official mandate is, "make every effort to enter that rest [of God, to know and experience it for ourselves]..." (Hebrews 4:11, AMP) The New King James Version says, "be diligent to enter that rest." Diligent in Greek means to strain every nerve.

We no longer have to work for our salvation; we no longer have to work for our healing; we no longer have to work for our conception and healthy pregnancy. We know this, right? According to scripture, though, the work we are instructed to do is to diligently strain every nerve to enter the rest of God (#oxymoron). How is this done? I will get there.

Now, when I think of straining every nerve, I imagine a weightlifter straining with all that is within to lift that crushing barbell overhead, grunting, groaning, breathing heavy, veins popping out, head looking like it's going to explode, etc. (#yougetthepicture.) So, if we are instructed to work that diligently to enter the rest of God, we can assume that it is either really difficult and heavy to get there or that there is something within that we must strain against (#readthatagain).

I eventually learned the religion in me was my barbell. In fact, my distorted core belief said I had to *do* something in order to receive the promises of God. This was in direct opposition to this state of rest. I've spiritually had to contend and labor and wrestle my core beliefs into receiving this promised rest of God (#takestime). And now that I have dropped weight (#akadroppedreligion), I can finally move forward.

Let's take a look at the Israelites who finally entered into the rest promised to them:

> *So the* L*ord* *gave to Israel all the land he had sworn to give their ancestors, and they took possession of it and settled there. And the* L*ord* *gave them rest on every side, just as he had solemnly promised their ancestors. None of their enemies could stand against them, for the* L*ord* *helped them conquer all their enemies. Not a single one of all the good promises the* L*ord* *had given to the family of Israel was left unfulfilled; everything he had spoken came true.*
> *Joshua 21:43-45, NLT*

The Israelites possessed their land, received their inheritance, and entered the promised rest. The same is offered to us. We possessed the land, but we must now receive our inheritance through the finished work of the cross. We must cease from our labors and make every effort to enter into His rest by believing and receiving.

We already believe, though, right? We got rid of the first obstacle, unbelief. The second obstacle is simply a matter of dropping weight, getting rid of religion, and receiving the finished work of the cross as a gift. Yes, this is actually as simple as it sounds. However, in order to truly grasp this principle, the Holy Spirit gave me two metaphors:

1. Bask in His "Yes"

We have seen that God's promises for us are "Yes and Amen"; we know that His promises have been fulfilled by Jesus; we know that they are a "Yes," because of His finished work on the cross; we know that there is absolutely nothing else we can do in order to receive these promises except to receive them as our own. How is this done?

By basking in His "Yes."

When we are at such a place of confidence, belief, and trust, our souls cannot help but relax and bask. We lie happily in the bright warmth and take pleasure in and derive enjoyment from His "Yes" (#howpoetic). Take the picture of my overweight, fluffy, pink-nosed kitty basking in the sunshine through my back door. He lies there sprawled out on the hardwood, practically glowing with the most contented look on his face. Sometimes, I just love to catch him in the act and gaze at him for a few minutes. He simply looks joyous. That, my friend, is basking at its finest. This is what God wants us to do in His radiant Son (#punintended). By basking in His presence, we find rest.

In Exodus, when Moses refused to go any further without God going with him, God responded, "My Presence will go with you, and I will give you rest." (Exodus 33:14, NKJV) His presence gives rest. I'm not going to lie though, this place of rest takes a higher revelation of the nature of God and of His love.

At the time of this writing, I've had dreams for the past six months of being in a wedding gown preparing for a wedding ceremony. In my dream, it seemed my anticipation was for my husband. After I woke up, though, I knew I was actually preparing to wed Jesus. We are, after all, the church, His bride, and He is our groom. Therefore, He loves us not just as His children. More than that, He loves us as His beautiful bride, not just as His friend, but as His beloved.

#sidenote: If you are curious about the intimacy of this kind of love, check out Song of Solomon. There is a reason this book is in the Bible, and it is not just to prove how we can enjoy the pleasures of the marriage bed.

Through these dreams and my Bible study into Song of Solomon, the revelation of who He is and His intimate love for me has been absolutely life-changing! I have now gone from servant of God, to daughter of the King, to friend, to bride and, to beloved (#happyinlovesigh).

My greatest heart's desire is to conceive and bear children. If my natural husband had the power to grant me anything, would he withhold my heart's desire from me? Of course not! He is not a cruel husband. In fact, he desires it for me more than I do! Dear friend, Jesus is not a cruel husband. He is not withholding anything from you. He loves you as His beautiful bride. He actually yearns to shower you with gifts, love letters, and affection (#andbabies).

#checkthisout: Did you know that you, in all your humanity, ravish His heart? (Song of Solomon 4:9) Did you know that He thinks you are beautiful (even when you make mistakes)? Did you know that He sees no spot in you? (Song of Solomon 4:7) He actually sees the longings and intentions of your heart to love Him and celebrates you for them, no matter how weak and frail they are. He always views you through the eyes of pure love and calls you lovely.

Because of this truth, we can bask in His love. We can bask in His "Yes." We can rest in His presence. And we can receive our inheritance.

2. Taste and See

Here is the tricky part, at least for me. Basking in His "Yes" made a bit more sense to me because of my cat metaphor. Resting in God's presence was simpler to understand because of the revelations I received of His intimate love as a husband. When He told me that all I have to do is receive His love as a gift, that's where I became unsettled again (#anyoneelse).

I am a giver. I like to give gifts, but I don't receive gifts as well from others (#workinprogress). So, for me to imagine opening up a big shiny package to receive His finished work, umm nope, it just didn't excite me. But then, a couple of weeks ago, I had yet another hallelujah moment (#drumrollplease #dumdumdum).

Eat.

I know. Weird, right? At least now I know why this word got stuck inside me! There's that Holy Spirit showing off as an amazing teacher again (#bestteacherever). So, what does this mean? Well, I don't just receive the gift of the finished work as a present; I can receive them as food.

Communion confirmed this to me the following Sunday at church. As I popped the little cracker in my mouth and began chewing, I gained full and complete understanding. Here is my journal entry from May 8, 2017:

Today, I partook in communion. As I ate the bread, I received the gift of my physical healing and fruitfulness. As I drank the blood, I received the gift of my forgiveness and righteousness. To receive the finished work as a gift requires partaking of it, eating it and accepting it inside my body, tasting it, chewing it, swallowing it, digesting it, receiving it in my body as a part of my cellular make up, transforming me from the inside out.

Now I know what the author of Hebrews is talking about, "For we have become partakers of Christ..." (Hebrews 3:14, NKJV) We receive His finished work like food! We eat it; we partake of it. We feast, share, and participate in what He has provided for us from the finished work of the cross. This means that because He died for my forgiveness, I partake of my forgiveness. He gave me healing, so I partake of my healing. He gave me fruitfulness, so I partake of my fruitfulness. He gave me righteousness, so I simply partake and receive my righteousness (#amen).

When it comes to the Lord's Supper, I believe there is a reason Jesus commanded His disciples to "do this in remembrance of me." Jesus foreknew that we would need to *constantly* remember what actually happened on that cross! So, another one of the steps I have taken in order to grasp this metaphor is to begin regularly taking communion. It has not been ritualistic, exhausting, or something where I am putting pressure on myself. I don't even take communion every day. But, I am going to continue until this revelation gets rooted down into my heart and becomes a settled reality in my soul. I am not just doing this act in order to conceive; I am doing it because I don't want any more room in my mind for religious thinking. I am doing this to *remember*. By partaking, eating, and receiving the finished work of the cross, religion becomes nonexistent (#boom).

I love this verse, "He escorts me to the banquet hall; it's obvious how much he loves me." (Song of Solomon 2:4, NLT) The banquet hall, or the table, is where He feeds us. He feeds us with who He is and from the finished work of the cross. He brings us here to celebrate and to feast on His love; to sustain and refresh us. "Oh, taste and see that the LORD is good; Blessed is the man who trusts in Him!" (Psalm 34:8, NKJV) Eat, taste, and then see how good He is.

Dear friend, if you don't get anything else from this section, I pray you'll get this: the true rest of God is completely nonexistent unless you are wholly in His presence All. The. Time. There is no rest outside of His presence. There is no rest apart from abiding in Jesus. There is no rest aside from His yoke. I mean, Jesus *is* rest. It is not a feeling or an emotion or an action; it is not a vacation or a good night's sleep; it is not even a designated sabbath day. Rest is Jesus. And Jesus is rest, "For the Son of Man is Lord of the Sabbath." (Matthew 12:8, NKJV) Jesus is Lord of rest!

I have noticed that anytime I look for rest outside of abiding in Jesus, it just doesn't happen. I could have the best night's sleep and still wind up in a funk the next morning. I could be on the most relaxing, exotic, secluded beach vacation, and peace is nowhere to be found. I could spend a rainy afternoon reading a good book and still be discontent. I could spend a day surrounded by the people I love the most and still be at unrest.

What is my point? Simply stated, the rest of God does not feel or look like the culture's definition of rest. If you seek what the culture offers, you will be sorely disappointed. I learned this the hard way. You see, I kept waiting for those feelings of peace and joy and the I-don't-have-a-care-in-the-world mentality to appear. And it would, for the first two weeks of the month. But then PMS would begin, and Aunt Flo would come for a visit. Suddenly, I am in despair again, trying to find that place of rest (#iknowiamnotalone).

Just yesterday, for example, as I was pouting and feeling oppressed, I kept talking to God, basically telling Him I just can't do this anymore. I am weak. I can't be all confident and act like my heart is not ripping in two every time AF (#auntflo) shows up. At the same time, though, another part of me is resolved not to grieve for something that has already been promised to me. Of course, you know what happens, Dr. Jekyll and Mr. Hyde make their famous appearance.

Anyway, in my rambling conversations with God, He brought to my remembrance the *fruit* of rest. He helped me realize that I am not going to feel and experience this fruit by culture's or even man's definition. You see, I was *still* depending on circumstances to bring me rest. And anytime my circumstances changed, I lost my rest.

Dear sister, circumstances do not bring rest. I am sorry to say that even if I received a BFP (#bigfatpositive) today, after all of the joy and excitement today would bring, I'd probably be freaking out and back to a place of unrest, worry, and anxiety, wondering if the baby was going to stick or worried about gaining too much weight tomorrow (#ohyeah). In other words, we cannot expect this rest of God to look anything like the world's definition of rest. The only place we will ever feel the fruit of rest is in the presence of God.

So, what does that mean for us? Well, if we bask in His "Yes," feast on who He is, and taste the finished work, then we will see His goodness all around and within us. His truth will get so deeply rooted within our hearts that before we know it, His truth is more of a reality than our own natural circumstances. This, my friend, produces fruit.

FRUIT OF REST

Although there is much fruit accessible to us this way, I will only focus on three. The following is the fruit available to us by resting in the finished work:

1. Peace

As you walk this out and begin to labor into rest, you will notice one of two things: A) You are wrestling and straining every nerve. Your process is not enjoyable, and you may want to give up. It doesn't feel like it, but this is a very good thing, so you cannot give up and need to keep pressing in; or B) You begin to feel peace; a weirdly confident peace that may not have ever been experienced before but can be discerned as wholly supernatural, "You will keep him in perfect peace, whose mind is stayed on You, because he trusts in You." (Isaiah 26:3, NKJV)

When we live a lifestyle of basking in His "Yes," resting in His presence, eating from the finished work of the cross, and remembering all we are and all we have, what can we expect? Our minds, when stayed on God, are in a state of perfect peace!

Let's go over peace again, only this time, more in-depth. In Hebrew, peace is translated *shalom*, meaning completeness, wholeness, peace, health, welfare, safety, soundness, tranquility, prosperity, perfectness, fullness, rest, and harmony. Umm, yeah, shalom is a great place to be! And here it is again; we cannot find rest or peace outside of Jesus. In fact, Jesus is the Prince of Peace, the Prince of Shalom (Isaiah 9:6). Let's take a look at peace in the New Testament:

> *Be anxious for nothing, but in everything by prayer and supplication, with thanksgiving, let your requests be made known to God; and the peace of God, which surpasses all understanding, will guard your hearts and minds through Christ Jesus. Philippians 4:6-7, NKJV*

I love that! The Greek translation for peace is *eirene*, meaning a state of rest, quietness, and calmness. Did you get that? A state of rest. The *rest of God* will guard our hearts and minds through Christ Jesus. There it is again! We cannot have rest without peace, and we cannot have peace without Jesus! (#amen)

So, this peace that we may be feeling is a fruit or a result of being in the promised state of rest. This is so exciting! In fact, in John, when Jesus is describing the Helper, He says, "Peace, I leave with you, My peace I give to you." (John 14:27, NKJV) What He's truly saying here is that He gives us rest. Through our Helper, the Holy Spirit, we can live and breathe and operate from a place of rest. He gave us rest, and He left us rest. We have the ability to do life from a place of rest, and this rest can only be found in Jesus from His finished work of the cross.

So, let's allow His peace to guard our hearts and minds from any fear, anxiety, or unbelief. Let's continue to bask in His "Yes" and feast on the finished work of the cross; then, we will not lose our peace (#shalom).

2. Laughter

The second fruit we may experience from resting in the finished work of the cross is laughter, joy, or extreme happiness. However, let's spend a moment and talk about two kinds of laughter. First, there is the laugh of unbelief exhibited by Sarah:

> *Then they said to him, "Where is Sarah your wife?" And he said, "There, in the tent." He said, "I will surely return to you at this time next year; and behold, Sarah your wife will have a son." And Sarah was listening at the tent door, which was behind him. Now Abraham and Sarah were old, well advanced in years; she was past [the age of] childbearing.* **So Sarah laughed to herself [when she heard the Lord's words], saying, "After I have become old, shall I have pleasure and delight, my lord (husband) being also old?"** *And the Lord asked Abraham, "Why did Sarah laugh [to herself], saying, 'Shall I really give birth [to a child] when I am so old?' Is anything too difficult or too wonderful for the Lord? At the appointed time, when the*

season [for her delivery] comes, I will return to you and Sarah will have a son." Then Sarah denied it, saying, **"I did not laugh";** *because she was afraid. And He (the* LORD*) said,* **"No, but you did laugh."** *(emphasis added) Genesis 18:9-15, AMP*

And yes, she really did try to lie to the Lord's face! Talk about a brave woman (#orstupid). That's how much she honestly didn't believe she was going to be a mother. Even after all of God's promises to Abraham, very specific promises might I add, she *still* didn't believe. And even as she was listening to God Himself speak that she would conceive, she scoffed! I marvel at her nerve, but dear sister, I have done the very same thing.

His promises are all throughout His Word, and yet I have chosen to laugh in unbelief; people have spoken into my life, whether in encouragement or through prophecy, and I have laughed in unbelief. They might have thought I was laughing from joy, but nope, deep down inside, I was scoffing "yeah right" (#anyoneelse).

The second kind of laugh is the laugh of belief. Let's look at how Sarah's laugh changed:

Abraham named his son Isaac (laughter), the son to whom Sarah gave birth. So Abraham circumcised his son Isaac when he was eight days old, just as God had commanded him. Abraham was a hundred years old when his son Isaac was born. Sarah said, **"God has made me laugh; all who hear [about our good news] will laugh with me."** *And she said, "Who would have said to Abraham that Sarah would nurse children? For I have given birth to a son by him in his old age." (emphasis added) Genesis 21:3-7, AMP*

Imagine the joy! A ninety-year-old woman pushing out an eight-pounder! Seriously. If you think about it happening today, so many people would literally laugh out loud. Sarah and Abraham named their son Isaac, which translated means "laughter" (#surprisesurprise).

Another example of this is from John the Baptist's mother, Elizabeth. Before John was conceived, Gabriel the Archangel prophesied to his father that, "You will have great joy and delight, and many will rejoice over his birth" (Luke 1:14, AMP). After John was born, Luke recorded, "Her neighbors and relatives heard that the Lord had shown His great mercy toward her, and they were rejoicing with her." (Luke 1:58, AMP) Hmm. Rejoicing? What do you think that looked like? Laughter! (#duh)

Now, both laughs of belief from Sarah and Elizabeth came *after* the baby was born. At least, that's how it was recorded. But you know, and I know from the many times we have witnessed our preggo friends, that there is extreme joy and laughter during the pregnancy too. From the positive pregnancy test, to the first time feeling the baby move, to the images viewed on the sonogram. Yes, lots of laughter. How can we, then, be expected to respond with laughter when we haven't even conceived yet? Easy. By resting in His promises and remembering who we have become: The Joyful Mother of children.

Let's look more in-depth at the word joyful. The Hebrew word *sameach* means happy, cheerful, rejoicing, and festive. The root of this word means to rejoice and to get happy. So, in other words, laugh! Get happy! If your experience is anything like mine, then you know that the laughter has already begun. It's not a forced laughter that we are doing out of faith; rather, it's a real laugh erupting from this deep, abiding joy within; the joy within that comes from basking, feasting, and resting in the presence of God.

3. Thankfulness

Remember when I explained the decree? I mentioned that we would know we were in the right place when our decree turned into praise and thankfulness. Well, just like basking and laughing, this one both naturally and supernaturally transforms into thankfulness. We truly cannot help but pray and sing praises to Him. Not only for our soon-to-arrive motherhood but also for authentic thankfulness in being His daughter; thankfulness for His presence; for His voice; for His shepherding; for creating us; for choosing us, etc. (#thatwasreallyhardtostop)

Just like the joyful laughter, thankfulness has completely overflowed in me in every area. I am probably making my husband and friends sick with how grateful and thankful I am for every single thing; a good parking spot, produce sales when I am grocery shopping, a yummy cup of coffee, a friendly cashier, a good hair day, a good song while I am cruising down the road, the sweetness of my son. Seriously. Every. Single. Thing. I am just so thankful!

Honestly? We need to just trust God; trust Him that He knows us and loves us and will keep His promises to us. Thank Him for that. In fact, I literally just finished busting out in a spontaneous song of thankfulness while I took a quick bathroom break. Seriously. It just erupts like this all day long (#punintended #harhar). Paul described it best:

> *Therefore as you have received Christ Jesus the Lord, walk in [union with] Him [reflecting His character in the things you do and say – living lives that lead others away from sin], having been deeply rooted [in Him] and now being continually built up in Him and [becoming increasingly more] established in your faith, just as you were taught, and* ***overflowing in it with gratitude.*** *(emphasis added) Colossians 2:6-7, AMP*

Me, The Barren Woman that everybody else sees, might just be the happiest and most thankful person in my circle. How can this be? Jesus, of course. In Him and through Him, all things are possible. Just as Luke recorded about Elizabeth's barrenness, soon and very soon, the woman they called barren will be in her six month (Luke 1:36, AMP).

There it is, dear friends; the fruit of resting in the finished work of the cross. Sounds exciting, doesn't it? Even if it's not exciting right now, or your laugh is forced, and thankfulness is hindered, your time is coming. This is a process. Just remember that circumstances do not bring you rest.

If we are doing this whole thing "right," then if or when we begin our periods this month, we should still be in this state of rest. Our peace, happiness, and thankfulness are not dependent on whether or not we conceive, but on our time in His presence, the remembrance of who He is, and what He has given us on the cross. The fruit of rest will always be accessible as long as we are abiding in Jesus (#amen).

Going Deeper:

- Do you need to "drop weight"?
- What is preventing you from entering into the promised rest of God?
- Study the book of Song of Solomon to discover a higher revelation of God's love for you as His Beloved. Record your process.
- Participate in communion and partake of the finished work of the cross.
- Are you experiencing any of the fruit of rest? If not, what steps will you begin to take?
- Scriptures to study: Mt. 11:28-30; Heb. 4:1-11; Ex. 33:14; Josh. 21:43-45; Song of Sol. 4:7-9; Heb. 3:14; Song of Sol. 2:4; Ps. 34:8; Mt. 12:8; Is. 26:3; Is. 9:6; Phil. 4:6-7; Jn. 14:27; Gen. 18:9-15; Gen. 21:3-7; Lk. 1:58; Col. 2:6-7; Lk. 1:36; Gal. 5:4.

Chapter fourteen
Tell Your Story

Welp. Here we are, halfway through; what a process (#literally), and I am not done yet; nope! Here I am to the "testimony" chapter, and guess what? Still no positive pregnancy test! Isn't that just like our God? He is such a comedian (#sarcasm). So yeah, I had to take a few weeks off because of the very fact written above. Still. Not. Preggo (#sigh). I did some questioning and had a much-needed come-to-Jesus meeting with, well, Jesus.

Once again, I am writing my story and am supposed to be sharing my testimony, but I still don't have a testimony to share, well, except what you've heard so far. You know what I mean, though. This is so crazy to me. You would think after several years I would be used to it, but no. Anyway, as always, my time off has been much more than I expected or planned (#staytuned).

#rabbittrail: Dear friend, I would like to suggest that when we are feeling restless deep down inside and have a lot of higher-level questions floating around, that maybe, just maybe, this is an open invitation to seek God until we find those answers. How many times do we just brush it off because the mystery is too great? How many times do we busy ourselves with distractions or empty works to ignore the restlessness? What if those very questions are an invitation to an intimacy with the

Father that we have never experienced before? Do we dare to go there? I did and got way more than I asked for! What a pleasant surprise it was! And now, here I am, ready to write in faith. Even though I may look crazy to most in our culture, Jesus smiles at me with pleasure (#thatsallthatmatters).

As we tell our stories (which we *all* have one), there are some things we need to know; that is the "what" and the "why." So, let's jump right in, shall we?

THE POWER OF THE TESTIMONY

Testimony contains power. Not just in warm feel-good fuzzies, but true Holy Spirit inspired power. "And they overcame and conquered him because of the blood of the Lamb and because of the word of their testimony…" (Revelation 12:11, AMP) The backstory of this scripture is talking about when Satan (the "him") was thrown out of Heaven and how he has been accusing and deceiving the citizens of Heaven still on earth for all of these years. Well, guess what? Just as the saints before us, we have already won! When we accepted Jesus and everything He did for us on the cross and in His resurrection, we already overcame the little, ugly guy! This is nothing new as we have come through the previous chapters, right? (#right)

But look what else it says: "because of the word of their testimony." What does this mean? Well, it is not just the precious blood that conquers the enemy. It is also the declaration of our testimony (#whoa). Our testimony is our witness, our proof, our evidence, and our experience. How powerful *is* our testimony? Devil-silencing powerful! How important is it to *tell* our story? Satan-defeating important! (#warriorprincessupinhere) This is especially true for The Barren Woman. Why, you ask? Well, along with the power of our testimonies releasing warfare on our enemy, they also have the power to release prophecy, "…Worship God! For the testimony of Jesus is the spirit of prophecy." (Revelation 19:10, NKJV) This is an angel speaking to John, who wrote the book of Revelation. He is telling him not to worship the messenger but instead worship God. He then speaks a complete and unshakable truth about Jesus: the testimony of Jesus is the spirit of prophecy.

But, what the heck does that even mean? To the best of my knowledge, the testimony of Jesus actively moving in our lives releases the spirit of prophecy. Any time our story points back to Jesus, we release prophecy. In other words, our testimony emits prophetic power into The Barren Woman's heart, making the impossible possible, the unreality reality, what was never considered now considered. Our testimony prophesies, *What He did for me, He can do for you* (#selah #readthatagain).

Is our testimony only prophetic regarding The Barren Woman? No way. Any time we share what God is doing in our lives, it has the power to release prophecy in someone else's. For example, to learn how to lay hands on the sick and bring healing, we need to find someone with a story; if we want to be debt-free, we need to find a story; if we want our husbands free from addiction, we need to find a story; if we want babies, we need to find a story. What could make more sense than that? And then, when we have found that story, we need to allow the testimony to do its prophetic work:

PROPHECY (TRUTH/PROMISE/TESTIMONY) + DECLARATION (THE VOICE) = DECREE (THE ACTION/LAW)

In other words, we receive it for ourselves and become what is spoken. But we need to remember to stay away from ritualistic confessions. The process above should flow naturally from our hearts, and above all, it should not compete with our desire for God.

YOUR MUSTARD SEED NOW

Remember that tiny seed we discussed back in The Faith Chapter? Our little mustard seed of faith? Well, what happens to a seed that gets planted into healthy, fertile soil? (#drumroll) It grows! So, if overcoming the enemy and releasing prophecy wasn't enough, our stories also have the power to plant seeds, water, and produce fruit in others. Even if they don't yet birth a child, they still birth *something* life-altering and revelatory. How cool is that?

As we tell our stories, we sow seeds in others which then has the potential to produce trees. Hang tight, these trees will make perfect sense once we get there. Just let Mrs. Windsor do her work:

1. The tree of life

> *Hope deferred makes the heart sick, But when the desire comes, it is a tree of life. Proverbs 13:12, NKJV*

Throughout this process, you have witnessed the healing of my sick heart. You have observed hope, true and abiding hope, develop in my life, so much so that I have expressed hope multiple times. And yeah, I'm still not done. Because as we tell our stories, guess what else it does? That's right! Our testimonies mend sick hearts and birth hope in The Barren Woman! (#getexcited)

This is not just a keep-our-fingers-crossed kind of hope. Rather, it is an actual gut-confident expectation. That's right. The Barren Woman becomes pregnant with expectation when she hears our story; she begins to expect good things; begins to expect a positive pregnancy test; begins to expect spiritual blessings and tangible blessings from the Daddy-God who loves her; begins to expect the desires of her heart to be fulfilled in every way.

How is this possible? Well, let's look at the above scripture again. When our desire comes, our hearts become a tree of life. Out of the abundance of our hearts overflows our story (Luke 6:45) and the fruit produced is hopeful expectation in whomever hears it (#somethingtothinkabout). And no, it doesn't matter if a BFP (#bigfatpositive) has not yet come. We *all* can still have this pregnant expectation.

Remember, there is prophetic power in the testimony. Plus, this kind of expectation rivals faith. Faith is the confirmation of things *hoped* for (Hebrews 11:1). So sometimes, we have to be pregnant with hope before we can be rooted in faith for our miracle (#thatsgood). What if that's all The Barren Woman is missing, then? How can we possibly stay silent when we have this amazing fruit-bearing story?

2. A tree by the waters

I am still barren. I don't like to call myself that because I definitely don't feel dry and empty. Since my womb has yet to conceive seed, then yes, I am still physically barren (#rollingmyeyes). But, the best news is that I am hugely pregnant with expectation! You see, this is what happens when we share our stories. Infertility will not seem as much of a reality because we truly realize there is hope, and this is where more fruit is produced. Take a look at this passage:

> *Blessed [with spiritual security] is the man who believes and trusts in and relies on the L*ORD*, And whose hope and confident expectation is the L*ORD*. For he will be [nourished] like a tree planted by the waters, That spreads out its roots by the river; And will not fear the heat when it comes; But its leaves will be green and moist. And it will not be anxious and concerned in a year of drought nor stop bearing fruit.*
> *Jeremiah 17:7-8, AMP*

Don't you love this? Seriously. I love how the author says, "whose hope and confident expectation *is* the Lord." How amazing is that? Not only is The Barren Woman pregnant with expectation, but her expectation is Jesus Himself. Remember how He has become my satisfaction, my contentment, and my hope in my process? Well, when we speak our testimonies to The Barren Woman, she learns how to make Jesus her expectation. She learns how to bask in His "Yes," yoke with Him, and be at rest. According to this passage, when The Barren Woman makes Jesus her confident expectation, she:

- is well-nourished; healthy of body, soul, and spirit
- has no fear of heat; does not fear pressure or hardship
- is not anxious in drought
- is fruitful all year long

Dear friend, this tree, whose roots are spread out by the river, might be my absolute favorite because its roots are strong and permanently grounded in the fountain of living water. Through our testimony, The

Barren Woman's hopeful expectation becomes rooted in Jesus. Jesus, our fountain of living water, who says that we too will have rivers of living water flowing out of our innermost being (John 7:38).

Could it be that our testimony is among those rivers of living water? Could it be that telling our stories can produce rivers of living water in The Barren Woman? Try it and see!

3. The mustard seed tree

...and of all the seeds [planted in the region] it is the smallest, but when it has grown it is the largest of the garden herbs and becomes a tree, so that THE BIRDS OF THE AIR FIND SHELTER IN ITS BRANCHES.
Matthew 13:32, AMP

The mustard seed is the smallest seed planted in the garden, but it grows tall enough to be labeled as a tree. Not only that, when it grows, it contains such an abundance of tiny seeds that it has the ability to spread quickly and widely. No wonder Jesus used this seed as an example! The seed's multiplication and fruitfulness are a perfect representation of the Kingdom. This, then, is the perfect representation of what our testimonies have the power to do within The Barren Woman (#whoa).

As we tell our stories, the goodness and faithfulness of God spreads quickly and widely from one barren woman to another. She is given seeds of truth that grow rapidly in the healthy, fertile soil of her heart. With this truth, she is unstoppable. She is fruitful, and she multiplies quickly and widely. Also, just as the birds of the air find shelter beneath the branches of this tree, so will The Barren Woman find shelter in the telling of our stories; she will find comfort in this sisterhood of truth; she will find comfort in the Comforter. How can we stay silent?

4. Trees of righteousness

So yeah, this tree was not in my outline for this chapter. It was literally just now added after a time of spontaneous worship. Seriously. Like, five minutes ago before writing this. God is *so* good. And, He is such an amazing teacher!

> *The Spirit of the Lord God is upon Me, Because the Lord has anointed Me To preach good tidings to the poor; He has sent Me to heal the brokenhearted, To proclaim liberty to the captives, And the opening of the prison to those who are bound; To proclaim the acceptable year of the Lord, And the day of vengeance of our God; To comfort all who mourn, To console those who mourn in Zion, To give them beauty for ashes, The oil of joy for mourning, The garment of praise for the spirit of heaviness; That they may be called trees of righteousness, The planting of the Lord, that He may be glorified. Isaiah 61:1-3, NKJV*

What does this mean? Well, first of all, these scriptures are a depiction of the essence of Jesus' ministry. Secondly, they are what we've inherited from Him as His church. Dear friend, *we* are anointed to preach the good news; *we* are anointed to heal the brokenhearted; *we* are anointed to comfort all who mourn. How? By the power of our witness, our testimony.

Our story births beauty from ashes, the oil of joy, and the garment of praise in The Barren Woman. Isaiah 61 in the New Living Translation reads, "In their righteousness, they will be like great oaks that the Lord has planted for his own glory." Dear sister, *we* are great oaks, deeply rooted and immovable, birthed for God's glory. Therefore, our stories are too. And, they have the power to do the same in The Barren Woman who hears them (#micdrop).

The BFP (#bigfatpositive) we will soon receive is great beauty from ashes. The happy tears that stream down our faces and the thankfulness overflowing in our hearts is the oil of joy replacing all our years of mourning. The movement of the baby in our womb is the garment of praise in exchange for the spirit of heaviness.

Friend, our time has come. We cannot stay silent. We must tell our stories and watch what happens. Even in this temporary season of barrenness, we are already a fruitful vine, a tree of righteousness, called to bear fruit and bring glory to the Father.

Going Deeper:
- What part of your story can you begin sharing with others?
- Find someone with a story of something you are believing for. Record your process.
- Are you pregnant with hope? Why or why not?
- Scriptures to study: Rev. 12:11; Rev. 19:10; Prov. 13:12; Lk. 6:45; Heb. 11:1; Jer. 17:7-8; Jn. 7:38; Mt. 13:32; Is. 61:1-3.

Chapter fifteen
Fruit That Remains

#RABBITTRAIL #VULNERABILITYALERT:

Here we go again. Still physically barren, I am writing about fruit. Not only that, I just ended another holiday season without a pregnancy or a baby, and I am going into another new year, which brings me here... a little shell-shocked and hurt. In fact, just a week ago, I had the worst emotional breakdown I have ever experienced. So bad that I found myself hyperventilating and dry heaving face down in the toilet. That's how bad I was crying, so bad that I made myself physically sick. And, I had a panic attack a couple of weeks ago, too. My heart was racing, I felt like I was dying, and I even prepared my son to call 911.

I thought for sure 2017 was the year, you know? It all made perfect sense. The pieces all fit. I mean, I experienced a tragic loss this summer when my sweet Grandma died just two days before my birthday. Then, in the fall, my old diabetic pug died, the same pug who had been my baby for the last thirteen years. I mean, these were *serious* losses. My pug's death was like a blow to my motherhood, really. My Grandma's death accompanied remorse that I never contributed to giving her more great-grandchildren, and now, with the fabric we picked out together, she will never get to sew my babies' blankets. Not only did I have to work through my grief, but I also had to process through the lies and torment that came with their deaths.

So yeah, see what I mean? The timing for a BFP (#bigfatpositive) could not have been any better. I thought, for sure, God was going to close out this year by restoring those losses and blowing my mind with His goodness (#butno). To make matters worse, 2017 was the year of Jubilee. According to the Jewish calendar, this is when all things lost or taken from you are supposed to be restored (#yeahdidnthappen). I'm nearly at the end of my book (#maybe #ithinkso), just waiting for the fruit. I mean, seriously. I already wrote about the testimony. The timing could not have been more perfect. And, to make you feel even more sorry for me, I had the weirdest cycle I have ever had and thought for sure I was pregnant. Even my body was confident. But no, Aunt Flo came late, and here I am, beginning 2018 completely shell-shocked. Thus, the reason for the emotional breakdown and panic attacks.

Do I still believe I am going to conceive and have children? For sure! But do I understand the timing of it all? No way! As always, however, in this adventurous life of following Jesus, amidst times of great turmoil, something beautiful was born. Not only did I experience true healing and comfort from the Comforter, but I also received great revelation and closure on this recent chapter. And oh, how sweet it is (#rabbittrailcompleted).

So, where do we go from here? Well, we talked about the fruit produced in The Barren Woman who hears our story. But what about us? What do we produce if it is not yet a baby?

Fruit that Remains.

I know, I know. Fruit that Remains is not nearly as exciting as a BFP (#bigfatpositive). Trust me. I've had to work through this. Fruit that Remains is, in fact, a big deal to God, so much so that He has a lot to say on the matter. Remember, this entire journey would not have even existed were it not for one small verse, "The entirety of your Word is truth." (Psalm 119:160) This one small verse was a tiny seed planted into my heart. You've experienced the journey of this seed first-hand. The discovery, the uprooting, the replanting, the pruning, the watering, the stretching, the fertilizing, the healing, the fighting, the resting, and now, the remaining. In fact, Jesus actually commissioned the journey of this little seed:

> *You did not choose Me, but **I chose you and appointed you that you should go and bear fruit, and that your fruit should remain**, that whatever you ask the Father in My name He may give you. (emphasis added) John 15:16, NKJV*

Remaining fruit is unseen. In fact, everything unseen is eternal, and everything seen is temporal (2 Corinthians 4:18). However, Fruit that Remains is Jesus' hope for us because He longs to reward us. This reward is not attained by effort, by works, or by striving. It is attained by fruit that lasts, fruit that is unseen yet eternal. It remains forever and into eternity. Another way to say it is, we receive seed from the Word, we bear fruit, our fruit remains, and then whatever we ask for and desire, He gives us. Let's look at this scripture again:

> *But without faith it is impossible to [walk with God and] please Him, for whoever comes [near] to God must [necessarily] believe that God exists and that He rewards those who [earnestly and diligently] seek Him. Hebrews 11:6, AMP*

Not only should we have faith that God exists, but we should also have faith that God rewards us both in the natural and the supernatural. Even Jesus walked this earth receiving temporal reward and knowing that He was going to receive eternal reward from the Father after He endured the cross (Hebrews 12:2). What is this eternal fruit, this Fruit that Remains, that brings great reward (#drumrollplease)?

Faithfulness!

Faithfulness is firmness, stability, fidelity steadiness, certainty, permanency, endurance, and steadfastness (#likearock #likeJesus). When we get to Heaven and stand face to face with Jesus, He will reward our faithfulness. This is confirmed in Matthew when he recorded "The Parable of the Talents." Jesus likened the kingdom of Heaven to a master taking a journey and going away for a time. This master entrusted his servants with portions of his possessions. To one, he gave five talents, to another, two talents, and to another, one talent. Now, talents were a measurement of weight for silver or gold. However, in this parable, they are symbolic of what Jesus has given us to steward. The one who received one talent did nothing with it. He buried it in the ground, not knowing God's nature to reward. While the master was away, the ones who received five and two talents doubled their portions. When the master came back, he said to them:

> *Well done, good and faithful servant. You have been faithful and trustworthy over a little, I will put you in charge of many things; share in the joy of your master... For to everyone who has, more will be given, and he will have abundance... Matthew 25:23, 29, AMP*

Dear friend, Jesus judges our faithfulness. And He rewards. As believers, we must come to a realization that one day, we all will be judged according to our faithfulness and stewardship of the seeds that have been sown (#yikes). This shouldn't be scary, but exciting! In fact, some of the beauty that came after my Grandma's death was realizing I wanted Jesus to look me in the eye and say, "well done, good and faithful servant," more than I wanted to conceive with my husband and have a baby. This is now my greatest and true heart's desire. I want to please Jesus. I want to fulfill all He envisioned and planned for me on earth. I don't want to waste any more time pursuing things to which He has not called me. I don't want to live for myself; I want to live for Him and be about *His* business.

So then, the seeds of truth we receive from the living Word of God are entrusted to us as His possessions. As faithful stewards, we learn to let these seeds do their work within us, multiplying and producing fruit:

> *The seed that fell into good, fertile soil represents those lovers of truth who hear it deep within their hearts. They respond by clinging to the word, keeping it dear as they endure all things in faith. This is the seed that will one day bear much fruit in their lives. Luke 8:15, TPT*

Clinging to the Word and enduring all things in faith; *that* is faithfulness. The Message renders it this way, "...the good hearts who seize the Word and hold on no matter what, sticking with it until there's a harvest." Holding on no matter what; *that* is faithfulness. The New King James reads, "...bear fruit with patience." Meaning, bearing fruit with patient endurance; *that* is faithfulness. In fact, Fruit that Remains is always, *always* birthed through endurance:

> *Be assured that the testing of your faith [through experience] produces endurance [leading to spiritual maturity, and inner peace]. And let endurance have its perfect result and do a thorough work, so that you may be perfect and completely developed [in your faith], lacking in nothing. James 1:3-4, AMP*

Friend, we have been producing endurance and have not even known it! This endurance produces perfection, maturity, and completion in our faith, lacking nothing. What is the outcome? Fruit that Remains; the fruit of faithfulness. If you refuse to give up on God's promises because you refuse to let go of the truth of God's Word, you will organically produce this fruit of faithfulness.

I am never giving up. No matter how many years I have to wait for that BFP (#bigfatpositive), I am not stopping. No matter how many cycles I endure, I'm still going to cling to what's been given to me through the finished work of the cross. No matter what, I am still moving forward in obedience and finishing this book. *This* is perfected faith; *this* is faithfulness.

How can I be so sure? Because the entirety of God's Word is truth. I have been sanctified and transformed by this very truth in my spirit, soul, and body. You have witnessed it first-hand (#frontrowseat). The Holy Spirit even confirmed this to me in my journal:

> *Fruit that Remains is a beautiful picture of endurance and faithfulness to each other. A picture of co-laboring at its finest. It is not about what I can do alone, but it is about what I can do in you and through you with a seed.*

So, how do you know when you've produced this fruit of faithfulness? The following attributes now form the cornerstones of your life. In fact, I could even add my name in place of faithfulness for each one of these attributes because that is how confident I am that I'm now exhibiting this fruit (#addyournametoo):

1. Faithfulness knows the nature of God
2. Faithfulness remembers the cross
3. Faithfulness holds fast
4. Faithfulness forgets what lies behind
5. Faithfulness is persistent
6. Faithfulness is of good courage
7. Faithfulness reaps a harvest
8. Faithfulness leaves a legacy

1. Faithfulness knows the nature of God

I will betroth you to Me in faithfulness, And you shall know the LORD. Hosea 2:20, NKJV

Along with the revelation of Jesus' husbandly love for me as bride and beloved came this betrothal in faithfulness. And, it is not just one-sided (#notanymore). Because we are betrothed to God in faithfulness, and because we know who He is, we can genuinely respond *back* to Him in faithfulness. In other words, we can remain faithful in serving Him, loving Him, and believing His Word all the days of our lives because Faithfulness knows the nature of God. Although He is unpredictable, He never changes. Although we cannot comprehend His timing, we know He is never late. Our security is not in circumstances or even what we see God doing in our lives. Rather, our security is in His consistent nature, "Jesus Christ is [eternally changeless, always] the same yesterday and today and forever." (Hebrews 13:8, AMP)

His consistent nature is why we can trust Him, because He never changes; He stays the same yesterday, today, and tomorrow; He is faithful. We never know how He is going to get us from point A to point B, but He will get us there because He is faithful and keeps His promises to us.

This is the solid foundation that we build our lives upon; the Rock; He is immovable, unshakeable. This faithfulness birthed in us can so clearly recognize this key attribute in our faithful God. And, it is this faithfulness that will receive its great reward. As you grasp this truth, it will change your life. You will truly be able to cast your cares and live a life of unstoppable faith.

No matter what comes against us, Faithfulness personally knows the Lord's unchanging nature. Faithfulness is so secure in knowing God and His goodness to believe for anything less than what He has promised. He is the same God of the Old Testament; He is the same God of the New Testament. The same God who gave babies to Sarah, Rebekah, Rachel, Hannah, and Elizabeth is the same God who will give us one (#boom #micdrop).

2. Faithfulness remembers the cross

Oh, that cross. I just can't get enough of it. Truly. It is so beautiful knowing that this amazingly consistent God sent Jesus to the cross for me, for relationship with me, for covenant with me, for eternity with me. I just can't come down from the high of the knowledge of what He did! Because, dear friend, Faithfulness remembers the cross; and Faithfulness knows that she is doubly guaranteed. We are not only guaranteed the promises because of the consistent nature of God and His Word but by the finished work of the cross. In fact, Jesus' broken body was physical evidence of *His* faithfulness. Because of this, we remember we can rest in the truth of what Jesus already bought.

The cross is our identity; the cross reminds us that we are not of this world, that we are protected and not affected by the results of sin because we have been washed by the blood, and by His stripes, we were healed over 2,000 years ago (#wewerehealed #pasttense)! So, anytime we become restless, Faithfulness remembers the cross, and we can find rest once again.

3. Faithfulness holds fast

Inasmuch then as we [believers] have a great High Priest... Jesus the Son of God, let us hold fast our confession [of faith and cling tenaciously to our absolute trust in Him as Savior].Hebrews 4:14, AMP

Faithfulness is evidenced by holding fast to our confession of faith. In other words, we cling tenaciously in faith to all we know to be true; cling tenaciously to the nature of God; cling tenaciously to the finished work of the cross, not by our own strength, but by *His*.

Faithfulness doesn't trust our symptoms or the inconsistencies in life, but we trust God's nature and hold on to this truth for dear life. We never let go, we never stop, and we push through and allow our Beloved to sustain us in weakness. We remain steadfast, unmoving, clinging to the Rock. Faithfulness says, "I will not give up on God. Ever."

Paul exhibited this kind of faithfulness. He was a prisoner under the guardianship of a centurion as they traveled to Rome, where he was to appeal before Caesar. Paul perceived that the voyage would end in disaster and tried to warn the centurion. He ignored Paul's warning and continued with the journey. Sure enough, a huge storm raged against their ship, and they were tempest-tossed for several days with no food. However, Paul said this:

But even now I urge you to keep up your courage and be in good spirits, because there will be no loss of life among you, but only loss of the ship. For this very night an angel of the God to whom I belong and whom I serve stood before me, and said, "Stop being afraid, Paul. You must stand before Caesar; and behold, God has given you [the lives of] all those who are sailing with you." So keep up your courage, men, for I believe God and have complete confidence in Him that it will turn out exactly as I have been told... Acts 27: 22-25, AMP

This was Paul's confession of faith. He confessed the nature of God. He remembered his identity, that he belonged to God, and he declared truth by confessing his belief and confidence in God. So, this is me. This is where I'm at. This is me saying, "Hold fast and do not quit!" You can believe God and have complete confidence in Him that it will turn out exactly as He says. *This* is faithfulness.

4. Faithfulness forgets what lies behind

...but one thing I do: forgetting what lies behind and reaching forward to what lies ahead. Philippians 3:13, AMP

Faithfulness forgets what lies behind. Instead, she reaches forward to the truth that is promised to her. Faithfulness remembers that each month is a new month. In fact, each day is a new day, and His mercies are new every morning. Faithfulness forgets the years of heartbreak and disappointments of previous cycles. Instead, she responds to each cycle with anticipation. Faithfulness declares with hope, "This could be the month!"

In other words, we intentionally forget and choose not to remember the former cycles and the former false alarms. Instead, we accept with hope the new thing that God is about to do, "Do not remember the former things, Or ponder the things of the past. Listen carefully, I am about to do a new thing..." (Isaiah 43:18-19, AMP)

#easiersaidthandone: Honestly, this can be a tough one. That's why this is an intentional choice. We must remind ourselves that it doesn't matter what happened yesterday or last month or last year or the last ten years. Faithfulness proactively chooses to forget and believes that this could be *the* cycle. What have we got to lose? We've already experienced the worst of it, knowing that crushing disappointment and what it feels like each month. But, God. He continues to sustain us. So, why not get our hopes up? Why not reach forward to this new thing? We might just be surprised with how simple it really is.

5. Faithfulness is persistent

Now Jesus was telling the disciples a parable to make the point that at all times they ought to pray and not give up and lose heart...Luke 18:1, AMP

This parable was about a persistent widow and an unjust judge. Basically, the widow kept coming before the judge to ask for justice and protection from her adversary. Each time, he would deny her request, but she kept coming and coming until finally, the judge said to himself, "Even though I do not fear God nor respect man, yet because this widow continues to bother me, I will give her justice and legal protection; otherwise by continually coming she [will be an intolerable annoyance and she] will wear me out." (Luke 18:4-5, AMP) Then, check out what Jesus said to wrap up the story:

> *Listen to what the unjust judge says! And will not [our just] God defend and avenge His elect [His chosen ones] who cry out to Him day and night? Will He delay [in providing justice] on their behalf? I tell you that He will defend and avenge them quickly. However, when the Son of Man comes, will He find [this kind of persistent] faith on the earth? Luke 18:6-8, AMP*

Hmm. Persistent faith is what, then? Praying day and night. Faithfulness is persistent; Faithfulness prays day and night and does not lose heart.

Another time that the disciples had just asked Jesus how to pray, He responded with what we know as "The Lord's Prayer." The conversation continued, and He then told a parable of a friend coming at midnight. The friend knocked on his neighbor's door in the middle of the night to ask for some bread to feed an unexpected guest. The neighbor responded with a big fat no because, of course, he was already in bed. I love what Jesus said next:

> *I tell you, even though he will not get up and give him anything because he is his friend, yet because of his persistence he will get up and give him as much as he needs. So I say to you, ask and keep on asking, and it will be given to you; seek and keep on seeking, and you will find; knock and keep on knocking, and the door will be opened to you.*
> *Luke 11:8-9, AMP*

Faithfulness is persistent. She keeps asking, keeps seeking, and keeps knocking. Faithfulness never quits. Jesus, Himself, was an embodiment of persistence when He was in the Garden of Gethsemane. Luke records that He was in such great distress and sorrow for what was about to come that He couldn't even stand on his feet and physically sweat drops of blood! He even prayed three times that God would remove this assignment. But, thank God He didn't! We know how the story ends. Jesus persisted through His humanity and walked out of the horror that was the cross. He remained faithful and earned His reward (#us).

Dear friend, amazing things happen when we persist! In fact, if we want anything impossible or amazing to happen in our lives, then we must allow persistence to be developed. David Diga Hernandez quotes, *"The faith that receives the impossible is persistent faith."*

Here is a stunning outcome of persistent faith. James, the brother of John, was just killed by Herod. Because Herod liked the attention so much, he also captured Peter to have him killed, "So Peter was kept in prison, but fervent and persistent prayer for him was being made to God by the church." (Acts 12:8, AMP) What happened next? Yep! The impossible! An angel appeared to Peter, removed his chains, told him to get dressed and put on his shoes, and then Peter followed the angel past all guard posts and through the iron gates of the city. These gates just happened to open of their own accord! He finally figured out what was going on and arrived at the doorstep of Mark's house. A girl named Rhoda was so excited he was there that she didn't even open the door! In fact, when she went to tell the rest of the disciples, they kept insisting that she was hearing Peter's angel. But Peter kept knocking, waiting to be admitted. Once they finally opened the door, they were astonished and realized they had just witnessed a miracle.

Incredible, right? So, what was the game-changer? Fervent and persistent prayer! Or what I like to call faithfulness. Even when we don't see our circumstances change immediately, we remain faithful. We don't lose heart; we don't quit! We know that our prayers, when in agreement with God's will, make the impossible possible!

#disclaimer: Remember, we do not have to plead and beg for a baby. We are not like the widow without a protector. We are not like the neighbor without bread. These examples show the power of co-laboring with God in persistent prayer. We do not, however, have to keep asking for a baby. God has already said "Yes" because of the finished work of the cross and the promises in His Word. Our conceptions, healthy pregnancies, and deliveries are our inheritance! So, we must not lose heart!

6. Faithfulness is of good courage

Be strong and courageous, do not be afraid or tremble in dread before them, for it is the Lord your God who goes with you. He will not fail you or abandon you. Deuteronomy 31:6, AMP

Faithfulness is of good courage. Good courage is present because we know God is with us. He will not fail or abandon us. Because of this courage, we can walk by faith and not by sight.

#allegoryahead: Faithfulness knows what enemies will come against her, and she tenaciously resists those enemies. She tramples fear, doubt, unbelief, and self-pity. In courage, she has battled the lion and the bear, so when the giant invades her land, she is fierce and resists him.

Faithfulness is of good courage. And with courage, she resists *anything* foreign to the kingdom. Courage allows Faithfulness to look fear in the face and rebuke it. Fear is common in her land, but it is not welcome. So with courage, she boldly confronts this fear and drives it out.

Courage helps Faithfulness actively resist doubt and unbelief that try to stealthily invade her territory. She ignores her own logic, her five senses, her own reasoning and courageously chooses to walk by faith. The truth of the sword of God's Word cuts down doubt and unbelief every time and conquers (#ohyeah). This same courage repeatedly defeats self-pity by helping Faithfulness remember who she is. She can recognize self-pity as an enemy of love and will fiercely defend and guard this love to the death of her flesh as she keeps her eyes on the cross in which lies her identity.

However, this courage is not flawless or seamless. In fact, courage can be messy and bumpy. It does not mean Faithfulness has perfect strength. Rather, courage will always push through even in the throes of weakness or pain. Faithfulness is of good courage, and good courage tells us that *God will never fail* (#amen).

7. Faithfulness reaps a harvest

And don't allow yourselves to be weary or disheartened in planting good seeds, for the season of reaping the wonderful harvest you've planted is coming! Galatians 6:9, TPT

Faithfulness experiences every process of planting from start to finish, from sowing to reaping. And because of this, Faithfulness receives a great reward. Because Faithfulness receives the promises of God:

*And we desire that each one of you show the same diligence to the full assurance of hope until the end, that you do not become sluggish, but **imitate those who through faith and patience inherit the promises.** (emphasis added) Hebrews 6:11-12, NKJV*

Faith and patience allow us to inherit the promises. And remember, children are our inheritance, just like every promise in the Bible through Jesus has become our inheritance! How do we inherit them? By faith and patience. Faith, we know, is trusting God and clinging to His truth. But, patience is so much more than waiting. It's forbearance, fortitude, and best of all, patient endurance:

For when God made a promise to Abraham, because He could swear by no one greater, He swore by Himself, saying, "Surely blessing I will bless you, and multiplying I will multiply you." And so, after he had patiently endured, he obtained the promise. Hebrews 6:13-15, NKJV

In other words, "Abraham stuck it out and got everything that had been promised to him." (The Message). Faithfulness stays the course, sticks it out, and gets everything promised to her. Because it is this very faithfulness that gets rewarded:

> *...without faith living within us it would be impossible to please God. For we come to God in faith knowing that he is real and that he rewards the faith of those who give all their passion and strength into seeking him. Hebrews 11:6, TPT*

What is this promised reward? Well, actually, there are multitudes of rewards, both seen and unseen. Most won't be known until eternity. In the following case, though, our reward is children! "Behold, children are a heritage from the Lord, The fruit of the womb is a reward." (Psalm 127:3, NKJV) The fruit of the womb is a reward.

Now, does that mean we "earn" the reward of children? No way! Why? Because we know the fruit of the womb is also our inheritance! However, there is no denying the truth that our faithfulness is most definitely rewarded. And, if Abraham can receive a child and descendants as his earthly reward, then so can we. So, remain faithful. Faithfulness *will* eventually reap a harvest.

8. Faithfulness leaves a legacy

> *Your faithfulness endures to all generations. Psalm 119:90, NKJV*

Because God's faithfulness endures to all generations, ours can as well. What we sow now and plant within our family line will eventually be harvested in our children and grandchildren. Thus, faithfulness leaves a legacy because she *endures all things*.

In the book of Matthew, Jesus described to His disciples the signs leading up to His second return. It's not pretty, y'all. Although He tells us not to be troubled, He goes on to list deceptions, wars, and rumors of famines, pestilences, earthquakes, tribulations, killings, betrayals, and lawlessness. *Not* pretty. Then, He says this profound statement, "But the one who endures to the end will be saved." (Matthew 24:13, NKJV) That is, the one who holds one's ground in conflict; the one who bears up against adversity; the one who holds out under stress; the one who stands firm; the one who perseveres under pressure. This one shall be saved. Faithfulness endures all things. We do not fear hardship or give up under pressure or conflict. Instead, we hold our ground and bravely endure anything that comes our way, never losing heart and never giving up (#amen).

As for me and my family heritage, I choose to be faithful. Because by faithfulness, we will endure to the end. When tribulation and hardship appear, my family will remain faithful; when great adversity and persecution come at the end of the age, my descendants will remain faithful.

As Billy Graham stated, *"My home is in Heaven. I'm just traveling through this world."* Everything seen is temporal, but everything unseen is eternal. The unseen is what matters in the end.

GOING DEEPER:

- Which attribute(s) of faithfulness currently form(s) the cornerstone of your life?
- Make a fresh commitment to remain faithful. Record your commitment in your journal.
- Is there any other Fruit that Remains you see blooming in your life?
- Scriptures to study: Jn. 15:16; 2 Cor. 4:18; Heb. 11:6; Heb. 12:2; Mt. 25:23,29; Lk. 8:15; Jas. 1:3-4; Jn. 17:17; Heb. 13:8; Heb. 4:14; Acts 27:22-25; Phil. 3:13; Is. 43:18-19; Lk. 18:1; Lk. 18:4-8; Lk. 11:8-9; Acts 12:5; Deut. 31:6; Gal. 6:9; Heb. 6:11-15, Ps. 127:3; Ps. 119:90; Mt. 24:13.

Chapter sixteen
IN THE DELAY

At the time of this writing, I am over four years into this journey. Mother's Day 2018 was just yesterday and, surprise, surprise, I began my period (#darnAuntFlo). Even now, while I am writing, I am contending with some cramping and exercising my decree for it to leave. Guess what? It's actually working! Even with something as "normal" as menstrual cramps, we do *not* have to accept it. Jesus took *all* sickness upon His body at the cross; He also took *all* pain! Cool, huh?

So, I have titled this chapter In the Delay. Up until this delay, I have been able to overcome unbelief and religion, I have been renewed and transformed in my mind, my head knowledge has become heart knowledge I wholly and truly believe, I have been exercising decrees at the same time as maintaining rest, and I am bearing fruit that remains and sharing my story! So, now what?

I wait.

And I keep allowing the Holy Spirit to shepherd and lead me into all truth. Oh, how tricky that can be. Because unfortunately, the delay can stall you out even further if you're not prepared for it. Yes, I am speaking from experience. I have learned this the hard way. You see, I'm not quite sure that I'm even supposed to be in a delay, that this was supposed to be plan A for me. But, because I got deceived and distracted, here I am, hoping to prevent you from making the same mistakes I did (#youarewelcome).

So, do not be deceived In the Delay, neither be distracted. Easier said than done, right? Because deception is deceiving and distraction is distracting. We don't even know if we have succumbed to it until our eyes are opened. And friend, my eyes are wiiiiiide open! I have fallen prey to both of these delays. As always, though, what the enemy meant for evil, God means for good (Genesis 50:20). And because the Holy Spirit led me into all truth, now I can help you! Here is what *to* do In the Delay:

1. Be on guard

Be sober [well balanced and self-disciplined], be alert and cautious at all times. That enemy of yours, the devil, prowls around like a roaring lion [fiercely hungry], seeking someone to devour. 1 Peter 5:8, AMP

Seriously. We have an enemy. And, he hates us. In fact, Jesus even informed us that the devil wants to steal from us, kill us, and destroy us (John 10:10). The truth is, he has no power to do any of that! Yes, the devil hates us because he is evil, but he really can't stand us because he's completely and utterly powerless. Seriously. Check this out:

Then Jesus made a public spectacle of all the powers and principalities of darkness, stripping away from them every weapon and all their spiritual authority and power to accuse us. And by the power of the cross, Jesus led them around as prisoners in a procession of triumph. He was not their prisoner; they were his! Colossians 2:15, TPT

Wow! Through the finished work of the cross, Jesus stripped away all weapons from the enemy. *All.* Now all he can do is prowl around like a roaring lion; all he can do is roar; all he can do is run his mouth (#getityet). The sneaky part, though, is that he searches for someone to devour. He roams around, searching for prey. Whom do you think he seeks? That's right, the weak ones and the ones weak of mind. He targets children and the rest of us when we are weak in our minds (#myopinion #takeitorleaveit).

For example, remember how I had panic attacks? My cycle was totally off, so I thought I might have been pregnant? Well, I was also battling fear. I began to have paralyzing fear that I was going to die if I was pregnant or if I ate certain foods. The panic attacks would happen while I was eating. It was always at different times of the day; there was no rhyme or reason; caffeine, no caffeine; at bedtime or during lunch. I was seriously being tormented. I especially didn't understand what the heck was going on because I had already overcome fear! Remember?

Some days I felt amazing, normal even, and was able to write, while other days, I was tormented and spent the whole day striving to get my thinking under control. This led to confusion and feeling ashamed because I was struggling with something that I thought I'd already overcome. I was miserable and desperate for a solution. I couldn't even sleep peacefully or take naps on Sunday afternoons. You guys, I would wake up in the morning and thank God I was still alive! That's how bad this had become. What did I do? I set myself before the Lord and renewed my mind again in this area. But nothing changed. In fact, it actually got worse (#saywhat).

Then, one day, my husband and I were talking and trying to figure out what was happening to me. He said this, "What if it's demonic?" I responded with, "But I've already overcome fear! And I don't think the enemy can touch me!" However, he had planted a seed. I began to study the Word and listen to a couple of messages on spiritual warfare. At the end of one of the messages, I felt led to speak out loud against the spirit of fear (#disclaimer). Now, I do not mean that I was demonically possessed. However, Christians *can* be demonized based on the lies we listen to and agree with.

So, after I spoke the words against the spirit of fear, nothing changed. I still felt the same. Later that night, however, I had a dream. In the dream, I was looking at myself in the bathroom mirror and noticed a huge whitehead pimple on my forehead (#gross). I leaned forward to squeeze it, and of course, out flowed the nastiness (#ewwmoregross). But then, a clear small snake the size of a worm also came out and dropped to the floor. I ran to my closet and grabbed a shoe to smash it. I whacked it on the head a few times, but it didn't die. Instead, it slithered into the commode and disappeared. Then, I woke up. I knew immediately that this dream was significant. But it wasn't until the next day that I received understanding.

You see, the Holy Spirit revealed to me what happened in the spiritual realm. He showed me that the clear snake was actually a parasite, a demonic parasite that hid itself in my mind bent on the path of total deception. And it had worked for a while. I was so deceived that I kept blaming myself when it was actually the enemy accusing me. I was so deceived that I didn't realize I was in unbelief because the parasite was whispering in my ear and making me question the true knowledge and authority of God and His Word. I was so deceived, I thought I was going to die because the parasite told me I couldn't trust God to protect me.

But I have good news! That spirit of torment was found out. I was set free! (#woohoo) Once I realized I wasn't wrestling against myself but against a spirit, I took authority, cast it away, and all fear ceased. All anxiety stopped, and the panic attacks were soon a thing of the past. Seriously. I've not had one since:

> *Listen carefully: I have given you authority [that you now possess] to tread on serpents and scorpions, and [the ability to exercise authority] over all the power of the enemy (Satan); and nothing will [in any way] harm you. Luke 10:19, AMP*

So, be on guard. Our enemy is searching for weakness to infiltrate our thoughts. At the end of 2017, I thought for sure I was going to get pregnant before the year was out, and when I didn't, I was devastated, and that was when the enemy struck. So, you need to be on guard and remember that the devil has no power over you! All he can do is run his mouth and plant deceptive thoughts. If you have any thoughts in your mind that go against truth, or make you feel condemned, or bring up past issues that you've already overcome, then that is your warning, and you can nip it before it gets worse.

2. Stay in truth

And you will know the truth, and the truth will set you free. John 8:32, NLT

Another delay we can encounter is to be distracted with everything else in life. To be totally honest, these may be really, really good things, such as things that require our attention and bear spiritual fruit. For me, it was my family and our ministry. Awesome things were happening! Unfortunately, however, this distraction led me to passivity on my journey to become The Joyful Mother of children. This made me vulnerable to unbelief and doubt. So, we must be careful not to get passive and distracted. Instead, we must stay in truth so that we can automatically be on guard. And not only that, if we stay in truth, we will be in a perpetual state of freedom, able to resist the temptation of doubt and unbelief every time. You will know the truth, and it will set you free. So, you can stay in truth and stay in freedom by doing the following:

- Continually renew your mind with truth- keep feeding and meditating on the Word, specifically on scriptures the Holy Spirit reveals throughout this season of barrenness. Remember, as you meditate, scripture is getting planted, watered, and fertilized in the soil of your heart.
- Read other faith-filled books and testimonies- find any books, blogs, or testimonies that encourage you to keep believing.
- Prophetically declare- keep declaring the Word and those scriptures that were revealed to you, as well as any prophetic words received. Remember, as you declare the Word, you have no doubt that what you are believing for is God's will.
- Decree- keep commanding your physical body to line up with truth. Command barrenness and whatever sickness or disease are causing it to go until God says to stop.

3. Remember

*I will remember the works of the L*ORD*; Surely I will remember Your wonders of old. I will also meditate on all Your work, And talk of Your deeds. Psalm 77:11-12, NKJV*

#sigh: I love Psalm 77. It so clearly gives voice to what I have been feeling. Because, I think the whole reason why I'm even In the Delay is that I *forgot*. I forgot I have an enemy, I forgot his tactic of deception, I forgot truth, I forgot who I am, and because of this, I have been delayed (#argh).

I mentioned previously that I don't think the delay was God's plan A for me. I know this because the delay has been filled with confusion, fear, and distraction, which are things I have already overcome. It's been filled with too many analytical questions instead of peace and rest. I love asking analytical questions and enjoy my deep conversations with the Holy Spirit. But, when the analysis leads to meditating on the impossibility of a situation versus the truth, well, then I have been deceived.

So, these next few points are crucial. Forgetting them may break you. Remembering them, however, will make you (#free #andpregnant):

- Remember truth

This seems easy enough. But, it's also easy for the deceiver to creep in and deceive if you don't *stay* in the truth. What is the truth, again? The entirety of the Word (Psalm 119:160); that is, *all* of the scriptures in the Bible promising and prophesying over you. As you meditate on these scriptures, the seeds sown into your heart will bear fruit through endurance and faith. Jesus said:

If you abide in Me, and My words abide in you, you will ask what you desire, and it shall be done for you. By this My Father is glorified, that you bear much fruit; so you will be My disciples. John 15:7-8, NKJV

So, let's remember truth and sow that truth down into our hearts. For eventually, we will bear much fruit, and God will be glorified.

- Remember the cross

Again, with the cross? Yes! It is our identity and our value, the stability and the rock of our lives. We need to remember the cross by remembering what Jesus has done for us through His finished work. He took *all* sin, sickness, and disease in our place. He healed us of barrenness, miscarriage, and *any* disease that is causing them. His finished work and all the promises in the Bible are "Yes and Amen!". He bought our inheritance with His precious blood, this precious blood that enables us to be at peace with God and to boldly decree with the authority of Heaven. We need to meditate on these truths so intently that they become alive in our hearts and transform our minds to places of rest and our bodies to places of manifestation (#readthatagain).

You then will notice that as these seeds bear fruit and the enemy tempts you to question the validity of your petition, you will more easily cast down the arguments, and you'll stay in truth. Likewise, the more of a reality these truths become, the more manifestation you will see in your body.

For example, I decreed normal, healthy cycles of 28-30 days, and it's been happening! I decreed no pain with my cycles, so any time cramping tries to rear its ugly head, I rebuke it, and the pain dulls. I have even been decreeing no allergies and colds, and as I rebuke them, the symptoms lessen! Remember, though; this is a process. We can find that our bodies actually respond to the decrees. So, let us continue to spend time meditating and thinking on the cross; always, always remember the cross!

- Remember creation

#saywhat: Remember how you were created; that God created you to be fruitful and multiply (Genesis 1:28). He gave you and your husband all the equipment and tools necessary to procreate. I could go into detail because I am definitely not afraid to talk about the baby dance (#letstalkaboutsexbaby). But I will refrain.

The point is, you already have everything you need. Your body was actually created to conceive and bear children. That's what it was made to do! It doesn't matter if it's broken or has missing parts or dysfunctional hormones, etc. It doesn't matter if your husband has some broken or missing parts either. Husbands and wives were created to create! God's job is done. He rested on the seventh day and didn't create another human being or animal or tree ever again because He gave all creation exactly what it needed to reproduce. It's all around us! In the trees, the grass, the flowers, the animals, the fish, the people, and even in the creepy, crawly insects!

This is why it's so important to remember the truth, which says that none shall be barren, male or female (Deuteronomy 7:14). This is a promise and prophecy we must receive! What if you've been told that you can't have children; what if your husband is shooting blanks? Well, this is why it is equally important to remember the cross! Jesus took *all* sickness and disease on His body. So, whatever is missing or broken in your body, Jesus has taken it on *His*! You are already healed and made new by the finished work of the cross. Jesus took sterility, barrenness, miscarriage, and whatever sickness or disease that is causing it on His back when He brutally died on that cross. Your body was created to create. You and your husband were born to be called "mommy" and "daddy." All you have to do is sow and God will bring the harvest! Seriously (#sowmeansdothebabydance).

As we remember this truth and as it bears fruit, we will be at rest like never before. We will no longer feel the need to strive or work; we will no longer analyze or predict how it's all going to happen. We just need to remember and trust that our bodies will do what they were created to do. This confidence can only come through meditating on and receiving all of the above. So, remember and trust how God made His creations. He will not let you down.

- Remember who you are

I was first deceived, then distracted, so that my soulish self wanted to resort back to false humility and a poverty mentality. However, this is the direct enemy to the truth of our identity. You see, my emotions love self-pity. It is so very comfortable and familiar to me. As the fog cleared, thankfully, the Good Shepherd led me into more truth and more revelation before I could continue writing. You will see those changes below. First, though, you must be on guard and remember who you are while In the Delay.

You have seen my progression of identity, from servant to daughter, to friend, to warrior princess, to beloved, and now the most recent revelation is to queen. I am royal. *We* are royal. We are not just His beloved (which is more than enough), but we are priestess-queens, "...God's chosen **treasure – priests who are kings,** a spiritual 'nation' set apart as God's devoted ones..." (1 Peter 2:9, TPT emphasis added). And, it is all because of what Jesus did for us through the finished work of the cross! We are transformed by the finished work of the cross; we have been called out of darkness into His marvelous light; we are new creations; we have become royalty! So, now we can imitate God and share the mind of Christ while seated in heavenly places! We can rule and reign with Jesus!

I am no longer Mandi Windsor, but I am Mandi Windsor, Christ in me! Insert your name here: I am no longer _____, but I am _____, Christ in me. This is who we are; co-heirs as He works in us and through us.

Because of the finished work of the cross, we know that fruitfulness is our inheritance. Fruitfulness is a byproduct of being royal. It is a given. Think about it. Royalty reigns, and fruitfulness just happens. Jesus already did the work! We get to sit back and reign; we get to pursue Jesus and act like Him because we are heirs to the throne. This is who we are! We are royalty! (#areyouconvincedyet)

To help me grasp this new revelation, I began to search out stories of royalty, specifically queens. Here is what I noticed: The queen is protected; she has bodyguards everywhere she goes. She may not be the prettiest woman, but her position and confidence make her beautiful and awe-inspiring. All of her needs are met and taken care of in abundance. Her requests are valued and honored. She is bold and courageous. People look to her for wisdom and guidance to lead. She surrounds herself with wise advisors. She is secure in her identity and authority. She is fearless and laughs without fear of the future. She dances and feasts. She is fruitful and multiplies. She is a servant-leader and gives to the poor and needy. She leaves a legacy and is known for a cause. She changes and imprints on history. She loves animals (yes, seriously; all queens that I studied had a great love for dogs).

Wouldn't it be so cool to *be* her? Well, you *are*! And, the best part about it is your royalty is not based on your family line or last name or even character. It is based on who Jesus is and the new creation you are in Him! Amazing, right? But, how do you actually *attain* this identity? Especially if you're just not feeling it (#goodquestion).

By coming to the end of yourself.

When you come to the end of yourself, you boldly state, "It is no longer I who live, but Christ who lives in me!" In other words, you *die*! It may sound morbid, but it's totally biblical. Mandi Windsor is dead. But Mandi Windsor, Christ in me, is more abundantly alive than ever before!

Also, you remember truth, you remember the cross, you remember creation, and you remember who you are. Check out my journal entry from June 14, 2018, as it describes this point of remembrance:

I am most myself when I am issuing a decree, when I am in authority, and when I am confident in who I am in Jesus. I am my best self, and it feels authentic and genuine. I have complete fullness and peace in my spirit, soul, and body when I am aligned with truth. I am free when I am in belief. I am at shalom when I walk by faith and not by sight. I can start my period on Mother's Day and on my husband's birthday and be okay! I can see others pop up pregnant and have babies and be okay! I can! Because I know, truly know, who I am to God. I know that He is not withholding from me. Instead, He brutally died so that I could live in complete salvation and wholeness (sozo)! He took sickness on His body. He took MY sickness. Whatever sickness or disease is in my body causing barrenness, He took it! It's gone and has died at the root! I truly believe this! I really do! We are joyful parents of children; we are fruitful, and we multiply; we are fruitful vines, and our children are like olive plants around our table.

None shall be barren or miscarry in our land, therefore body, conceive and be pregnant! Do what you were created to do! You are healed! You are free! You are in perfect health to do what you were created for! Thank You, Jesus. Thank You for taking it all for me. Thank You for giving me the authority and bringing me up to Your heavenly throne. You are so generous to share with me and to anoint me as queen and co-heir! Wow! Thank You, Beloved. I am amazed by You and in awe of Your love for me. Holy Spirit, remind me of truth any time I begin to miss the mark. May I always stay in this place with You – at my best and most authentic.

So, remember, dear friend. Remember. And as you do, the delay will not be such a delay any longer, but a bridge; from faith to faith; from glory to glory; from The Barren Woman to The Joyful Mother of Children (#amen).

GOING DEEPER:

- Do you feel like you are in a delay?
- Describe a time when you were deceived.
- Describe a time when you were distracted.
- Have you struggled with passivity on your journey?
- If you haven't already, begin exercising your decree over your cycles, cramps, bodies, etc.
- Come to the end of yourself by declaring, "It is no longer I who live, but Christ who lives in Me! I am _____, Christ in me."
- Scriptures to study: Gen. 50:20; 1 Pt. 5:8; Jn. 10:10; Col. 2:15; Lk. 10:19; Jn. 8:32; Ps. 77:11-12; Jn. 15:7-8; Gen. 1:28; Deut. 7:14; 1 Pt. 2:9.

Chapter seventeen
Now is the Time

Those who sow their tears as seeds will reap a harvest with joyful shouts of glee. They may weep as they go out carrying their seed to sow, but they will return with joyful laughter and shouting with gladness as they bring back armloads of blessing and a harvest overflowing!
Psalm 126:5-6, TPT

What actually happens when we come to the end of ourselves? What happens when we surrender to who we are, or think we are, to whom we truly are in Christ? What happens when we choose to put on the new man and clothe ourselves in our true identities as queens? What results when we meditate on these truths until they become a reality (#whatwhatwhat)? We bear fruit in the form of harvest!

Yes, the harvest has come. What we have sown in tears, we now reap with joy. Our season of sowing is complete. Now, I don't mean that we stop "sowing seed" with our husbands or stop planting seeds of truth in our hearts. I mean, the time has come. The time is now. Fruitfulness is here!

As I discern the signs of the times, I realize the season has shifted from one of sowing to one of reaping. God, in His infinite mercy, confirmed this in two tangible ways. The first is, my husband got recruited and offered a really great job! We didn't even have time to pray and ask for what we needed. God orchestrated it and set all the pieces into motion without any help from us. Secondly, the very next day, after journaling the above, we got a phone call announcing our application for a pug puppy was accepted! This was a huge deal because we hadn't been able to afford a puppy from a breeder. We were in a place of desperately wanting a puppy. However, the outcome seemed hopeless. When we saw that this puppy had come through the rescue organization as a breeder release, we thought we would simply apply (#sowingseed). Well, we now have a precious twelve-week-old pug puppy! God brought the harvest! We named our new pup Percy. He is just the sweetest thing and such a huge blessing.

Now, these examples may not seem like a big deal, but God used them for me as evidence of the times. The time is now. The harvest has come. What I have sown in tears, interceded for in tears, I now reap with joy. As I accepted and received this revelation in my heart, the Holy Spirit gave me even more insight and truth by His Word.

#question: How many times have we heard people talk about "in God's perfect timing" this or "in God's timing" that? Well, what if I said that times could be changed; that we have the ability to receive "God's perfect timing" as *now* time? Throughout this journey, there has been the temptation to wait on "God's perfect timing." But what if *He* has been waiting on *me*, has been waiting for me to boldly demand my inheritance? What if? What if this is how co-laboring works? What if this is actually what God is seeking from His people? For us to know our identities and realize we are royalty, ruling and reigning with Him, infused with the power from Heaven to decree laws and change time! What do you think? If I'm crazy for thinking this way, then I guess I rank right up there with Esther, Ruth, Hannah, Mary of Bethany, and Mary, the mother of Jesus. And I am more than happy to join them.

Let's start with Esther. In a nutshell, her story tells about a young Jewish woman who found favor and became queen. Her Uncle Mordecai discovered a plot to wipe out all the Jewish people and informed Esther so she could make supplication for their people. Esther initially responded to Mordecai by reminding him of the glaring fact that anyone who went into the inner court of the king without being summoned would be put to death. Mordecai responded:

> *...if you remain completely silent at this time, relief and deliverance will arise for the Jews from another place, but you and your father's house will perish. Yet who knows whether you have come to the kingdom for such a time as this? Esther 4:14, NKJV*

Esther then replied, "I will go to the king, which is against the law; and if I perish, I perish!" She stuck to her word. She put on her royal robes and faced the king. She did find favor in his sight. And, he listened to her petitions. There's a lot more to the story, but Esther and Mordecai ended up saving all the Jews because of Esther's boldness. Esther put on her royal robes and reminded herself that she had the authority to boldly approach the throne and declare what she wanted. Friend, God is beckoning us to do the same. We have attained royalty for such a time as this.

Another example of this kind of boldness comes from the story of Ruth. Ruth was not a Jew; she was a Moabitess. She had become a widow, and instead of staying in her homeland, she remained faithful and stayed with her mother-in-law Naomi. Naomi returned to her people, the Jews, and Ruth went to work gleaning in the fields for food. She happened upon the field of Boaz, who heard of her faithfulness to Naomi. He offered her provision and protection. After the harvest, Naomi told Ruth to wash and anoint herself, put on her best garment, and boldly enter the threshing room where Boaz would be sleeping after preparing the grain. Not only did she enter the room, but she brazenly risked her reputation by uncovering his feet, lying down by them, hoping he would wake and see her. Once he woke up, she said, "I am Ruth, your maidservant. Take your maidservant under your wing for you are a close relative." (Ruth 3:9, NKJV)

Yes, that's exactly what it looks like! Ruth threw herself at his feet. Literally (#wowsers). She basically proposed! Boaz, the gentleman that he was, though, protected her reputation and honorably arranged their marriage, "So Boaz took Ruth and she became his wife; and when he went in to her, the Lord gave her conception, and she bore a son." (Ruth 4:13, NKJV #happyending) Friend, Boaz was *not* planning to pursue marriage with Ruth. In fact, the passage alludes that Boaz was possibly older and surprised that Ruth would even want him. But, by Ruth's boldness, she turned a possibility into an actuality, a someday into a now!

So, Esther and Ruth both went to see the king/leader without being summoned. They used their royalty, their identity as a faithful and virtuous woman, and declared their requests. They boldly approached the throne with threats of death and loss of reputation. They came to the end of themselves for their people; Esther for the Jews and Ruth for Naomi.

Next, let's talk about Hannah again. Hannah was one of the two wives of Elkanah. Peninnah was the other who was able to get pregnant. Hannah remained barren and was provoked by Peninnah. Year after year, it was the same. They would travel to the tabernacle to make offerings. Hannah, in her grief, would weep and not eat. Maybe she would go into the tabernacle and pray, maybe not. But, there came a year that, for some reason, she decided enough was enough. She went into the temple, prayed, wept in anguish, and made a vow to the Lord that if He gave her a son, she would return him back to His service. She poured out her soul before God until there was a shift in her countenance until she knew God heard her and answered her prayers. And He definitely answered. In fact, Hannah's prayer moved the heart of God (#saywhat). How? Israel desperately needed her son, Samuel. God knew this, and yet, He didn't just make it happen alone (#thinkaboutthat). Perhaps, this time, He knew Hannah would boldly approach Him and make her request. Once she did, He moved mightily.

Mary of Bethany is another example (John 11). Jesus knew her brother Lazarus was sick before he died, but He stayed where He was for two more days (#makessense #ummno). Then, when Jesus knew that Lazarus "slept," as He called it, He finally arrived on the scene. By this time, Lazarus had been in the tomb for four days! Martha, Mary's sister, met Jesus on His way in and said to Him, "Lord, if You had been here, my brother would not have died." She then went on to concede that it must have been God's will. Jesus told her that her brother would rise again, and Martha agreed that he would rise again at the resurrection. She had already accepted Lazarus's death, which is not necessarily a negative thing, it just wasn't what Jesus was looking for (#hmm). Martha then told Mary that Jesus was there. When Mary got to Jesus, she fell down at His feet and said to Him:

> *"Lord, if You had been here, my brother would not have died." And then she began to weep. Therefore, when Jesus saw her weeping, and the Jews who came with her weeping, He groaned in the spirit and was troubled. And He said, "Where have you laid him?" John 11:33-34, NKJV*

Mary's tears and the tears of the Jews moved Jesus to act! He asked, "Where have you laid him?" He wanted to know because He had every intention of resurrecting Lazarus! Martha had said the exact same words. She had the correct theology about Lazarus rising again in the resurrection, but Jesus wanted someone to boldly believe and petition for the *now*! He didn't want His friend to be dead! But He wouldn't just raise Lazarus on His own timing. He moved when He was moved by Mary's tears (#dowegetityet).

Dear friend, Jesus is looking for faith! That's all this boldness is! And the even better news is that we already *have* this faith. In fact, we have something even greater. We are post-cross, New Covenant believers. What Hannah and even Mary of Bethany had to contend for, *we* just get to receive. We no longer have to beg God to move on our behalf. He already moved when He sent Jesus to the cross! Remember, Jesus was the answer to everything we could ever need. He took all sickness, disease, barrenness, and miscarriage on *His* body.

So, when we approach Him with boldness and faith, we are not doing so in order to make Him move. He can move no more than what He already did when He sent Jesus (#Healreadymoved). Furthermore, God does not respond to our faith; instead, our faith and tears of boldness are *responses* to God. Now is the time because God's timing was actually over 2,000 years ago!

However, if this is true, then what about the warring and struggling and angst we feel deep within our hearts? What is that all about? Well, it is because we have this incongruity of what Jesus already accomplished for us, God's nature, His Word, and what is actually happening in our bodies. It *should* torment us to tears! Because we know His heart! We know His Word! We know what He did for us! Just like Mary knew Jesus didn't want Lazarus to die, we know He wants to give us children! We. Know. His. Heart. He doesn't want us waiting until the resurrection or when we're in our new bodies; He doesn't want us to concede to a life of sickness, infertility, or miscarriage. He wants us to believe and receive the miracle *now*! Not tomorrow, but *now*! Not next year, but *now*!

#checkit: Studies show that about 7.4 million women in the U.S. have had difficulty getting pregnant or staying pregnant. That's approximately twelve percent of *all* women in the United States![1] It may not seem like a lot in the grand scheme of things, but that's 7.4 million women who are in a constant state of grief and mourning; 7.4 million women who possibly hate their bodies; 7.4 million women who are questioning if God really loves them, questioning if there even *is* a God! That's not even including all the women of the world! I am not okay with this!

These facts have moved me to physically weep, to groan inside myself. Imagine what it does to Jesus. Especially when He created *all* women to be fruitful, multiply, and enjoy the gift of motherhood. Especially when He already provided the answer over 2,000 years ago.

So, what do we do? Well, after groaning and interceding on behalf of all The Barren Women, I have gotten to a confident place in my relationship with God. It may seem like arrogance. It is not. It is righteousness, a right standing; it is a knowing that I can boldly approach His throne because I know His heart for me; His heart for The Barren Woman. And I know He has to stay faithful to His Word, or else He be called a liar. He is not. He is true and good and merciful and kind and loving.

---

1 https://www.huffingtonpost.com/.../infertility-statistics-stats-about-infertility_us_571f8

And He loves me, The Barren Woman. He loves *you*, The Barren Woman. He desires to give us children more than we desire to have them. He desires that we are fruitful and multiply more than we do. He desires to bless our wombs more than we want it. So, because I *know* Him, because I know that the barren womb and the abundance of miscarriages make Him groan, I have chosen to partner with Him from my place in Heaven; from my place of authority as priestess-queen, as royalty. This is how I have been praying:

> *You brought me out of my fear; You brought me out of my religion; You brought me out of my shame; You brought me out of my unbelief; You brought me out of my doubt; deception, and self-pity; You brought me out of every hindrance! You healed me; You healed my husband! You healed my soul! Now hurry! Now God! Now! Now is the time! I demand my inheritance of fruitfulness! You promised it! You spoke it! You died for it! You bought it with Your blood! You said The Barren Woman becomes The Joyful Mother of children! You said none shall be barren or miscarry! You prophesied to me! So now, Abba! Let it be done to me according to Your Word, now!*

It sounds sacrilegious or like blasphemy speaking to God, the Almighty One, with such demands, doesn't it? Seriously though, what did He die for? Why would He even exhibit His power and authority on earth if He didn't want us to be able to do the same? Why would He call us co-heirs if He didn't expect us to rule and reign with Him? Why would He tear the veil in two if He didn't want us to co-labor on this earth to make things happen? It's all throughout the Bible! History has proven that times can be changed; *Now is the time*.

Look at Mary, the mother of Jesus. She recognized this truth. We know she knew the heart of her Son more than anyone else on earth. In fact, it was Mary who moved Jesus to perform His first visible miracle:

> *On the third day there was a wedding in Cana of Galilee, and the mother of Jesus was there. Now both Jesus and His disciples were*

> *invited to the wedding. And when they ran out of wine, the mother of Jesus said to Him, "They have no wine." Jesus said to her, "Woman, what does your concern have to do with Me? My hour has not yet come." His mother said to the servants, "Whatever He says to you, do it" John 2:1-5, NKJV*

Jesus even told Mary that it was not yet time. Did she listen? Nope. She simply knew her authority as His mother and told the servants to obey Him in expectation. Isn't that awesome? It's time for us to step into our true identities, not just as The Joyful Mother of children, but as royalty. And as a queen, we declare fruitfulness in our kingdoms. *Now.* What Jesus provided over 2,000 years ago, we receive *now*. We proclaim liberty to the captives, healing to the brokenhearted, comfort to all who mourn, beauty for ashes, the oil of joy for mourning, and the garment of praise for a spirit of heaviness. We declare that instead of shame, we will have double honor; instead of incongruity, we will rejoice in our portions; and in our land, we shall possess double; everlasting joy will be ours (Isaiah 61)!

So, what time is it? Harvest time! What we have sown in tears, we now reap with joyful shouts of laughter and singing.

Going Deeper:

- Have you been told that you will have children "in God's perfect timing"? Record how that made you feel.
- What was your first reaction to hearing how times can be changed; that we can believe for "now timing"?
- God's timing was over 2,000 years ago. Record your thoughts about this truth.
- Read the stories of Esther, Ruth, Hannah, Mary of Bethany, and Mary the mother of Jesus. Record any revelations.
- As a queen, begin boldly decreeing over your land. Record.
- Scriptures to study: Ps. 126:5-6; Esther 4:14; Ruth 3:9, 4:13; Jn. 11:33-34; Jn. 2:1-5; Is. 61.

Chapter eighteen
THE SONG OF VICTORY

Blessed be the Lord. Because He has heard the voice of my supplications. The Lord is my strength and my shield; My heart trusted Him, and I am helped; therefore my heart greatly rejoices, and with my song I will praise Him. Psalm 28:6-7, NKJV

In "Sing, Oh Barren," we talked about the songs of praise and battle. Well, the Holy Spirit reminded me that we still hadn't discussed The Song of Victory. Earlier, I had not experienced full victory, so I actually didn't even know what or how to sing at that time. However, God doesn't want me to wait for my positive pregnancy test before moving forward.

I always thought that I would get pregnant during the process of writing this book, especially so near the end. Well, I am pregnant... in spirit. This has been confirmed through a dream I had on the same night as my husband. It is only a matter of time before my physical body will demonstrate this reality. But, if God wants me to move forward in the whole book-writing process, I need some closure.

So, the Holy Spirit reminded me of a loose end, a.k.a. The Song of Victory. But I had a problem. You see, when I completed the previous chapter, I felt a shift in the signs of the times, but I still felt the same emotionally. Here I was, supposed to be excited and free from mourning, but there was no joy. How was I qualified to write The Song of Victory when there wasn't the emotion to match it? It just wouldn't come. This confused me. I felt like a fraud. I didn't doubt at all what I was discerning, but I didn't understand why I wasn't experiencing the emotional feelings of joy. So, I asked, sought, and knocked. And I went to battle because I was most definitely experiencing resistance (#grrdevil).

However, what I discovered was that *I* was contributing to the resistance of this breakthrough because *I* didn't believe. Not that I didn't believe God, or the promises, or the signs of the times, rather I still didn't believe in *myself*. I still didn't believe that I was enough, that I was worthy, that I could walk out this testimony and message He wants me to deliver to others.

At the same time, I discovered I didn't know how to worship God and serve Him without being The Barren Woman. I mean, I have spent my whole adult life in grief and mourning. I didn't know how to move forward without it. I didn't even know how to worship God without it. I felt lost. In my journaling, I even wrote, "I don't know what to do. I don't know where to go from here." And I didn't. I was bereft without this identity as The Barren Woman. How was I to move forward? I knew the time had come. I was no longer barren, but I felt naked and exposed and vulnerable. And, because I felt so out of control, I was holding onto it, which of course, is sin. For real, I knew my time of mourning had ended, but I kept trying to *extend* that mourning. Then, it came to me. I had more faith in the lies than I did in the truth. This revelation just about broke me. I began to weep and repent for the years of extended unbelief and mourning; for the years of believing the lies over the truth; for the years of embracing the spirit of heaviness; for the decade-plus that I had spent identifying as The Barren Woman.

Then something amazing happened. As I repented and cried and made the choice to step out into the unknown, I began to laugh. Tears rolled down my cheeks, but I was still laughing. I was experiencing the oil of joy physically for the first time in my life. It was beautiful. I was belly laughing and crying; my stomach didn't even hurt after the fact. I was clean. Whole. Holy. And, Healed. My heart was healed. The oil of joy washed away all my years of mourning. It sealed up all the broken pieces of my heart. Every crack, every crevice, all of it was healed.

I was so victorious over this first resistance. But there was a second. The enemy was coming at my thoughts hardcore, wanting me to agree with his lies and partner with a false identity. It kept coming, but I resisted. I sang or chanted the lyrics the Holy Spirit gave to me as my Song of Victory, *"I'm not going back anymore because it's not who I am anymore. I'm not looking back anymore because it's not who I am anymore."* I just repeated this over and over again anytime the enemy tried to whisper something else.

You see, I know, that I know, that I know, that I am no longer The Barren Woman. It is just not me. The time is now, and I have crossed over from death to life, from barrenness to fruitfulness. But I still was not feeling the emotions of joy. And it still felt like I was battling every hour until I received a picture in my mind as I was singing and chanting those lyrics.

The Holy Spirit showed me what was taking place in the spiritual realm. There was an image of a dark jail cell or cave with cement walls from floor to ceiling. I saw myself covered in a gray, tattered and torn, dusty cloak, kneeling on the ground. My hands were bound in chains on both sides of me, and I was hunched over. But then, I began to stand. I broke free from the chains on my right side, then my left, and I stood up fully and threw the dusty, heavy cloak off of my back and stood straight and tall and radiant as I looked up to the ceiling. At that moment, light shone down upon me, and I was absolutely stunning. I had my hands raised in freedom and received the light. Then, I saw myself clothed in a red royal cloak, with a tiara and a scepter. A white spiral staircase appeared, and I walked up the stairs.

Dear friend, this picture was the very image of the spirit of heaviness being broken off from me and replaced with garments of praise (Isaiah 61, Psalm 30:11). He broke off the chains that kept me bound to reproach, rejection, shame, and self-pity. My good, good Daddy actually gave me these supernatural experiences as evidence of His healing in my life. And it was after these two demonstrations that the joy finally came (#abouttime).

I can't stop smiling. I can't stop saying "Thank You." I can't stop singing. I can't stop looking at myself in the mirror and loving who I see. I am actually in love with who God made me to be! This is foreign to me! I am worthy and beautiful, and it has nothing to do with my body! I can clearly see myself in His image and through His eyes because the spirit of heaviness and the lenses of mourning are gone. They are gone! I am free! I am free to sing my Song of Victory ("I Won't Go Back" by William McDowell. Check out the lyrics here: https://bit.ly/3O8DyBU.)

These lyrics are so similar to the words the Holy Spirit gave me before discovering this song. My husband introduced me to it when I told him about the phrase I kept singing. As soon as I heard it, I wept (#yes – iamacrybaby). I had been asking for a song to decree during this time, and He answered me. This is my Song of Victory. Because here's the deal, I will *not* go back. It's that simple. I am no longer The Barren Woman. She is dead. God has given me the oil of joy in place of my mourning, garments of praise for the spirit of heaviness, my healing is complete, my journey is complete. The Joyful Mother of children has been resurrected!

So, get excited! You are about to be blown away by the healing that takes place within *your* being and how He actually does it. He will blow your mind. There is a shift coming. Your time is now. You still may have resistance; you still may have some scrapes and barely healed wounds. The enemy knows this and will continue to resist your complete healing. But God. He arms you with a song and gives you supernatural experiences that you'll never forget. He did it for me just to confirm and seal *my* healing and what I already know in my spirit. He will do it for all of us. How amazing is that?

So, here I am. Completely healed and pregnant in the spirit. I sing my Song of Victory because I know that what is happening in the spirit will soon be manifested in the natural. I rejoice and know that what I have sown in years of tears will reap a joyful harvest; mourning and grief are over; the heaviness is gone; the chains have been broken; I am free. I am free to be Mandi Windsor, Christ in me, The Joyful Mother of Children.

Going Deeper:
- Are you contributing to the resistance of your breakthrough?
- Are you still holding onto the identity as The Barren Woman? If so, record your process of repentance.
- Ask the Holy Spirit to give you a Song of Victory. Feel free to steal mine if you want!
- Scriptures to study: Ps. 28:6-7; Is. 61; Ps. 30:11.

Chapter Nineteen

YOU ARE WHAT YOU SEE

I will get straight to the point. How do we walk in this place of victory without seeing movement in the natural? How is our joy sustained if we don't see things change? In other words, what if there is still no manifestation of what we know to be true? I mean, we can know what the Bible says; can wholly and completely believe that we are healed body and soul; can know that we are no longer The Barren Woman but are The Joyful Mother of children; we can be pregnant in spirit. But what happens if we *still* don't see the BFP (#bigfatpositive)? Do we rest? Do we continue to rejoice and sing our Song of Victory? Do we continue to contend and decree? Do we keep boldly approaching the throne room and demanding our inheritance? What do we do *now*? Good question. And one I grappled with for a while. Thinking I was finished writing, I turned this manuscript into my current editor. I was truly changed and even felt different physically. I still didn't have closure, though; I still didn't have a BFP. I was having trouble maintaining my victory.

Back in the previous chapter, where I had imagined myself walking up the white staircase, I knew I had overcome. I knew it was time to reign. I knew I was sitting in heavenly places, but my mind continued to be stuck here on earth. I was having trouble seeing what was in front of me or which direction to take. I was having trouble *seeing* what could be; I was having trouble *seeing* truth, and not just because I hadn't yet received my BFP.

After submitting my manuscript, I attended a women's retreat that same weekend. One of the ladies gave me a prophetic word, "think higher." Of course, she had no more explanation (#grr), and I'm like a dog with a bone when I can't figure out what God is trying to tell me. So, I gnawed on that bone and tasted a big juicy steak instead. In that steak, I found more profound truth, more revelation.

#checkitout: I am pregnant in spirit, right? And I am healed in my body, healed in my soul (my mind, will, and emotions). But, as with any sort of traumatic experience, my mind continued to remember who I used to be. So, even though I aligned my will with truth, my mind and emotions still remembered the trauma of being barren. Yes, even after being healed, renewed, and transformed. Why is that?

Well, Google defines trauma as a deeply distressing or disturbing experience. So, think about it… fourteen years (give or take) is a *loooong* time to experience trauma over and over again every single month. That's approximately 5,110 days of disappointment, mourning, and grief (#yikes). That's called trauma, sister. In fact, when I look at it that way, no wonder I've been writing this book for so many years; no wonder it's taken me so long to be renewed and transformed in my thinking and identity! No wonder my mind has struggled to grasp truth!

So anyway, as I sought wisdom and conversed with the Holy Spirit, He revealed to me that He wanted me to *imagine* with Him. *This* is how I was to think higher. *This* is how I can see truth. *This* is my next step. *This* is how I become the Word that's been promised and prophesied. God revealed to me that I must first become the Word in my mind before it manifests in my body. I must conceive it in my mind before I conceive it in my body. It is already true in the spirit, but how do I *become* truth in my mind?

By imagination! By thinking higher.

So, then I wondered, how long had it been since I last allowed my imagination to dream? How long had it been since I imagined what it would be like to announce my pregnancy? How long had it been since I imagined what it would feel like to be pregnant? How long had it been since I imagined what my babies would look like? I mean, how long had it been?! Too long. I had stopped doing so several years ago. It just hurt *way* too much.

In fact, I was in a place where I couldn't even fathom a BFP scenario. So much so that experiencing pregnancy and childbirth or even holding my own babies seemed like such an unreality to me because I had suppressed my imagination for so long. This was not okay! My imagination was literally stunted and corrupted because of previous trauma. In contrast, I would worry and become easily fearful with no issues. I created scenarios in my mind that may never come to be. But I had more difficulty imagining hopeful scenarios based on truth. What did I do? I sought God for revelation. Girl, did *He* deliver! Here is what I learned:

1. Imagination heals trauma

What do we dwell on the most, our past or our future? One of these will be the focus of our imagination, whether we know it or not. We can be receiving all sorts of amazing aha moments and experiencing true healing where there's been pain, but the fact remains that our life goes where our most dominant thoughts go.

Our memories can reign supreme, linked with strongholds. Our dreams and imaginations can be linked with hope or fear. If we are not imagining and hoping for the future, then we will probably be consumed by fear or worry. This is because our imagination has been corrupted, or our minds automatically revert to those memories (#defaultmode). In order to renew our minds, we need to cast down those imaginations of worry, fear, or any other thought that stands against the knowledge of God (1 Corinthians 10:5). But how do we move past the trauma? We look to the future and conceive new hopeful memories over the old. A memory for a memory. How is this done? We use our imagination to visualize and dream.

You see, our souls still remember the past years of grief, mourning, and trauma. But because this is not who we are anymore, we must conceive a new memory to replace the old, a *new* reality, a *heavenly* reality. We must see ourselves in our imaginations as we truly are, as God says we are, as His Word says we are. Why? Because our imagination ignites our souls, thereby activating our minds, wills, and emotions. In other words, imagination and visualization engage the soul and align it with truth. In a nutshell, we can use our imaginations to write our own endings! We imagine how *we* would do things so that the Father can do it even better. After all, that's what He promises:

> *Never doubt God's mighty power to work in you and accomplish all this. He will achieve* **infinitely more** *than your greatest request, your most* **unbelievable dream**, *and exceed your* **wildest imagination**! *He will outdo them all, for his miraculous power constantly energizes you. (emphasis added)* Ephesians 3:20, TPT

What does this look like practically? Well, take a plunge and bravely list every traumatic memory associated with being barren. You can label these traumatic memories "soul wounds" because they are wounds in the soul. These are the same wounds that have been exposed and infected all of those years of barrenness. Recall every single memory that's been floating around in your mind for years. For me, this was ugly. And I admit I was down the rest of the day. But I knew I had to *acknowledge* the trauma before God could fully heal it. Then, I could conceive a new memory.

#fact: Jesus paid for our *complete* healing on that cross. He doesn't just want us healed in our bodies. He wants us fully healed in our souls. So, after we acknowledge the soul wounds and move on throughout the day, it will be a pretty quick process to replace those memories with truth. After all, the truth has already set us free. We just need to get our memories onboard (#allaboard).

After making the list of soul wounds and filtering those memories through what you now know to be true about yourself and God, then you can make another list. This time, you make an "I see…" list. This list contains imaginations and dreams you hope to see; basically, the antithesis of the soul wounds. They are full of truth, hope and get more detailed and bigger and better than you can ever imagine.

This was so much fun! Who knew I could still dream like this? It was freeing and exhilarating! Best of all, it felt completely authentic, like I was *born* to dream and imagine with God!

2. Imagination is walking by faith

For we walk by faith, not by sight. 2 Corinthians 5:7, NKJV

If we are to live life by what we know to be true and not by what we see in the natural, then we need to have something called an enlightened mind. This is basically a renewed, transformed, and healed mind that is able to see truth in our imaginations. Therefore, seeing truth in the imagination is walking by faith. Let me break this down even further:

That the God of our Lord Jesus Christ, the Father of glory, may give to you the spirit of wisdom and revelation in the knowledge of Him, the **eyes of your understanding being enlightened; that you may know** *what is the hope of His calling, what are the riches of the glory of His inheritance in the saints. (emphasis added)*
Ephesians 1:17-18, NKJV

In the above scripture, Paul is praying for the eyes of our understanding to be enlightened. In Greek, the word for understanding is defined as mind, insight, perception, and meditation. The Amplified writes it a little differently:

And [I pray] that the **eyes of your heart [the very center and core of your being] may be enlightened [flooded with light by the Holy Spirit], so that you will know** *and cherish the hope [the divine guarantee, the confident expectation] to which He has called you, the riches of His glorious inheritance in the saints (God's people).*
(emphasis added) Ephesians 1:18, AMP

In Greek, "heart" can also be translated as mind, character, inner self, will, intention, or center. How do enlightened eyes of our hearts and an enlightened understanding mean the same thing as walking by faith?

Simply stated, because *we are what we see*. What we see through our mind or heart is who we are because that is our innermost being, "For as he thinks in his heart, so is he." (Proverbs 23:7, NKJV)

We all have an image of who we are on the inside of us. For years, I have been The Barren Woman, so that's how I continued to see myself, cloaked in grief, mourning, and shame. Because our soul responds to the image we have within our heart, we then take on those negative or positive emotions associated with how we see ourselves. But, once we are enlightened, we now know who we are in Christ, and we know the power we contain within us (#akatruth). When this happens, things change.

We start to dream and imagine. And through the eyes of our hearts, we can actually *see* ourselves healthy. We see ourselves as The Joyful Mother of children. We see ourselves reacting to the BFP (#bigfatpositive); we see ourselves looking at the sonogram; we see ourselves announcing our pregnancy; we see ourselves pregnant when we look in the mirror; we see ourselves holding our babies. We feel it too! We actually *feel* pregnant! We are excited and expectant and hopeful! We now find that our emotions respond to what we see in our minds more than our outward circumstances. This is amazing, friend! Because we *know*, we know that we know, that we know, that we are finally walking by faith. We finally believe, and there are no more traces of unbelief because our souls fully and completely align with the truth we can see in our hearts (#whoa).

Jesus spent His time on earth living like this. In fact, He was able to endure the cross because He saw His circumstances through the eyes of His heart:

> *Keep your eyes on Jesus, who both began and finished this race we're in. Study how he did it.* **Because he never lost sight of where he was headed** *– that exhilarating finish in and with God – he could put up with anything along the way: Cross, shame, whatever. And now he's there, in the place of honor, right alongside God. When you find yourselves flagging in your faith, go over that sto-*

ry again, item by item, that long litany of hostility he plowed through. That will shoot adrenaline into your souls! (emphasis added)
Hebrews 12:2-3, MSG

Jesus became who He saw through the eyes of His heart. He never lost sight of where He was headed. Even though He endured the shame and disgrace of the cross, the eyes of His understanding only saw His reward (#us). This is called walking by faith and not by sight. Seeing with the eyes of our hearts is seeing truth through faith. Therefore, when we use our imagination to *see* we are walking by faith (#likeJesus).

3. Imagination is becoming like a child

Learn this well: Unless you dramatically change your way of thinking and become teachable, and learn about heaven's kingdom realm with the wide-eyed wonder of a child, you will never be able to enter in.
Matthew 18:3, TPT

As I began to exercise walking by faith and using my imagination, I found myself so full of hope, excitement, and anticipation. Here I was, not only pregnant in spirit but also pregnant in my soul. I truly believed that anything was possible! My whole countenance transformed before my very eyes! And, although I had forgotten what it felt like, this feeling wasn't completely unfamiliar to me because I was experiencing how I felt as a child! I felt like a little girl again! That's when I knew imagination is becoming like a child (#lightbulb #hallelujahmoment).

A child hopes, dreams, imagines, and believes that anything is possible; a child trusts and expects miracles; a child is a good receiver. She can continue to hope and dream even after getting wounded because she receives the comfort and healing kisses of her Daddy. She keeps dreaming and hoping and expecting. She gets lost in the fantasy of her pretend play, so much so that it feels more real to her than what's in front of her natural eyes.

When we dream with God and walk by faith, the hope we experience is child-like hope, where what is true in our spirit and soul becomes more real to us than what we see. And our emotions are engaged, so there is absolutely no swaying us any longer. We are absolutely, positively, 100% convinced.

After I recognized that imagination is becoming like a child, I received more revelation. Our dreaming and imagining also give God the permission to come into any situation with His power, "Now to Him who is able to do exceedingly, abundantly above all that we ask or think, **according to the power that works in us…**" (Ephesians 3:20, NKJV emphasis added) When we dream and imagine with God, He does more than we can ask or imagine; that is, according to the power that works in *us*. Our dreaming and imagining give God the permission to come into the situation with His power working through *us*. He works His power through *us*, so we have to be willing participants. We do that through our imagination and child-like faith.

If we continue to withhold our imagination from Him, the desires of our hearts will not be fulfilled because we are unknowingly preventing Him from working His power through us. We create a dam instead of a floodgate, and we hinder the Word from coming to pass. We become the clog or the barrier within our own lives due to our barren imagination. Remember, we must conceive in our minds before we can conceive in our bodies.

So, there I was, decreeing, meditating on the truth, and even receiving confirming prophetic words. But I was still hindering the Word from being manifested because of my barren mind! Think about it. He is the ultimate artist, but we are His hands. We are the tools He uses to create and demonstrate His creative power on earth. So, if we prevent God from moving through our imagination, then we have essentially cut off His hands. He died on that cross to make us co-heirs, empowering us with the same spirit that raised Him from the dead! We are not powerless vessels! We must cooperate with Him to make things happen on this earth, and the primary way we do so is by conceiving in our minds, seeing truth through the eyes of faith, imagining, and dreaming.

This was confirmed through a dream I had many months ago where I woke up in a white hospital room. I was lying in the hospital bed and next to me stood a man wearing all-white scrubs. At the end of the bed was an ultrasound machine with the sonogram of my womb. I squinted and peered into it, looking for a baby, but instead, I couldn't see anything but a barren womb. I told this man, "I can't see anything." He responded and said, "Not yet." Then I heard laughter in the background and looked off to my left to see several female nurses giggling with excitement. The doctor shushed them, and they looked contrite, but they still had smiles on their faces.

When I woke up, I knew this was significant. First, I knew the doctor was Jesus, and the giggling nurses were angels. Second, I knew something had happened on that hospital bed, like a procedure of some sort. Third, I knew there had been something wrong because I couldn't see anything in my womb; it felt like I had not passed the test. Now, I don't mean that something was wrong physically. I knew right away this dream had everything to do with the spiritual. So, I wrote it down and pondered it for the months to come.

As God continued to heal me and reveal these truths to me in this chapter, He took me back to that dream during one of my quiet times. This was after I had received the revelation that I had denied Him access to my imagination, the most creative part of my being. I then had a vision about the same dream. In this vision, He woke me up, His hands on my face while I was in the hospital bed. Before I could say anything, He asked me, "What do you see?" I looked at the sonogram of my womb and didn't see anything at first. It wasn't until I allowed my desires, what I know to be true, to appear in my imagination, that I saw them; two embryos, two babies; two different sacs; fraternal twins; my son, and my daughter (#myheartsdesire). I smiled as they came into focus. I looked at Jesus and said, "I see two. Multiplication." He grinned from ear to ear and said, "Yes."

He then let the angels freely giggle with excitement while I pulled Him down by His neck and wept in His arms. He leaned back and kept wiping my tears with His hands. I repented for the years of doubt and unbelief, for my lack of imagination, for the years of hindering His Word from coming to pass in my life, for the years of blocking His creative power being demonstrated on this earth through me. And I rejoiced and praised Him through my weeping. When I stopped, He surprisingly bowed over my hand and asked me to dance. He was now clothed in an all-white suit, and I was barefoot in a white flouncy dress. So, I danced and rejoiced in my Beloved's arms, and oh how beautiful it was! He basked in my adoration and just simply enjoyed watching me praise and celebrate and worship Him.

Do you see that? See how He asked me what I saw? He wants us to participate with Him! The power and the ability to do so are already there within us! I received confirmation of this from the book of Jeremiah. Jeremiah expressed to God that he could not walk out his prophetic mandate because he was too young. God corrected and encouraged him and then put His hand to Jeremiah's mouth to fill him with His words (#holdup). Are we, too, filled with God's words? Yes! We are filled with His Spirit, and His Word has been sown into our hearts. Later, God asked, "Jeremiah, what do you see?" After Jeremiah responded, God said, "You have seen well, for I am ready to perform My word."

Dear friend, Jesus is *so* ready to perform His Word! *What do you see?* Jesus is ready to work His power through us and do exceedingly, abundantly more than *all* we can ask or imagine! He is ready! It is *done*. But it is our unbelief that hinders Him. In this case, it is our lack of imagination and child-like faith that hinders this power from operating within and through us.

What power am I talking about? His creative power! His resurrection power! In fact, that's what happened to me! In my vision, I woke up to Jesus caressing my face, but with that caress, I knew He resurrected me as Mandi Windsor, Christ in me, The Joyful Mother of children. While I was "asleep," He had healed me. When I woke up and had begun to dream and imagine, resurrection power just began to flow in me and through me. Because I dream and imagine with God; because I walk by faith and not by sight; because I am pregnant in spirit and pregnant in my soul, I bring life to dead situations. I carry resurrection power within me wherever I go (#micdrop).

What do *you* see when you imagine and dream? Will you let yourself become like a child once again? I hope so. For then, you too will carry resurrection power in you and through you.

4. Imagination is meditation

But his delight is in the law of the LORD, *And on His law [His precepts and teachings] he [habitually] meditates day and night. Psalm 1:2, AMP*

Now, before I get started explaining what I mean for this section, I want to remind you that the meditation spoken of in this book has nothing to do with new-age practices. I am speaking of Biblical meditation and only that. So, with that firmly in mind, how is imagination meditation?

In a nutshell, imagination is visual meditation of the Word. It is conceiving an image of ourselves and seeing ourselves in the promises of God. We have the truth to decree, we've memorized the words, but we can take it a step further and conceive an image *as the* Word. Once we have an image, nothing can stop us because it feels so real. Because then our emotions line up to what we see in our imaginations versus what we see in the natural. We then have hope and joy because the truth has already set us free.

We are no longer limited by what we see in front of us. Instead, we are free to dream. We become so excited because we know God is going to do even more than we can ask or imagine; because we *believe* Him; because His Word is truth; and we believe in ourselves; we see ourselves through the eyes of truth; we see ourselves through the eyes of faith; through an enlightened mind. What we see is real, and nothing can take it away. Period (#amen).

Just think, God even gave Abraham an image when he received His promise of fruitfulness. In Genesis 13, God promised Abraham that his descendants would be as plentiful as the dust of the earth. In Genesis 15, God again promised Abraham that his descendants would be as abundant as the stars. Abraham received these promises, these words. More than that, God engaged his imagination by giving him the images. Think about it. Abraham lived in a tent in the middle east. He was outside all the time, washing the dust off his feet and eating his meals under the stars. God gave him full permission to meditate on the words of His promises as well as the images He had given him. God wanted Abraham to look at these images because God knew the power of imagination. He knew that imagination is meditation, and meditation is how we become the Word (#readthatagain).

Now, what does this look like, practically speaking? This is more than just using our Pinterest boards to get our hopes up as we did in a previous chapter. Imaginative meditation is seeing through the eyes of the heart, which is directly linked to our faith. All we are doing is fantasizing if we don't yet know the Word, have it sown in our hearts, and are allowing it to renew our minds.

So practically, get scriptures in front of you. You *must* know the truth before it can set you free. Next, get a picture. Yes, it is as simple as making a vision board or an "Imagination Board." I copied and pasted pictures of a positive pregnancy test, a sonogram, a pregnant belly, and two cute babies. Then, in the same document, I wrote the promises that I had been meditating on for years. So now, anytime I look at this board, I see images with my promises. Before bed, or when I am in prayer, the images will come to my mind as I am speaking life and prophesying over my body. I can now imagine that those are *my* BFPs (#bigfatpositives), and that's *my* sonogram of *my* children, and that's *my* pregnant belly, and those are *my* newborn babies.

Through the activating of my imagination coupled with scriptural meditation, the promises are no longer just words to me; now, I have found that I *am* those promises! I already *am* The Joyful Mother of children! I already *am* the fruitful vine! My children are *already* around my table! I have *already* been blessed with the fruit of my womb! I am *already* multiplying! It is done! It has *already* happened! Because by His stripes I *was* healed! (1 Peter 2:24) Past tense. It has already happened in the spirit. It has already happened in my mind. And now, it is just a matter of time before it manifests in my body.

When it does, it will no longer be a surprise because I have already seen it through the eyes of my heart; I have already seen my reaction to the BFP; I have already seen myself rejoicing with my husband and son; I have already seen the reactions of my parents, family, and friends. I have already felt myself heavily pregnant; I have already seen my newborn babies; I can already hear their cries; I can already smell their soft, beautiful skin; I can already see myself kissing their downy heads; I can already *see* what is coming in the natural. It's real! It. Is. Real. And it is all because I began activating my imagination while meditating on the scriptures I have had memorized for years.

So, after you make your "Imagination Board," you then hang it in a spot to be seen often throughout the day. While in your quiet/prayer times, eliminate all distractions, sit, and imagine. Let the Holy Spirit take you on an adventure in your imagination. For example, imagine yourself healthy; imagine taking a walk pushing the baby stroller; imagine announcing your pregnancy in front of your husband; imagine giving birth or breastfeeding; imagine feeling the baby kick in your womb; see the BFP on your bathroom counter. Anything goes. But remember, you must have the Word sown and known in your heart before you are able to do this through faith.

If this sounds weird or new-agey, it is not. We can do this with any scripture in the Bible! To understand the David and Goliath story, we can use our imagination; to understand the parting of the Red Sea, we can use our imagination; to understand Jesus raising Lazarus from the dead, we can use our imagination! We can imagine ourselves in each of these scenarios; imagine ourselves *as* the Word. And once we have that image, these Bible stories we've had memorized since childhood now become real and potent. Think about it. As a kindergarten teacher, I couldn't teach a *thing* without having a visual to go with it. Children need images to learn! So do we! It is not just about memorizing or knowing scripture; it is about meditating on the Word so that it becomes absolute truth in our hearts and minds (#areyouconvincedyet).

Here's another way to look at it. Scripture is a seed sown into our hearts. Consider, then, imaginative meditation as the water and fertilizer that makes the seed grow and bear fruit. This happens because as the seed is sown into our hearts, meditation becomes the catalyst to the transformation and renewal of our minds. So, we know *information* by memorizing the scriptures, but it becomes *revelation* and *understanding* when we meditate. It is this revelation of truth that sets us free, enlightens our minds, and activates us into child-like faith.

5. You are just not there yet

What if it hurts to dream and imagine and sends you into despair instead of hope? Simply stated, you are just not there yet (#saywhat). Your imagination has most likely been used in the wrong way. You may have given the enemy ground, and the lies have corrupted your imagination through his deception. You may not be able to see clearly through the eyes of your heart because your mind still needs to be renewed and transformed.

Tearing down strongholds in your mind that have been built up over months and years can take time. That is why they are called strongholds and fortresses (#theytaketimetobuild #itisaprocess). So, you must seek God and ask Him to reveal to you what you are struggling with. What is hindering the Word from being fulfilled or manifested in you? What is the lie or mindset you have focused on for so long that it's a part of your identity instead of what you know to be true? Sorry to say, but it is not God; it is us.

Remember, He is faithful. He is "not a man that He should lie" (Numbers 23:19). We can decree all we want, we can believe all we want, we can hope and pray all we want, we can demand all we want, but until we uncover the fortresses or lies that are still built up in our minds, God's hands are held back in manifesting His Word in our womb. That may be hard to hear. We would much rather blame God, but He has already done His part when He put Jesus on the cross and raised Him back up again.

Find out what is hindering the Word. Ask, seek, knock; contend and go after your mind until it only knows and thinks about the truth; contend for the Word of God and the enlightenment of your heart; tear down those strongholds and replace them with truth; meditate on truth until your mind is transformed and new fortresses of truth are in place; repent and allow for more character development; submit to the process and engage in the fight. You must do whatever you have to do! Because as Paul says:

> *... we long to see you passionately advance until the end and you find your hope fulfilled. So don't allow your hearts to grow dull or lose your enthusiasm, but follow the example of those who fully received what God has promised because of their strong faith and patient endurance.*
> *Hebrews 6:11-12, TPT*

GOING DEEPER:

- List each and every one of your soul wounds or traumatic memories from the past years of barrenness (once they are written down, don't spend a lot of time thinking about them. Quickly move on to the next step).
- Make an "I see..." list, filtered through what you now know to be true, to create new memories over the old soul wounds.
- Gather scriptures in front of you to use for imaginative meditation (hint: these will be the promises you have been using throughout this journey).
- Get pictures and create your "Imagination Board."
- If you find that "you are just not there yet," ask God to reveal the strongholds, lies, and mindsets you are still agreeing with. Allow Him to take you through more renewing of your mind.
- Scriptures to study: 1 Cor. 10:5; Eph. 3:20; 2 Cor. 5:7; Eph. 1:17-18; Prov. 23:7; Heb. 12:2-3; Mt. 18:3; Jer. 1; Ps. 1:2; Gen. 13; Gen. 15; 1 Pt. 2:24; Num. 23:19; Heb. 6:11-12.

Chapter twenty
YOU WILL HAVE WHAT YOU SAY

As we conceive in our minds and see ourselves through the eyes of faith; as we begin to walk in this conception of knowing who we are and the power we contain; as we begin to enact imaginative meditation, we will notice something shift. The way we pray will drastically change. Why?

Because we know what is ours!

It is already done! We know we carry resurrection power! So, anything less than the Word in *all* areas of our life begins to drive us crazy. Seriously. I mean, I *am* who the Word says I am! I am The Joyful Mother of children! I am the fruitful vine! My children are like olive plants around my table! This is truth, and it is *my* truth! It is *my* reality! So, I refuse to accept anything less than this, and all other hindrances and obstacles better get the heck out of the way!

Yes, you read that right. I am angry. I am righteously angry. I am done. I am done accepting lack or barrenness in any area of my life any longer. It is just not allowed, not when I know who I am and the power I have within me through Jesus; not when I know I am in full faith and unbelief is a thing of the past. So yeah, my prayer life has drastically changed. And yours will, too (#getexcited).

Not only am I walking in this confidence produced by faith, but I am also walking in peaceful authenticity. I feel *normal* for the first time in a decade! Ha! There is no doubt in my soul or guilt in my conscience warring and bringing unbelief. I cannot feel an ounce of the enemy; it is as if any heaviness or oppression has been completely obliterated. I am free. And I *feel* it. I feel like my best self. It is completely authentic. This is not fake-it-until-I-make-it. This is legit! I have been resurrected. I feel the most at peace; the most joyful I ever remember feeling in my entire adult life.

So, when you have a transformation like this, *everything* changes. You now have a new perspective on prayer because you pray from an authority and power operating from within you. You now pray from your seat next to Jesus in Heaven. As this is my process, your way of praying might look different, but here is what I have been doing:

1. Thanking

Enter His gates with a song of thanksgiving And His courts with praise. Be thankful to Him, bless and praise His name. Psalm 100:4, AMP

Because my prayers have already been answered and what I see in my heart and mind is more real to me than what I see in the natural, I am already thanking God for the gift of pregnancy, I am already thanking Him for my son and daughter, I am thanking Him for His Word, I am thanking Him for healing me and for setting me free, I am thanking Him for this journey, and I am thanking Him for loving me. I am already filled with so much thanksgiving!

And here is the best part, He has then responded and thanked *me* for trusting *Him*! He thanks *me* for choosing Him and surrendering to this process. He thanks *me* for loving Him and being faithful to Him. And then, there we are, both of us in a thanksgiving war like two annoying love birds. "I thank you." "No, I thank you." "No, I thank you." "No, I thank you." (#yougetthepicture)

2. Decreeing

This one is nothing new. But as I sing and decree about who I am, there is no battle behind it anymore. There is no warring against the enemy. There is no warring against my soul or five senses. I decree who I am and prophesy what is coming and know that it is already mine. For example, simply decree something like this, "I am The Joyful Mother of children. I am the fruitful vine. I am fruitful, and I multiply. My children are like olive plants around my table. None shall be barren or miscarry, so I am not barren, and I will not miscarry!"

Just decree truth! Decree the Word! As you hear it out loud, your mind will be continually renewed to walk by faith and not by sight.

3. Speaking

*For assuredly, I say to you, whoever **says to this mountain**, "Be removed and be cast into the sea," and does not doubt in his heart, but believes that those things he says will be done, **he will have whatever he says**. (emphasis added) Mark 11:23, NKJV*

After we enter into His courts with thanksgiving, after we decree, it is a natural progression to begin speaking to the mountain. *Speak* to the obstacle! Speak to the sickness or disease that is causing barrenness in your body and tell it to go away! Tell it to be removed and cast into the sea! Tell it to go back to hell where it belongs! Get *angry*! This is *your* inheritance! Jesus bought your complete health and fruitfulness! It is already yours! Tell the obstacle, sickness, or disease that is causing barrenness or miscarriage, to leave!

Yes, it is that easy. I feel so silly that it's that simple, but as you know, I had to go through this whole process in order to get rid of unbelief. The mountain is only moved if we do not doubt in our hearts. I was filled with so much doubt and unbelief I had to renew my mind for a while to be rid of it. Here I am, though, full of faith and belief. And I really do believe what I say! I believe there is power in my words because I carry His resurrection power within me! I believe that when I tell the sickness or disease that is causing barrenness in my womb to go, *it will go*!

More than that, life and death are in the power of our tongue. We can bring life or death to any circumstance. With that said, we need to curse and kill that obstacle with our words! How will this sound? The Holy Spirit will lead the way, but here is how I began, "Sickness or disease in my body that is preventing me from conceiving, I command you to go in the name of Jesus. Barrenness, I kill you in the name of Jesus. You are dead. Abnormal hormones or anything abnormal in me or my husband's body, I curse you and command you to go in the name of Jesus. By His stripes, we *were* healed! I release healing and life to my womb and reproductive organs in the name of Jesus."

You can get as detailed as you want, especially if you know of specific diseases that are in you or your husband's bodies. Call it by name and tell it to be removed and cast it out to the sea! It has absolutely no power over you because of the power that is within your being.

4. Commanding

After we speak to the mountain, we are then filled with this undaunted power to begin commanding *anything* that is not lining up to truth (#withinreasonofcourse). So, I began commanding my body, "Body, you are fruitful. Womb, you are pregnant. Womb, you conceive my son and daughter. Body, you multiply. Body, you *were* healed by the stripes of Jesus." And this is where you could get into detail with each of your reproductive organs.

But that is not *all* we can begin to command. We can even speak to our homes (#weirdiknow)! I have been commanding, "Home, you *will* have the sound of children's laughter echoing throughout your walls. Home, you are a house of the Lord, so you *must* be fruitful!" I have even begun speaking to my kitchen table and commanding it, "Table, you *will* have children like olive plants around you!" And I have told the nursery, "Nursery, you *will* be filled with children!" And to the living room floor, "Floor, you *will* have baby toys all over you!" Sounds crazy, right? But at this point in my journey, it is crazier for me *not* to command these things. Remember, I feel the most authentic I have ever felt in my life.

5. Calling

So they took away the stone. And Jesus raised His eyes [toward heaven] and said, "Father, I thank You that You have heard Me. I knew that You always hear Me and listen to Me; but I have said this because of the people standing around, so that they may believe that You have sent Me [and that You have made Me Your representative]." When He had said this, **He shouted with a loud voice, "Lazarus, come out!"** *Out came the man who had been dead, his hands and feet tightly wrapped in burial cloths (linen strips), and with a [burial] cloth wrapped around his face. Jesus said to them, "Unwrap him and release him." emphasis added) John 11:41-44, AMP*

This resurrection power makes you think about what else can possibly be resurrected.. Not dead bodies, although I personally am aiming to resurrect at least three dead people in my lifetime. Resurrection power is within us and working through us, so through our words, we have the power to resurrect dead things. I know I will conceive a son and a daughter. I know their names. So, in a nutshell, all I am doing is calling them by name and telling them to come forth (#easypeasy).

6. Resisting

So submit to [the authority of] God. Resist the devil [stand firm against him] and he will flee from you. James 4:7, AMP

As we continue to operate in this power and faith, the enemy will continue to come against us through our thoughts. But guess what? We have the power to reject any thought that we don't want in our minds. This is called free will. So that is what we do. We resist those thoughts. Then, the enemy will run away from us (#withhistailbetweenhislegs).

Seriously! It seems like the enemy has truly run away from me! There is no sign of him anywhere. This is the way it's supposed to be! Dear friend, he has no power over us! And even if he tries to plant thoughts, all we need to do is resist him! And he flees! Yes, it is that simple.

If any doubt or unbelief creeps in from our soul, from what we view or hear through our five senses, we can still resist that crap! Yes, you are correct. You hear righteous anger again in my voice. You must become almost militant in your stance against anything that tries to creep into your thoughts. You literally have to guard your mind to the death of your soul. And it *can* be done, especially as we recognize and walk out this power that is working in us and through us.

7. Rejoicing

So, victory after victory after victory, resisting thoughts, staying in faith, we can't help but rejoice some more. Seriously. I have broken into song more times than I can count while writing this chapter. And I keep erupting into hysterical laughter. Not only that, but I find myself dancing around my house! The joy is already here! I am The Joyful Mother of children! It is oozing from every part of my being! I just can't help but rejoice!

8. Nesting

And then, suddenly, I began to prepare. I began staying on top of taking my prenatal vitamins, working out hardcore, and putting cocoa butter on my stomach. Before I even knew what had happened, I lost ten pounds! It is like the spirit of heaviness literally melted off me (#supernaturalweightlossdoesexist).

There I was, suddenly, taking such pride in my body and realizing how precious it is to me. I love my body! And I am preparing it for pregnancy and delivery. I'm strengthening my arm and shoulder muscles so I can carry those car seats. I am strengthening my abs and pelvic floor muscles for labor and delivery. And it is effortless. Like, I am enjoying it immensely! Really, I have not enjoyed working out since I was in my mid-twenties. Do you hear me? I am enjoying doing *abs* (#whaaat)! This is *huge*! If this is not evidence that I am truly healed body and soul, then I don't know what is.

I have literally gotten my joy back in every single area. I would say that I don't even recognize myself anymore, but that's not true. This is who I was always meant to be. I was just buried under the spirit of heaviness for so many years.

I also began putting my house in order. I painted that room that needed paint, I organized various things, and I stayed on top of cleaning, budget, etc. Again, it was effortless. Before this, I had to give myself a pep talk to get stuff done around the house. Now I have this very genuine desire to keep it in order. I even took down Christmas decorations way sooner than when I normally do. In the past, it would have overwhelmed me, but not this time. I was eager to get them taken down and put my house back in order. Then it hit me (#drumrollplease).

I am nesting!

I am already nesting! Because it's done. I have already conceived in my spirit and in my mind. It is done. That's why I am full of excitement and expectation; that's why I am preparing my body and preparing my house. I am pregnant! And I'm experiencing the expectation and preparation that comes with it! How cool is that?

9. Praying

Lastly, along with this nesting and physical preparation comes prayer. Not only have I prepared for my children physically, but I have also begun to prepare spiritually. I made a list of every single one of my desires for my pregnancy, birth, and my children. For example, I desired no high blood pressure or sugar, perfect implantation, no crazy hormones, no extreme weight gain, baby weight to stay all in my belly, no swelling in my hands and feet, cervix to stay shut, water to break on its own, etc. I listed it all. Every big or small thing that I wanted. It turns out that all that fertility expertise came in handy after all.

Once I made my list, I began to decree and speak to my body and my babies. For example, "I decree that I am in perfect health. Hormones, you will be at normal levels in the name of Jesus. You will be at peace and use self-control. Cervix, you will stay tightly shut until it is time to deliver. Babies, you will not come early. Babies, you will get in the right position for delivery and stay there. Babies, you are in perfect health, etc." I then let myself imagine each one of these desires coming to pass. I meditated on these desires coupled with what I know to be true in the Word until they were conceived in my mind.

Now when the natural pregnancy comes to fruition, I will not want to settle for anything less than what I have already prayed, decreed, and spoken. If fear tries to tempt me or if the midwife or doctor says something contrary to what I prayed, then I will be able to stay in faith because the truth in my mind is already a fortress. Plus, I have the image to go with it. *Nothing* can sway me from what I now know is my portion (#boom)!

Going Deeper:

- Because we are all in various stages of this process, ask God how He wants your prayer life to begin changing.
- If you are not already, begin speaking to the mountain and commanding.
- Have you noticed it is getting easier to resist the devil? Why or why not?
- Make a prayer list of everything you desire in your pregnancy, labor, delivery, and babies. Start praying as if it is already done (because it is).
- Scriptures to study: Ps. 100:4; Mk. 11:23; Jn. 11:41-44; Jas. 4:7.

Chapter twenty-one
BLESSED ARE THOSE WHO MOURN

Blessed are those who mourn, for they shall be comforted. Matthew 5:4, NKJV

At the time of writing this chapter, Mother's Day 2019 has come and gone. Two of my family members have just delivered their babies, and another one will deliver this summer. Not only that, but two of my friends recently told me they are expecting. Thankfully, they told me before announcing it publicly, which usually softens the blow and makes me feel honored (#sometimes). However, as much as I am being transformed and as far as I have come in my journey, I have recently succumbed to weakness. Needless to say, I write this truly humbled and repentant (#vulnerabilityalert).

There have been so many thoughts coming against me simply because of Mother's Day. Coupled with all of the deliveries and announcements, I was, of course, beginning my cycle. Well, need I say more? So yeah, I totally was tempted to revert to the old mindset, the old man, the old nature of The Barren Woman (#dundundun).

Honestly, it felt like an out-of-body experience as I observed myself returning to grief and mourning. I fought against the emotions as long as I could. Eventually, however, I succumbed. I knew the truth, yet I still succumbed to the unfairness of being left out *again*, I succumbed to the grief of Mother's Day, and I succumbed to the self-pity.

It wasn't until I was able to get alone and cry out to the Lord that the reasons why were revealed to me. The Holy Spirit brought to my remembrance a recent dream in which I was sitting in a basement with people who were mourning the loss of their loved ones. In dreams, basements can symbolize something hidden or suppressed. The people with me in the basement symbolized grief and mourning. I realized, then, I *still* had a stronghold of mourning in my mind, a lie or mindset with which I still agreed, which steered my emotions in the absolutely wrong direction. Because my emotions went so out of control, I knew there was some area I had not yet allowed the Comforter to comfort; I was in extended mourning.

#sidenote: As much as we want to ignore our emotions, we must also pay attention to them. Think of them as the indicator lights on a dashboard. Emotions are a good indicator of what thoughts we are allowing to penetrate our minds. In other words, emotions are the byproduct of our thoughts.

What happens if we stay in extended mourning? A stronghold can be built upon a foundation of self-pity, and self-pity is just another form of pride (#ouch). I know, I know. I get it. In our pain, we don't want to hear that we are prideful. In fact, we associate pride with arrogance or boastfulness, *not* with mourning. But *extended* mourning can soon become pride if we continually wallow in our pain and remain hardened to comfort. Why? Because extended mourning creates a hardened heart, whether against God or people. A hardened heart is a selfish heart, turned inwards and focused only on self. For example, was I able to truly rejoice with my friends when they announced their pregnancies? I said all the right things, yes, but what did I *feel* in my heart? To be honest, I felt envy, jealousy, and even anger. I thought, *It was supposed to be my turn, not theirs!* How ugly is that? I could hear the selfishness written all over those reactions, and that is *not* okay!

The emotions of grief and mourning plus my reactions revealed to me loud and clear that I *still* had a stronghold; I was *still* reacting out of my carnal and fleshly self. "...For where there are envy, strife, and divisions among you, are you not carnal and behaving like mere men?" (1 Corinthians 3:3, NKJV)

Dear friend, we are not mere men! We are in Christ, and He is in us! We cannot be in continual grief and mourning if we are in Christ. It is impossible! Why? Because the fruit of the Spirit, which is the evidence of Christ within, is love, joy, peace, longsuffering, kindness, goodness, faithfulness, gentleness, and self-control (Galatians 5:22-23).

Are we joyful when we are in mourning? Are we at peace when we are in mourning? Do we have self-control over our emotions? Do we love our neighbors and serve them? If the honest answer is no, then we are not in the Spirit. We are not allowing "Christ in us" to dominate. Instead, we are acting carnal. In this state, our flesh will continue to experience the emotions of grief and mourning when our cycle comes; it will continue to react to others' announcements in a selfish or envious manner because we have not yet torn down that stronghold, and we can only tear it down *in Christ:*

> *For though we walk in the flesh, we do not war according to the flesh. For the weapons of our warfare are not carnal but mighty in God for pulling down strongholds, casting down arguments and every high thing that exalts itself against the knowledge of God, bringing every thought into captivity to the obedience of Christ... 2 Corinthians 10:3-5, NKJV*

We destroy this stronghold of mourning by casting down lies and every thought higher than the knowledge of God and by taking every thought captive. In other words, we take each thought as a prisoner of war (#warriorqueen). If it is an enemy of truth, then we make it submit. If it does not submit, then we kick it out of our minds.

We are not victims of our thoughts.

We do not have to receive and accept every thought that filters through our minds. We can *choose* what we want to keep or reject (#scientificfact). Likewise, when we surpass the healthy mourning stage and begin to wallow in self-pity and envy, we can take those thoughts captive as well.

You see, the process is supposed to be an exchange: We mourn, we get comforted; we mourn, we get comforted; we mourn, we get comforted (#repeat). We express our emotions at the same time as reminding ourselves of what is true. We align our minds with His truth and become one with Christ. This is also called strengthening ourselves in the Lord (1 Samuel 30:6). We remind ourselves who we are, what the finished work of the cross did for us, that we are *not* lacking anything, that we are already pregnant, that we are already mothers, that our negative emotions do not reflect the truth but are based on a lie, etc.

We. Do. Not. Stay. In. Mourning.

We allow the Comforter to comfort us and give us *His* perspective. We are blessed when we mourn because we have the opportunity to receive a greater encounter with the Comforter and go places in the Spirit that we would not be able to go otherwise.

#hereisthekey: If we *receive* from Him, the Comforter will enter our circumstances and absorb our grief and pain. This is what He did on the cross, remember? He took our grief and pain, so we do not have to carry them (Isaiah 53). He will also gently (#butbluntly) remind us to forget the former things, to let go of the past once and for all (Isaiah 43:18). Paul, who suffered numerous amounts of trauma, hardship, and even physical beatings, said:

> *...I do not count myself to have apprehended; but one thing I do,* **forgetting those things which are behind and reaching forward** *to those things which are ahead,* **I press toward** *the goal for the prize of the upward call of God in Christ Jesus. (emphasis added) Philippians 3:13-14, NKJV*

How did Paul survive such trauma during his ministry? By forgetting those hardships and reaching *forward!* We are supposed to reach forward and press toward those things which are ahead. However, we cannot do so if we are constantly looking back and wallowing in the pain, heartache, and injustice. We cannot reach forward and press toward those things ahead if we remain focused on ourselves. One of our promises we reach for, in fact, is redemption and restoration of all these years of barrenness:

> *Do not fear, for you will not be ashamed; Neither be disgraced, for you will not be put to shame; For **you will forget the shame of your youth, and will not remember the reproach** of your widowhood anymore. (emphasis added) Isaiah 54:4, NKJV*

Not remembering is a gift from the Comforter *if* we let Him; *if* we remember what He has done for us through the finished work of the cross; and *if* we remember that we are made new, "Therefore, if anyone is in Christ, he is a new creation; old things have passed away; behold, all things have become new." (2 Corinthians 5:17, NKJV)

We are a new identity, a new person, a new species even. We are no longer The Barren Woman, so we cannot keep doing the same things over and over again, or keep reacting the same way. If The Barren Woman (the old, carnal nature) is dead, then those old memories and emotions should be dead and buried as well. If I keep resurrecting my carnal self and the emotions that go with it, I will continue to be double-minded. But I am past that. In fact, the emotions of grief and mourning are false; they are not reality. They do not represent who I am anymore, thus the reason for the out-of-body experience.

So, let us choose to let go of the past once and for all. Let us choose to receive comfort from the Comforter, and let us receive the redemptive promise of forgetting the shame of our youth.

Going Deeper:

- Do you still have a stronghold of mourning hiding somewhere in your heart? Emotions and/or reactions to pregnancy and birth announcements are a good indicator of this.
- If so, cry out to the Lord, repent for a hardened heart that has prevented comfort from the Comforter. Record this process in your journal.
- Using 2 Corinthians 10:3-5, destroy the stronghold of mourning by taking every thought captive and making it submit to truth.
- Record in your journal the process of receiving comfort from the Comforter (i.e., pray and ask Him to absorb your grief, your pain; be honest with how you feel and then let it go; receive the redemptive promise of forgetting the shame of your youth; receive your identity in Him).
- Scriptures to study: Mt. 5:4; 1 Cor. 3:3; Gal. 5:22-23; 1 Sam. 30:6; Is. 53; Is. 43:18-19; Phil. 3:13-14; Is. 54:4; 2 Cor. 5:17; Jas. 1:7.

Chapter twenty-two
THE NEW MAN

#THEJOYFULMOTHEROFCHILDREN. #REVIEW:

As we have come to see, barrenness and infertility severely affects our identities as women. It is not just a physical issue. When struggling with barrenness (or any illness) for an extended length of time, it can poison us from the inside out, perverting our sense of identities, wrecking our emotions, mental state, and physical bodies.

It is obviously of great importance, then, for our Healer to heal us from the inside out, to reveal who we are in Him in order to receive our complete and lasting healing. Remember, we can see in the Word how easy it is for God to give women children. Plus, we know that all creation is created to create! We already have all the tools necessary, as discussed previously. Simply stated, motherhood is a done deal when standing on faith in the Word.

However, when we choose to stand on the Word and commit to our healing journeys, God will take us through a transformation process. This process will be based on the truth of who we are in Him, *regardless* of our natural circumstances. As we submit to this process, it will end with our complete transformation of soul and body. We will birth who we truly are no matter how things look in the natural. We will even birth a great love for Jesus that we may not have chosen to pursue otherwise.

#happysigh: So here I am. Marveling, rejoicing, and shaking my head in awestruck wonder. Not because I am looking at a BFP (#bigfatpositive), but because I am looking at *myself*. I am looking at myself in Christ, at how far I have come. I thought this journey was all about contending for my family. I thought it was all about becoming a mother and living out my dream. But this journey has been so much more than I could have ever imagined! Where I have been pursuing healing so I can conceive and give birth to my children, I have actually birthed *my true self* instead. I look back at the multiple levels of identity through which God has led me. From servant, daughter, friend, to warrior, beloved, queen, and co-heir, to now Mandi Windsor, Christ in Me. It has been a journey of healing, discovery, transformation, and renewing, and I am so very pleased with the outcome.

Getting the BFP is no longer the goal (#saywhat). Getting pregnant in the natural is just a by-product of who I am; I know it is coming. The goal for this chapter is to equip you to keep your carnal self dead and buried; to stay in your new man; and to stay in your new identity as _____, Christ in Me, The Joyful Mother of children (#insertname).

Because, let's be real, these last few months have been up and down. I have been going back and forth between my carnal self and The New Man, between The Barren Woman and The Joyful Mother of children. The stronghold of mourning lingered, yes, but even after taking care of that, I kept losing my peace and forgetting how to *stay* in The New Man, The Joyful Mother of children. It was a tug-of-war; I knew I had already overcome this struggle; I knew who I had become, but learning how to *stay* in that new identity evolved a whole new chapter of life.

Likewise, I kept trying to force-finish this book. I finally had to put it on hold yet again and just receive. I have been at this long enough to know when the Teacher wants to teach me something. I thought to myself, *what else could I possibly need to learn regarding conceiving and bearing children through faith?* That's when it hit me! This whole journey has been about so much more than becoming a mother! It is about being transformed into who we were always meant to be (#Christinus #thehopeofglory)!

Because we have ultimately crossed over from death to life, from barrenness to fruitfulness, from The Barren Woman to The Joyful Mother of children, from our carnal self to The New Man, we must know how to sustain this identity in order to stay in our freedom regardless of the natural circumstances. Here are five ways to sustain our identity in Him:

1. Every day is a new day

Give us this day our daily bread. Matthew 6:11, NKJV

As we choose to forget what lies behind us and as we forget the shame of our youth, we must create a new mindset that every day is a new day. We cannot take the battles from yesterday into today. Likewise, we cannot take the victories from a week ago into today. This means any joy, sorrow, frustration, or excitement from the previous days are put behind us (#eventhegoodemotions). Each day is brand spanking new; each day offers its own daily bread. I know it may not seem like a big deal, but this is a huge key to the success of living in our new identity.

Every day, we start fresh and receive *first* from the Holy Spirit. Remember, "We love Him because He first loved us." (1 John 4:19, NKJV) Before we ever exhibit any sort of love and commitment to Jesus, He has first given it to us. Before I get out of bed, I am acknowledging the Holy Spirit and welcoming Him into my day. I am even asking Him what part of His nature He wants to reveal today.

Who does He want to be for us? *Receive* from Him for that day. Sometimes He is Beloved, Defender, Provider, Recalibrator, Friend, your El Shaddai, or your Healer. But whatever He says He wants to be for us that day, He will show up and be our strength in that day's weakness. It's the coolest thing! (#tryitandsee)

2. Put off the old man

*...**put off**, concerning your former conduct, **the old man** which grows corrupt according to the deceitful lusts, and **be renewed in***

the spirit of your mind, *and that you put on the new man which was created according to God, in true righteousness and holiness. (emphasis added) Ephesians 4:22-24, NKJV*

When we start fresh every day, we can then make a choice to put off the old man, which is our carnal, fleshly self. Remember, we are a spirit, soul, and body. Our spirit is one with Jesus, perfect and complete at salvation. Our soul contains our mind, will, and emotions, which are not yet perfect and complete. Our soul is in the process of being transformed by the renewing of our mind, and it will continue to be so until we leave this earth or Jesus returns. With all that said, the choice to put off the old man comes from remembering that our old man is dead. Dead. Dead. Any carnal and fleshly negative emotions are dead as well (#deadasadoornail).

For example, if we see another pregnancy announcement on our social media feed and find ourselves leaning towards jealousy and envy, we have resurrected the old man. If we start another cycle and weep with despair, we resurrected the old man. If we start feeling sorry for ourselves because all of our family and friends keep having babies, it's the old man. Self-pity and the emotions that come with it become a false mindset because our *self* is supposed to be dead. We end up living a lie, becoming tormented in our emotions and unsettled in our conscience.

How on earth do we even endure? How do we cope with the pregnancy announcements, births, and negative emotions that will continue to come our way? By daily crucifying the old man:

My old identity has been co-crucified with Messiah and no longer lives; for the nails of his cross crucified me with him. *And now the essence of this new life is no longer mine, for the Anointed One lives his life through me – we live in union as one! (emphasis added) Galatians 2:20, TPT*

Pretty awesome scripture, right? Practically, this is about starting fresh every day, receiving from the Holy Spirit for that day, and testing our thoughts. We think about what we are thinking about and ask, *is this thought the old man or The New Man? Does this thought inspire hope or despair, foreboding or freedom, envy or unity, etc.? Does this thought produce life or death?* If it is the old man and we exhibit carnality, then we become renewed in the spirit of our mind by taking that thought a prisoner of war. We submit the thought to the truth as discussed in the previous chapter. The choice of putting off the old man is one we will make every day, all day long, monthly even, with pregnancy announcements and more babies. Can it really be done? Yes ma'am. In fact, I have had a lot of practice, and I am happy to say that it really does work!

Here is what I do: after I start the day fresh with the Holy Spirit, I close my eyes and picture myself putting off the old man. In my imagination, I go back to the dark jail cell from a previous vision I have had, and I see myself shucking off that old dusty gray robe of heaviness. I didn't know it at the time, but that vision was also the image of me putting off the old man. If those emotions of envy, jealousy, self-pity, or despair come roaring back to life, I will say out loud, "No! You are dead! The old man is dead! So stay there!" I might have to keep saying that over and over again, or I might even have to yell. But it works. How? Because the negative emotions attached to the thoughts of the old man do not have power over me any longer. I can nip them in the bud, remind myself of truth, and freely rejoice with those who are rejoicing.

3. Put on The New Man

*By living in God, love has been brought to its full expression in us… because **all that Jesus now is, so are we in this world.** (emphasis added) 1 John 4:17, TPT*

If becoming more empowered over our thoughts and emotions isn't enough, here is more good news. Each day after we receive from the Holy Spirit, after we put off the old man, we then put on The New Man. Who is The New Man? Christ! This means that every day we give our independence to and rely solely on Jesus.

For every thought that tries to come back to life from the old, carnal man, we resist, replace it, and put on Christ. If fear, we replace it with love; if anxiety, we replace it with peace; if shame, we replace it with identity; if envy, we replace it with rejoicing. If we don't know, then we ask Him, "What do You want to give me in place of _____?" We can do this in *all* circumstances for *all* emotions.

As He is, so are we in this world; currently; not when Jesus comes back; not when we get our new bodies, but *right now*. As He is, so are we. He is fruitful, so I am fruitful. He is joyful, so I am joyful. He multiplies, so I multiply. He is patient, so I am patient. He has many children, so have I *many* children. He is kind, so I am kind. He is at peace, so am I at peace. He heals the sick, so I heal the sick. Have we got it yet? As He is, so are we!

We already contain the full expression of who Jesus is because we are one with Him. To put on The New Man is to put on Jesus, His thoughts, attributes, character traits, actions, etc. Every circumstance, every scenario, we *step* into it as Christ in Me, "But we have the mind of Christ [to be guided by His thoughts and purposes]." (1 Corinthians 2:16, AMP) We are already in Him, and He is in us.

By the way, this is another guarantee that we are already fruitful and pregnant because The New Man has no lack or barrenness present because lack or barrenness does *not* exist in Jesus! With that said, we no longer "battle" against infertility, sickness, grief, anger, etc. If we feel like we are striving or battling, that means we haven't yet put on and started walking in The New Man for that day. Yes, it is that simple. Yet, it takes a renewing of the mind comprehend the simplicity of it.

That is what we need to do. We need to keep receiving from the Holy Spirit each day; putting off the old man, putting on The New Man, allowing our minds to be renewed in who we are in Him, living in all that He is *now*, not when our circumstances change or when our long-awaited dreams come to fruition. As He is, so are we in this world *now*.

4. Walk in the Spirit

If we live in the Spirit, let us also walk in the Spirit. Galatians 5:25, NKJV

If we live as The New Man in Christ, let us also begin walking in The New Man in Christ. Easier said than done, right? Wrong. Well, it *is* easy. However, it takes a laser-like focus to do so. As *He* is, so are we. We walk in His character, attributes, thoughts, actions, etc. In a nutshell, this means that we banish *all* negativity completely. Any negative thought or emotion gets resisted and rejected, banished from our emotions and thoughts forever. *Forever.* FOR.EV.ER. Why? Because negativity keeps us chained to the soul realm (#selah).

When we hear or see that next pregnancy announcement, when Mother's Day rolls around, if we go into the BWD (#barrenwomandepression), it is because we are partnering with the lies of the old man. When we succumb to self-pity, we are succumbing to the old nature; when we begin to envy and look around at the amazing life that pregnant friend has compared to us, we are resurrecting the carnal man. We are acting carnal instead of being one with Jesus. We are acting like mere men, and that is just not who we are!

Think about it. As Jesus is, so are we. Does He feel sorry for Himself? Does He have any negative emotions or thoughts? Does He feel hopeless? Does He look around at others and wish He had their life? Heck no! This is us, then! We have the ability to *live* life this exact same way because we are one with Him!

#warning #sillymetaphorahead: Think of your soul as a treehouse. Instead of a sign that reads, "No Boys Allowed," you make one at the entrance of your soul that says, "No Negativity Allowed." You make a firm, laser-like resolve to allow only hope and expectation into your emotions and thoughts. The sign now reads, "Only Hope and Expectation Allowed."

Likewise, you hole yourself up in that treehouse with just Jesus and you. Meaning you keep your eyes fixed solely on Him. You become a student of who He is, and you emulate Him in every facet of your life. You fix your mind on *Him*, you only express emotions that *He* would express, you only do what *He* would do, and you only speak what *He* would speak. When Jesus walked the earth, He lived in this same way with regard to the Father "...Therefore, whatever I speak, just as the Father has told Me, so I speak." (John 12:50, NKJV).

You are no longer just yourself; you are no longer a mere human; you are no longer The Barren Woman. She is dead and buried. The New Man has been resurrected and raised to life with Jesus. But, walking in this new life takes intentional, laser-like focus on Him to forget what lies behind, to press toward the prize, to live in the fullness of Jesus in the here and now.

5. Practice expecting

Peter and John, looking straight into the eyes of the crippled man, said, "Look at us!" **Expecting a gift, he readily gave them his attention.** *Then Peter said, "I don't have money, but I'll give you this – by the power of the name of Jesus Christ of Nazareth, stand up and walk!"*
(emphasis added) Acts 3:4-6, TPT

#review: Every day that we receive from the Holy Spirit and start off fresh, we forget what lies behind and put off the old man. We put on The New Man and step into Christ for each situation, and lastly, we walk in the Spirit with laser-like focus of whose we are in Jesus, completely breaking free from the soul realm. Then expectation (#yesyouareexpecting).

In the above scripture, the crippled man would sit in the same spot every day, asking for resources in order to live. He was essentially a beggar by trade and had no way of working to support himself. He lived in daily expectation of receiving from people. It is this expectation that got him his miracle. Did he get what he was expecting? No. He got something even better! He got healed! Instead of one handout to last for the day, he received a lifestyle change. He obtained the ability to work and make his own way. Notice, though, that he had to keep his eyes on the one providing the gift (#hinthint).

Therefore, to practice expecting is to expect favor and blessing each day; to look for God's hand in every situation or circumstance; to look for what God wants to give you or to be for you each day. You see, we have this new mindset that *anything can happen!* We expect something good each and every day for each and every scenario. We can do this even if the scenario is negative. For example, let's say we get cut off in traffic and have to slam on our brakes to keep from rear-ending the very car that cut us off (#grr). At this moment, we have a choice. We can either resurrect the old man or stay in The New Man and, with expectation, look for God in this circumstance. We can ask, "Jesus, which part of your character do you want to reveal to me at this moment? What do You want me to glean? Show me the good." He will reveal it to us. Yet, let's say we resurrect the old man and fly off the handle (#guilty). What do we do then? We simply repent and continue growing up into Him; no condemnation or guilt; we move on in expectation (#easypeasy).

Likewise, we reach a place in our faith where we no longer ask, we *expect*. This is not based on our decisions or successes or failures for that day; it is based on who Jesus is within us. We know God wants to give gifts to us and rain down His blessings upon us because of Christ in us:

> *Every spiritual blessing in the heavenly realm has already been lavished upon us as a love gift from our wonderful heavenly Father, the Father of our Lord Jesus –* **all because he sees us wrapped into Christ.** *This is why we celebrate him with all our hearts! (emphasis added)*
> Ephesians 1:3, TPT

Every blessing has already been lavished upon us because God sees us wrapped into Christ! Isn't that just amazing? Every spiritual blessing and promise are already ours! We are already carrying! We are already expecting! This just confirms even more so how we can already be pregnant in the spirit.

What's next, then? Well, this expectation turns into thanksgiving because everything we could ever need or want is already ours because of Christ in Us! We *pray* from this expectation; we *live* from this expectation; we *walk* in this expectation; therefore, we *will* walk into blessings, fruitfulness, motherhood, etc. We just *walk* into it. No striving. No battling. No warring. We just expect good, and good happens.

#disclaimer: Let me be clear. This is not a magic formula, nor is it the law of attraction. This is simply walking in The New Man in a posture of expectation and hope. This is the way Jesus walked. He wasn't fearful or full of foreboding; He wasn't worried or anxious; He wasn't annoyed and frustrated by His family or neighbors (#exceptforthepharisees). Wherever He walked, He expected signs, wonders, and miracles. He expected His father to bless Him and exceed His expectations. Even in His death, He expected the ability for the whole world's redemption to be worked. He lived a lifestyle of expectation! And we can too!

GOING DEEPER:

- Do you feel like you are becoming who you were always meant to be? Why or Why not?
- Every day, start brand new by forgetting the successes or failures from the previous day. Practice receiving from the Holy Spirit first. Journal this process.
- As you put off the old man (the carnal/fleshly self of the soul realm), walk in each new day testing your thoughts before God. Don't let a thought stay there without judging whether it is from the old man or The New Man.
- Begin putting on The New Man by thinking, talking, and walking like Jesus. Study Him in the gospels and let Him work in you His will for each circumstance. As He is, so are you!
- Pay attention to and then banish each thought that inspires negative emotions. Allow only hope and expectation into your thought life by focusing on Jesus. Journal how this changes you.
- Practice expecting each day. Expect favor and expect that God will reveal His goodness to you in every situation. Record what you receive from Him.
- As you begin to see yourself as The New Man, start looking at your fellow brothers and sisters as The New Man, as well, instead of as mere humans. Record any revelations in your journal.
- Scriptures to study: Mt. 6:11; 1 Jn. 4:19; Eph. 4:22-24; Gal. 2:20; 1 Jn. 4:17; 1 Cor. 2:16; Gal. 5:25; Jn. 12:50; Acts 3:4-9; Eph. 1:3-6.

Chapter twenty-three
The Birthing

*B*ut whatever former things were gains to me [as I thought then], these things [once regarded as advancements in merit] I have come to consider as loss [absolutely worthless] for the sake of Christ [and the purpose which He has given my life]. But more than that, I count everything as loss compared to the priceless privilege and supreme advantage of knowing Christ Jesus my Lord [and of growing more deeply and thoroughly acquainted with Him – a joy unequaled]. For His sake I have lost everything, and I consider it all garbage, so that I may gain Christ, and may be found in Him [believing and relying on Him], not having any righteousness of my own derived from [my obedience to] the Law and its rituals, but [possessing] that [genuine righteousness] which comes through faith in Christ, the righteousness which comes from God on the basis of faith. And this, so that I may know Him [experientially, becoming more thoroughly acquainted with Him, understanding the remarkable wonders of His Person more completely] and [in that same way experience] the power of His resurrection [which overflows and is active in believers], and [that I may share] the fellowship of His sufferings, by being continually conformed [inwardly into His likeness even] to His death [dying as He did]. Philippians 3:7-10, AMP

#rabbittrail: Wow. Just wow. I am sitting down to write, at a loss for words, which is a tricky thing considering words are how I am communicating this book. Thankfully, Paul explained it best in the above scripture "...whatever former things were gains to me [as I thought then], these things... I have come to consider as [absolutely worthless] for the sake of Christ [and the purpose which He has given my life] ... I count *everything* as loss compared to the priceless privilege and supreme advantage of knowing Christ Jesus my Lord."

In other words, I am *so madly, deeply in love.*

The New Man, Christ in me, The Joyful Mother of children, is in love with her beloved and best friend, her greatest reward. Everything else is moot; all the promises, the blessings, the gifts. None of it matters compared to knowing and being in relationship with Jesus. *He is my everything.* He is my gift, my reward, my promise fulfilled, my greatest blessing. Nothing compares, and I don't need anything else but Him.

Many years ago, when I first began writing this book, my hopes were to conceive and give birth to my children, but even back then, I also felt God's heart for The Barren Woman. I knew not being able to fulfill the command to be fruitful and multiply was not His best for humanity. I knew that if I was this depressed and broken, there were many, many more women feeling the same way. I wrote this book for them, for *you*. I submitted to my healing journey and process of transformation out of obedience and to teach what I have learned to others. Little did I know that God would use this journey as a way to woo my heart; little did I know that He would romanticize me through His Word; little did I know He would make me fall in love with Him to the point of death; little did I know that being raised to life with Him and *knowing* Him would become my greatest reward.

So, friends, as much as I want you to become The Joyful Mother of children in the natural, I want you to become *one* with Jesus even more. With this love and knowledge of Him comes *everything*. I pray that through reading this book, you will get a taste of it. I pray that as you continue to submit to your own process of transformation, you allow your heart to be healed and wooed into intimacy with Jesus. I pray that reading this chapter will open your eyes and spark a fire in your heart to experience these same blessings (#rabbittrailcompleted).

#backtoTheBirthing: After I wrote the previous chapters, I came to a pause in the flow of my writing due to some very distracting dreams; distracting in a good way, of course; distracting in a *God way*. I now very clearly see the purpose for them, even if I still don't have a full understanding of their meaning. Both dreams had connotations of God's intimate and jealous love for me. So, I just took some time to meet Him there and enjoy His presence. I basked in His love. And, on the other side of this love, I experienced a massive shift, a shift from faith to a deep, abiding *knowing*. And like the last piece of a puzzle, it has almost felt like an audible "click" in the spirit. I am no longer just in faith. I am in the *knowledge of the truth*.

What does this mean? Because it's not like I have achieved perfection. It's not like I have officially arrived into the fullness of representing Jesus here on earth. I only know that I have left where I came from. I've left the past, my old identity, my old memories, my old expectations (#orlackthereof), my old corrupted imagination, my old way of speaking, my old emotions; and my old way of thinking. I have become The New Man, Mandi Windsor, Christ in Me, The Joyful Mother of children. And *something* has shifted; *something* has changed; the mystery has been solved:

> *There is a divine mystery – a **secret surprise** that has been concealed from the world for generations, but now it's being revealed, unfolded, and manifested for every holy believer to experience.* **Living within you is the Christ** *who floods you with the expectation of glory! This* **mystery of Christ, embedded within us, becomes a heavenly treasure chest** *of hope filled with the riches of glory for his people, and God wants everyone to know it! (emphasis added)*
> Colossians 1:26-27, TPT

This secret surprise, also known as the mystery, is a true experiential knowledge of "Christ in me." It is a renewed mind transcending the realms of revelation and understanding. It is a deep, inner *knowing* of being one with Jesus, "But he who is joined to the Lord is one spirit with Him." (1 Corinthians 6:17, NKJV)

In this oneness, in this knowledge, there has been a deposit, and implantation has occurred. I am pregnant with the blessings and promises of God, yes, but I am also pregnant with Jesus Himself, with the Word (#saywhat). His seed remains in me; therefore, I *carry* the presence of God everywhere I go (1 John 3:9). As I carry the presence of God, I also give birth to who He is and the blessings He has provided for me. However, these blessings are not just for me. Likewise, the secret surprise, the mystery, is not just mine to solve. He has unfolded these truths for *every* believer to discover because He "desires all men to be saved and to come to the knowledge of the truth." (1 Timothy 2:4, NKJV).

And. Oh. My. Goodness. Talk about discovery! Wow! Solving this mystery and experiencing this knowledge has literally felt like the unearthing of secret treasures. This inner peace and joy are incomparable to anything I have ever experienced. I am living each day in a state of supernatural rest. Also, this may sound silly, but I feel like a superhero. Seriously. Nothing is impossible, and I can overcome *anything!* I am no longer putting any limits on God or myself; I know I am one with Jesus, and together we are unstoppable.

Furthermore, my eyes have been opened to a clear understanding of the Word. Where I had questions and confusion, I now have clarity and understanding. My dream life has increased exponentially, and I am even receiving prophetic dreams for the corporate body. It is like my spiritual senses have come alive! I have greater discernment, greater wisdom, greater exhibition of the fruit of the Spirit, and I have this boldness, this tenacity, to speak up and stand up for truth no matter the cost. I am His. He is mine. We are one (#yesyesyes).

The following "babies," then, are what has been birthed from my oneness with Jesus; from entering into the knowledge of the truth. Additionally, these "babies" are anyone's for the taking (#hinthint).

STAGE 1: EARLY LABOR & ACTIVE LABOR

The Robe of Righteousness

> *I will greatly rejoice in the* LORD, *My soul shall be joyful in my God; For He has clothed me with the garments of salvation,* **He has covered me with the robe of righteousness,** *As a bridegroom decks himself with ornaments, And as a bride adorns herself with her jewels. (emphasis added) Isaiah 61:10, NKJV*

In the chapter of The New Man, I spoke about the dusty, ratty cloak of heaviness, the cloak of the old man. We shucked it off to put on The New Man, and we have been walking in our new man ever since. I forgot to mention, however, that The New Man is not walking around naked (#duhMandi). The New Man is clothed in garments of salvation and covered with the robe of righteousness. This robe is not a substance or a title; it is oneness with the person of Jesus. It carries His presence; it is being wrapped in the secret place with Him, cloaked and hidden in Him.

If we are hidden in Jesus, this robe of righteousness offers us two different kinds of divine protection. The first one is physical (#letsgetphysicalphysical #ohbrotherherewegoagain):

> *He who dwells in the* **secret place of the Most High Shall abide under the shadow of the Almighty.** *I will say of the* LORD, *"He is my*

*refuge **and my fortress**; My God, in Him I will trust." Surely He shall **deliver you** from the snare of the fowler and from the perilous pestilence. **He shall cover you with His feathers, and under His wings you shall take refuge;** His truth shall be your shield and buckler. You shall not be afraid of the terror by night, nor of the arrow that flies by day, nor of the pestilence that walks in darkness, nor of the destruction that lays waste at noonday. A thousand may fall at your side, and ten thousand at your right hand; but it shall not come near you. Only with your eyes shall you look, and see the reward of the wicked. **Because you have made the L<small>ORD</small>, who is my refuge, even the Most High, your dwelling place, no evil shall befall you, nor shall any plague come near your dwelling; for He shall give His angels charge over you, to keep you in all your ways.** In their hands they shall bear you up, lest you dash your foot against a stone. You shall tread upon the lion and the cobra, The young lion and the serpent you shall trample underfoot. **"Because he has set his love upon Me, therefore I will deliver him; I will set him on high, because he has known My name. He shall call upon Me, and I will answer him; I will be with him in trouble; I will deliver him and honor him. With long life I will satisfy him, and show him My salvation."** (emphasis added) Psalm 91:1-16, NKJV*

#loveit: I obviously had to include the whole chapter because it is just so, so good. I have prayed this chapter over my family for years. We even have it written on the foundation of our house. I prayed it over my husband while he was in Iraq. I speak it over my son before he goes to school every day. I spoke it over my classroom and students. We pray it any time we travel in the car or by plane. We speak it over our fur babies. You name it; we pray it. And guess what? We are supernaturally protected! It works! And that was just when I was using it as a proactive weapon. Now that I know I am hidden in Christ, now that I am one with Him in the secret place, I have even more peace and more security knowing that I am preserved and protected from absolutely *anything*!

The second kind of divine protection is in the soul realm (mind and emotions). Simply stated, the robe of righteousness protects our hearts from getting wounded. If I am rejected, it is because they reject *Him*; if I am persecuted, it is because *He* is persecuted. We are truly free from offense and pain. Remember, Mandi Windsor is dead. Yes, I have been resurrected, but I am now *hidden* in Christ. This robe protects me! In fact, maybe that's what Paul meant when he spoke of the armor of God, "Stand therefore, having girded your waist with truth, having put on the breastplate of righteousness" (Ephesians 6:14, NKJV)

The breastplate of righteousness protects our heart and vital organs; therefore, I can wrap this robe around me to guard my heart. And when things don't turn out like I think they should or when someone lets me down, I can step into the secret place and receive comfort and protection. When another pregnancy announcement or delivery comes my way, I can nuzzle down deep into my robe and receive His identity and truth (#thinksnuggie). I am worthy because He is worthy; I am not lacking anything because He is not lacking anything. This is how we can even keep from getting offended and wounded in everyday life! It is not I who live, but Christ who lives in me (Galatians 2:20). I am covered in His robe of righteousness which frees me up to love and live as He did.

The Rest of Righteousness

> *I want you woven into a tapestry of love,* **in touch with everything there is to know of God. Then you will have minds confident and at rest, focused on Christ,** *God's great mystery. All the richest treasures of wisdom and knowledge are embedded in that mystery and nowhere else...(emphasis added) Colossians 2:2-3, MSG*

I love this scripture! This is Paul exhorting the church of Colosse to attain everything there is to know of God. In other words, when we come into the knowledge of God and solve the mystery of Christ in us, we will have minds confident and at rest. So then, after we put on this robe of righteousness, we birth the *rest* of righteousness. Here is a journal entry describing this rest:

Wow. Wow. Wow. I am so free! This is what Christianity is supposed to feel like! It is not about me. I don't have to have the perfect formula or the perfect amount of faith or the perfect process. I just get to lean into You. I get to keep my peace and be at rest. I don't have to hurry or rush around. I don't have to feel guilty or condemned. I don't have to be fearful or worried. I just get to be me in YOU. You take all the pressure. You already took it all! I just get to rest. As You are, so am I. I move in favor and expect blessings to flood every area of my life. I swim in favor and blessings! And it doesn't depend on me! That's the most amazing part! I am awesome because You are awesome, and Your heart's desire is to bless the Jesus in me. I just get to receive. (June 17, 2019)

#happysigh: In the rest of righteousness, we are free from performance. We *know* it is not about us. Blessing, favor, and the promises of God come our way because of who Jesus is. We can be a total failure for the day, and God will still want to rain down blessings and give us what we've asked. We are truly free from guilt, condemnation, and self-induced pressure. We are free from wrestling and striving to believe. We are worthy because He is worthy (#saythattoyourselfoverandoveragain).

I am free to simply rest in my oneness with Jesus in the knowing that it is finished. My healing, my motherhood is already secure; it is already done. I don't have to keep asking or commanding or decreeing. I have surpassed those stages of the wrestle and have fully *received* my children. In fact, that was the implantation, the "click" in my spirit. The shift from faith to knowing was the shift from believing to receiving. In other words, it is done. It. Is. Finished.

Furthermore, we can transfer this rest of righteousness to our relationships. We no longer have expectations of anyone (#saywhat). Seriously. We are at rest in our relationships because nobody owes us a thing (#moreonthiscomingsoon).

A NEW NAME

> *For Zion's sake I (Isaiah) will not be silent, And for Jerusalem's sake I will not keep quiet, Until her righteousness and vindication go forth as brightness, And her salvation goes forth like a burning torch.* **The nations will see your righteousness and vindication [by God], And all kings [will see] your glory; And you will be called by a new name which the mouth of the** L<small>ORD</small> **will designate. You will also be [considered] a crown of glory and splendor in the hand of the L<small>ORD</small>, And a royal diadem [exceedingly beautiful] in the hand of your God.** *It will no longer be said of you [Judah], "Azubah (Abandoned)," Nor will it any longer be said of your land, "Shemamah (Desolate)";* **But you will be called, "Hephzibah (My Delight is in Her),"** *And your land, "Married";* **For the L<small>ORD</small> delights in you,** *And to Him your land will be married [owned and protected by the Lord]. (emphasis added) Isaiah 62:1-4, AMP*

In the chapter Fight for Your Testimony, I wrote about activating prophetic declaration and the decree in order to become what is spoken. You have heard me call myself "The Joyful Mother of Children" over and over again. So, yes, she has been born. And we know that The Joyful Mother of children metaphorically represents The New Man, Christ in me. Likewise, we know it represents our natural motherhood.

However, this name I am about to explain to you is even more closely connected to our identity. In fact, I believe this name is specifically birthed after the *knowing*, the shift, the "click" in the spirit realm. I believe this name is eternal. Although I don't quite understand it, I believe this name is given by Jesus Himself:

> *He who has an ear, let him hear and heed what the Spirit says to the churches. To him who overcomes [the world through believing that Jesus is the Son of God], to him I will give [the privilege of eating] some of the hidden manna, and* **I will give him a white stone with a new name engraved on the stone which no one knows except the one who receives it.** *(emphasis added) Revelation 2:17, AMP*

Earlier in the year, I actually had a dream in which I was pregnant with my new name, my eternal name, my name as His bride (#sorry-canttellyou #itisoursecret). Although it was a legit name, I had never heard it before and had to research its meaning. When I did, I was blown away because this new name so clearly represented the fullness and completeness of the person of Jesus. As you can probably imagine, I stayed quiet about this revelation and just sat and meditated for a while.

To be honest, the above passage in Isaiah is the most similar name I could find in the Word that matched the one He gave to me–Hephzibah (My Delight is in Her). Dear friend, this can be your new name. You, as Jesus' bride, have been birthed, "I am my beloved's, And his desire is toward me." (Song of Solomon 7:10, NKJV)

#warning #propheticalert: At the time of this writing, many in the body of Christ are coming out from deep wrestling with God for His promises. In fact, if you are reading this book, then you have most likely been in this same wrestle. Many of us went into this wrestle contending for the Word of God and what is promised to us, but in that wrestle, we met the person of Jesus instead. And from knowing Him, we have come out of this wrestle birthing these very things written in this book. In intimacy with Jesus, we have birthed our identity as His bride, the same bride that He is returning for. We are healthy, whole, beautiful, and transformed, soul and body. We love God with all of our heart, soul, mind, and strength, and we live to serve and love others.

What if *you* have not yet felt this knowing or "click" in the spirit? Begin calling yourself Hephzibah. His delight *is* in you; your new name *is* coming quickly, and you *will* soon be so unrecognizable that people will be saying, "…Who is this coming up from the wilderness, Leaning upon her beloved?" (Song of Solomon 8:5, NKJV)

The Fragrance of Jesus

> *But thanks be to God, who always leads us in triumph in Christ, and* ***through us spreads and makes evident everywhere the sweet fra-***

grance of the knowledge of Him. For we are the sweet fragrance of Christ [which ascends] to God, [discernible both] among those who are being saved and among those who are perishing:... (emphasis added) 2 Corinthians 2:14-15, AMP

We birth the fragrance of Jesus because we *are* the fragrance of Jesus. We should also be spreading and making evident everywhere the sweet fragrance of the knowledge of Him. This is what our lives are all about, Jesus and growing up into the knowledge of Him! We then come into a place of what the Bible calls maturity. In fact, a mature bride is so important to Jesus that He even gave us gifts to attain it:

Now these are the gifts Christ gave to the church: the apostles, the prophets, the evangelists, and the pastors and teachers. Their responsibility is to equip God's people to do his work and build up the church, the body of Christ. ***This will continue until we all come to such unity in our faith and knowledge of God's Son that we will be mature in the Lord, measuring up to the full and complete standard of Christ. Then we will no longer be immature like children.*** *We won't be tossed and blown about by every wind of new teaching. We will not be influenced when people try to trick us with lies so clever they sound like the truth. Instead, we will speak the truth in love,* ***growing in every way more and more like Christ****, who is the head of his body, the church. He makes the whole body fit together perfectly. As each part does its own special work, it helps the other parts grow,* ***so that the whole body is healthy and growing and full of love.***
(emphasis added) Ephesians 4:11-16, NLT

This healthy body, this unified church, is why Jesus is coming back. He wants a mature bride with His fragrance on our breath, "Like an apple tree among the trees of the woods, So is my beloved among the sons. I sat down in his shade with great delight, And his fruit was sweet to my taste." (Song of Solomon 2:3, NKJV) We achieve this maturity through intimacy and oneness with Jesus. In other words, the more time we spend in the shade of His apple tree, the more we take on His fragrance (#ahamoment).

I recently had a dream in which a man was escorting me and my husband around his property. We were riding in a horse-drawn wagon. As he drove us around to see everything, he told us about his fiancé and how they were remaining pure before the wedding. There were many outbuildings, and everything was beautiful. But he made sure to point out the only incomplete building on the property, which was still under construction. He called it the perfume factory.

As I pondered this dream in prayer, the Holy Spirit revealed to me that the man was Jesus. His fiancé was the bride of Christ, and the beautiful property was symbolic of His kingdom. As His bride, we know we are pure because of the Word that's been spoken to us (John 15:3) and because of the Word made flesh, sacrificed, and resurrected. However, it took me a little longer to receive the interpretation for the perfume factory. Initially, I thought, *What the heck is that?* But darn it, my best friend who knows me knows I like a good mystery to solve!

So, Detective Mandi went to work and discovered that the perfume factory actually represents the immature bride of Christ. It represents our lack of fragrance, our lack of the knowledge of Him, and our lack of intimacy and oneness with our Bridegroom. Everything in His kingdom is beautiful and established, but the perfume factory is still young and under construction. Intimacy is still being built up in His body. In other words, His bride is still growing up into the knowledge of Christ.

This is where we are right now in history. Jesus is beckoning His gifts (the apostles, prophets, evangelists, pastors, and teachers) to equip the body and build up the saints in the knowledge of the truth. Remember, the knowledge of the truth is birthed through intimacy and oneness with Jesus; this knowledge is the solved mystery of Christ in me! We cannot achieve it without Him. Likewise, we cannot be a productive factory without being built up in Him. Think about it. A factory manufactures a product for the consumer. We are the fragrance of Jesus, but we are to spread this fragrance everywhere. We are to become more and more like Jesus, but we do so in order to fulfill His work here on earth. A factory has output! We are meant to be productive; we are meant to bear fruit.

So here I am, smelling like my beloved. I have birthed the fragrance of Jesus. His perfume is on my lips. I have become productive and useful for His purposes. However, if you feel like you're not there yet, please know that you *will* be if you keep seeking Him and loving Him with all your heart, soul, mind, and strength.

The Garment of Light

> *You are the light of the world. A city that is set on a hill cannot be hidden. Nor do they light a lamp and put it under a basket, but on a lampstand, and it gives light to all who are in the house. Let your light so shine before men, that they may see your good works and glorify your Father in heaven. Matthew 5:14-16, NKJV*

Wow. So, if birthing His robes of righteousness and rest, receiving His bridal name, and smelling like the fragrance of Jesus wasn't enough, here is something that will really light your fire.

We learned that at salvation, we received all of the spiritual blessings. We have also received the light of Jesus because we have received new life (John 8:12). Furthermore, we have the *information* knowledge at salvation, but it eventually becomes *revelation* knowledge as we commit to our transformation journey and, therefore, spiritually mature. In other words, it isn't until we come into the knowledge of the truth that we shine:

> *Even if our gospel message is veiled, it is only veiled to those who are perishing, for their minds have been blinded by the god of this age, leaving them in unbelief. Their blindness keeps them from seeing the dayspring light of the wonderful news of the glory of Jesus Christ, who is the divine image of God. We don't preach ourselves, but rather the lordship of Jesus Christ, for we are your*

servants for Jesus' sake. **For God, who said, "Let brilliant light shine out of darkness," is the one who has cascaded his light into us – the brilliant dawning light of the glorious knowledge of God as we gaze into the face of Jesus Christ.** *(emphasis added)*
2 Corinthians 4:3-6, TPT

As we gaze into the face of Jesus, as we enter into intimacy with Him, we begin to shine. As we take on His fragrance, we also take on His appearance, "Bless the LORD, O my soul! O LORD my God, You are very great: You are clothed with honor and majesty, Who cover Yourself with light as with a garment…" (Psalm 104:1-2, NKJV)

Remember, as He is, so are we. As He is clothed in light, so are we. And, as we continue to come into the knowledge of the truth, our garments of light will shine even brighter. Why? Because His light includes His glory and splendor. In fact, the same glory that was in the cloud by day and the fire by night can rest upon us; the same glory that filled Solomon's temple can fill *our* temple:

Arise, shine; For your light has come! And the glory of the LORD is risen upon you. *For behold, the darkness shall cover the earth, And deep darkness the people;* **But the LORD will arise over you, And His glory will be seen upon you.** *The Gentiles shall come to your light, And kings to the brightness of your rising. (emphasis added)*
Isaiah 60:1-3, NKJV

Pretty amazing, huh? However, just as Jesus said that the cares of this world can choke the Word and cause us to be unfruitful, so too can our light become choked by the same cares (Matthew 13:22). Loving the culture and being carnally minded dulls our light; it drains our oil. But, when we are in intimacy with Jesus, our oil is filled. The Holy Spirit makes us *burn*, "For You will light my lamp; The Lord, my God, will enlighten my darkness." (Psalm 18:28, NKJV) Once we burn for Him in the true light of the knowledge of Him, we begin to shine fully. When we shine this brightly, we effortlessly birth good works that glorify God.

A Mature Love

If you [really] love Me, you will keep and obey My commandments.
John 14:15, AMP

"*You just want to be loved!*" I cried out to the Lord one day in prayer. And He does. He just wants to be loved. He doesn't force us into a relationship with Him because He wants our *voluntary* love. He wants us to *choose* Him, even in our own weak and broken way. Our choice to love Him is so precious to His heart.

So, when I created the outline for this chapter, He revealed to me how my love had been transformed and renewed. Where in the past I obeyed His promptings out of a sense of duty (#likethisbook), I now noticed a burning desire in my heart to obey out of love; to be in service to the Lord, not because I had to, but because I *wanted* to.

Through intimacy with Jesus, this love I have birthed motivates me to obey His commands. What are His commands? Well, we know the greatest one is to love God with all our heart, all our soul, all our mind, and all our strength. He just wants to be loved! He just wants our all. And as we come into the knowledge of the truth, our love grows for Him and births a mature love.

Loving Him wholeheartedly becomes our destiny and our greatest passion. Where it used to be a discipline and chore to spend time in prayer and the Word, it has now become the time we can hunger and thirst for above anything else. We cannot get enough of communing with our best friend; we cannot get enough intimacy with our lover. We cannot receive enough of His love for us and the joy we find in giving it back to Him. Praise is always on our lips. Thanksgiving rolls off the tongue. *We are so in love,* madly, deeply, passionately, with all that we are and all that we have. It is our heart's desire to do His will and obey Him in all things. We have become consumed by love; thus, we have *become* love (#saywhat).

Out of the overflow of this mature love, we become love itself. We are, then, motivated to love others. We desire to obey the second greatest command. We begin to manifest this love for others, especially as defined in the great "Love Chapter":

> *Love endures with patience and serenity, love is kind and thoughtful, and is not jealous or envious; love does not brag and is not proud or arrogant. It is not rude; it is not self-seeking, it is not provoked [nor overly sensitive and easily angered]; it does not take into account a wrong endured. It does not rejoice at injustice, but rejoices with the truth [when right and truth prevail]. Love bears all things [regardless of what comes], believes all things [looking for the best in each one], hopes all things [remaining steadfast during difficult times], endures all things [without weakening]. Love never fails [it never fades nor ends]. 1 Corinthians 13:4-9, AMP*

#disclaimer: We do not become totally perfect in how we love others because we are all still in the process and working out our salvation (Philippians 2:12). But, in our interactions with people, we start seeing our love manifested as in the above passage. And it is usually confirmed through peace in our hearts because we are no longer convicted by our conscience. In fact, we see ourselves shining even more brightly because, "He who loves his brother abides in the light, and there is no cause for stumbling in him." (1 John 2:10, NKJV) Consequently, we could deduce that evidence of walking in that light is by how well we love, "But if we walk in the light as He is in the light, we have fellowship with one another..." (1 John 1:7, NKJV)

We have fellowship with one another, a true brotherhood where we are fully free from seeking our own. We don't require or need anything from anyone else in a demanding and selfish manner. We serve others, and we wash their feet. When they hurt us in their humanity, we continue to serve them and wash their feet. We can do this without expecting anything in return. We will not burn out because our hearts are deep wells of love, constantly being replenished in intimacy with Jesus and by the return affection of Him through others. We always have something for one another to draw from, and it becomes our greatest joy to give and receive love from our Beloved and to give selfless love to one another, "... Freely you have received, freely give." (Matthew 10:8, NKJV)

Going Deeper:

- Do you feel like you have been wooed into a love affair with Jesus on your journey? Why or why not?
- Have you given birth to any "babies" from your intimacy with Jesus? Ask the Holy Spirit and then list them in your journal.
- Begin decreeing Psalm 91 over yourself and your family every day. Imagine His robe covering and protecting.
- In regard to your motherhood, have you shifted from believing to receiving? Why or why not?
- Meditate on Isaiah 62 and begin calling yourself *Hephzibah*. Journal this process and how it changes you.
- Do you hunger and thirst for prayer and the Word? If not, seek God for what is hindering this love from being birthed?
- How well are you loving others? Are you still selfishly expecting from them, or are you free to love sacrificially? Journal your honest thoughts.
- Scriptures to study: Phil. 3:7-10; Col. 1:26-27; Is.61:10; Ps. 91; Eph.6:14-18; Gal.2:20; Col. 2:23; Is. 62; Rev. 2:17; Song of Songs 7:10; 2 Cor. 2:14-15; Eph. 4:11-16; Song of Songs 2:3; Mt. 5:14-16; Jn. 8:12; 2 Cor.4:3-6; Ps. 104:1-2; Is. 60:1-3; Ps. 18:28; Ps. 119:105; Jn. 14:15; 1 Cor. 13; 1 Jn. 2:10; 1 Jn. 1:7, Mt. 10:7-8.

STAGE 2: THE BIRTH OF YOUR BABIES

The Vessel for Honor

> *But in a great house there are not only vessels of gold and silver, but also of wood and clay, some for honor and some for dishonor. Therefore **if anyone cleanses himself** from the latter, **he will be a vessel for honor, sanctified and useful for the Master, prepared for every good work**. (emphasis added) 2 Timothy 2:20-21, NKJV*

My labor was plugging along beautifully until I came to this massive surprise of a "baby." The bigger the baby, the bigger the stretch and the longer the labor. This process has been a true wrestle and labor of love, a labor from love; a labor to His love (#itwillmakesenselater). I definitely was not expecting this one, nor did I see it coming. But, after months and months of intense labor, I am happy to announce the birth of the vessel for honor. In fact, I have become the vessel for honor.

I had thought becoming The Joyful Mother of children, with or without the baby, was the end goal. I thought this identity represented the fullness of where the Spirit was taking me. But I was wrong. The vessel for honor was always the goal, and *you* are invited to become one too.

Becoming the vessel for honor is the process of sanctification. We agreed to this process when we said "yes" to following Jesus. This does not just happen on its own. We have to surrender to it, to choose it. And, as the above scripture describes, we have to *participate* in it by cleansing ourselves. This is also called consecration; that is, being separate from the world and unto the Lord (#readthatagain).

#review: At salvation, we became a new creation, and our spirits became one with Jesus. We were washed clean and made pure as The New Man in our spirits. Our souls, however, were still mixed with the old man in our negative mindsets, thoughts, memories, habits, emotions, actions, etc. This is why we were born again and sealed as Christians, yet nothing immediately changed in our characters and choices. Our souls must go through the process of sanctification to manifest the fullness of what Jesus has provided through His finished work. Paul described this best:

> *...because God has chosen you from the beginning for salvation through the **sanctifying work of the Spirit [that sets you apart for God's purpose]** and **by your faith in the truth [of God's word that leads you to spiritual maturity]**.... so that you **may obtain and share in the glory of our Lord Jesus Christ**. (emphasis added) 2 Thessalonians 2:13-14, AMP*

Salvation is both the sanctifying work of the Spirit for God's purposes *and* faith in the truth of God's Word. In other words, salvation consists of sanctification by your faith in God's Word. This results in spiritual maturity or preparation and the ability to share in the glory of Jesus as He uses us for His purposes. Our part is to believe the Word and feed on His Word. As we do, the Holy Spirit will shepherd us into sanctification, which is complete salvation spirit, soul, and body. How do I know? Because the Greek word for salvation is *soteria*, derived from sozo. Sozo means to deliver, save, heal, preserve, and rescue both spiritually and naturally:

> *Now may the God of peace Himself **sanctify you through and through** [that is, separate you from profane and vulgar things, make you pure and whole and undamaged – consecrated to Him – set apart for His purpose]; and **may your spirit and soul and body be kept***

complete and [be found] blameless at the coming of our Lord Jesus Christ. (emphasis added) 1 Thessalonians 5:23, AMP

Remember, Jesus is returning for a bride who has made herself ready, "'Let us be glad and rejoice and give Him glory, for the marriage of the Lamb has come, and His wife has made herself ready.' And to her it was granted to be arrayed in fine linen, clean and bright," (Revelations 19:7-8, NKJV) Even Paul in exhorting the Corinthians said, "For I have betrothed you to one husband, that I may present you as a chaste virgin to Christ." (2 Corinthians 11:2, NKJV) The bride makes herself ready for the return of Jesus by consecrating herself; being arrayed in fine linen, clean and bright; becoming holy, sanctified, and chaste:

*...that He might **sanctify** and **cleanse** her with the washing of water by the word, that He might present her to Himself **a glorious church**, **not having spot or wrinkle** or any such thing, but that she should be **holy** and **without blemish**. (emphasis added) Ephesians 5:26-27, NKJV*

Did you catch that? "...that He might sanctify and cleanse her with the washing of water by the *word*." The Word washes us! Not only should we be clean and holy, prepared for the return of Jesus as His bride, but God commanded that we be holy simply because *He* is holy (Leviticus 19:2). Peter later elaborated on this command:

*Therefore gird up the loins of your mind, be sober, and rest your hope fully upon the grace that is to be brought to you at the revelation of Jesus Christ; as obedient children, **not conforming yourselves to the former lusts**, as in your ignorance; but as **He who called you is holy, you also be holy in all your conduct**, because it is written, "Be holy, for I am holy." (emphasis added) 1 Peter 1:13-16, NKJV*

So, we can be holy, not just in our spirit man as one with Christ (which occurred the moment we believed and confessed His name). We should also be holy in all our conduct, our behavior, our good works, and in the motives of our hearts. If we do this, we make ourselves vessels for honor, useful and prepared for Him to work through us. Remember, *everything* Jesus provided for us is within our spirits. Yet, we are powerless to receive it for ourselves and release it to others unless we become a vessel for honor.

#disclaimer: I am not saying we have to be holy vessels in order to receive a baby or in order for God's Word to work in our lives. History proves time and time again that God is good to His people and faithful to His Word even when we are not. However, we have also learned that if our souls (mind, will, emotions) are unrenewed, we won't likely receive nor be able to release what Jesus made available to our bodies and to others because we are in unbelief. Remember, unbelief isn't an intentional choice; it is simply the direction our natural mind will go if not renewed, transformed, and cleansed by the Word.

Back in 2011, when the Holy Spirit asked me if I believed the entirety of His Word was truth, I unknowingly submitted to this process of sanctification. I've called it different titles throughout the book: a transformation, a journey, the process, the wilderness, my story. Other terms might be the process of sanctification, the process of becoming the vessel for honor, submitting to His Word, cleansing the soul through the renewing of our minds, and allowing His Word to transform us from the inside out into vessels that God can fully use. *This* is the end goal!

Prior to the time of this writing, I had seemingly hit a wall and felt like my labor was stalled. Honestly, I still felt so powerless, and it was driving me crazy. What is the point of living in The New Man but not walking in the same power as Jesus? I couldn't stand the tension between being where I was as opposed to where I was *supposed* to be. Thankfully, my Great Midwife (#akaHolySpirit) knew this. I kept having cleansing dreams every week even (i.e., dreams of going to the bathroom or cleaning). At the same time, we had some crazy things happening around our house, which I'll get to in a moment, but this is why we can never put God in a box. He can do anything, and He can use anything to speak to us and lead us into truth.

For example, our Dyson vacuum stopped working and needed to be repaired. After contacting Dyson, we received a quote from them, but never had to use it. After my husband commanded the vacuum to come back to life, it did! Later, our dishwasher began backing up with water and even flooded onto our wood floors. It kept doing this, so we had to unplug it several times per week to make it drain properly. Thinking we were going to have to purchase a new dishwasher, we thought we had better first try speaking to it and commanding it to do its job. Guess what? It began to work normally! And, our wood floors were not ruined as we had supposed. They returned to normal once dry, as well. Lastly, our washing machine stopped working mid-wash, and it wouldn't switch to the next cycle. I turned it off, spoke to it, and commanded it to work. Ten minutes later, it was back to normal! We haven't had any issues with any of these appliances ever since! Crazy, huh? What's even crazier is that they are all *cleansing* vessels! Coincidence? I think not! The vessel for honor, then, has been birthed. And she is made up of two primary components:

1. A living sacrifice

> *I encourage you to **surrender yourselves to God to be his sacred, living sacrifices. And live in holiness, experiencing all that delights his heart.** For this becomes your genuine expression of worship. **Stop imitating the ideals and opinions of the culture around you, but be inwardly transformed by the Holy Spirit through a total reformation of how you think.** This will empower you to discern God's will as you live a beautiful life, satisfying and perfect in his eyes. (emphasis added) Romans 12:1-2, TPT*

All those many years ago, after saying, "yes," to the process of sanctification, after choosing to consecrate myself unto the Lord, I unknowingly threw myself on the altar. As I grew through study and meditation of His Word, little did I know what the Holy Spirit was doing. All along, I have called it the transforming and renewing of the mind. I was, however, in the process of becoming a living sacrifice, growing in true love and worship to my Beloved.

As you know, it did not begin that way. It did not begin as a love affair. It began with a desire to be a mom, simple Bible disciplines, and dutiful obedience. However, I chose to believe His Word and surrendered to a journey of laying down my brokenness, my logic, my jealousies, my bitterness, my fear, my self-pity, my religion, my unbelief, and my humanity to wholly embrace His truth. I have had an overhaul literally from the inside out. And it all started with obedience to His Word:

> *Now, **because of your obedience to the truth, you have purified your very souls,** and this empowers you to be **full of love** for your fellow believers. So express this **sincere love** toward one another passionately and with a **pure heart**. (emphasis added) 1 Peter 1:22, TPT*

Love. It all comes back to love. Love is the goal. Anything less than love from a pure heart is empty or dead works with unclean motives. Additionally, every work, every act of service, every financial gift, every time we minister from a pure heart is remembered by God. Thus, He will reward us. Why? Because we built our house on Jesus with lasting materials that have been tested and purified:

> *For we are God's fellow workers; you are God's field, **you are God's building**... **But let each one take heed how he builds on it. For no other foundation can anyone lay than that which is laid, which is Jesus Christ.** Now if anyone builds on this foundation with gold, silver, precious stones, wood, hay, straw, each one's work will become clear; for the Day will declare it, **because it will be revealed by fire; and the fire will test each one's work, of what sort it is. If anyone's work which he has built on it endures, he will receive a reward.** (emphasis added) 1 Corinthians 3:9, 10-14, NKJV*

Now, what does this have to do with becoming the vessel for honor? To be the vessel for honor is to be prepared for His good works! The motive of His good works is *always* to love from a pure heart. Love is purified in the fire, love never fails, and love endures forever:

> *If I were to speak with eloquence in earth's many languages, and in the heavenly tongues of angels,* ***yet I didn't express myself with love, my words would be reduced to the hollow sound of nothing more than a clanging cymbal.*** *And if I were to have the gift of prophecy with a profound understanding of God's hidden secrets, and if I possessed unending supernatural knowledge, and if I had the greatest gift of faith that could move mountains,* ***but have never learned to love, then I am nothing.*** *And if I were to be so generous as to give away everything I owned to feed the poor, and to offer my body to be burned as a martyr,* ***without the pure motive of love, I would gain nothing of value… Love never stops loving.*** *It extends beyond the gift of prophecy, which eventually fades away.* ***It is more enduring*** *than tongues, which will one day fall silent.* ***Love remains*** *long after words of knowledge are forgotten. Our present knowledge and our prophecies are but partial, but when love's perfection arrives, the partial will fade away… Until then,* ***there are three things that remain: faith, hope, and love – yet love surpasses them all. So above all else, let love be the beautiful prize for which you run.*** *(emphasis added) 1 Corinthians 13:1-3, 8-10, 13, TPT*

Because love is the goal of being a living sacrifice, we need to rid ourselves of any mixture and impurities that hinder this love. We must *humbly* choose to stay on the altar and submit to the process of sanctification because it has some added death and suffering, which we will see in a moment. First, let's look again at the key passage in this chapter:

> *But more than that, I count everything as loss compared to the priceless privilege and supreme advantage of knowing Christ Jesus my Lord [and of growing more deeply and thoroughly acquainted with Him – a joy unequaled].* ***For His sake I have lost everything, and I consider it all garbage,*** *so that I may gain Christ, and may be found in Him [believing and relying on Him], not having any righteousness of my own derived from [my obedience to] the Law and its rituals, but [possessing] that [genuine righteousness] which comes*

> *through faith in Christ, the righteousness which comes from God on the basis of faith. And this, so that I may know Him [experientially, becoming more thoroughly acquainted with Him, understanding the remarkable wonders of His Person more completely] and [in that same way experience] the power of His resurrection [which overflows and is active in believers]*, **and [that I may share] the fellowship of His sufferings, by being continually conformed [inwardly into His likeness even] to His death [dying as He did]**... (emphasis added)
> Philippians 3:7-10, AMP

Before we can share in the power of His resurrection, that is, before we can release His power and glory in its fullness, we must crucify everything else that is competing to take its place. Think about it; if we want signs and wonders, we simply cannot be carnal (fleshly/natural); we *have* to become supernatural. We have to allow the fire of God to purify every part of our souls. Our souls will not be bypassed in this process of manifesting His power. Our souls contain the on/off switch, or they contain the filter. They *must* be pure; must be sanctified, "Sanctify yourselves [for His purpose], for tomorrow the Lord will do wonders (miracles) among you." (Joshua 3:5, AMP)

A living sacrifice willingly allows the fire to expose and purge. And friend, this is *not* a pretty process. It is deeply, deeply painful, but it is necessary. You see, we cannot mix our self-absorbed souls with the purity of His Spirit. Our motives and intentions must be pure for His glory to manifest, and I have recently discovered that mine wasn't.

I mean, I *thought* I was pure and holy in my soul. Shoot, I have been at this long enough. I was doing all the right things and saying all the right things, but the Holy Spirit soon revealed to me how ugly my heart really was, "The heart is deceitful above all things, And desperately wicked; Who can know it?" (Jeremiah 17:9, NKJV) Jesus even taught:

> *"These people draw near to Me with their mouth, And honor Me with their lips,* **But their heart is far from Me**"*... When He had called the multitude to Himself, He said to them, "Hear and understand:* **Not what goes into the mouth defiles a man; but what comes out of the**

> *mouth, this defiles a man… Do you not yet understand that whatever enters the mouth goes into the stomach and is eliminated?* **But those things which proceed out of the mouth come from the heart, and they defile a man. For out of the heart proceed evil thoughts, murders, adulteries, fornications, thefts, false witness, blasphemies. These are the things which defile a man"** *(emphasis added)*
> Matthew 15:8, 10-11, 17-20, NKJV

Pretty intense, right? What is even more intense is that right around the time I began to ponder these things, I received this passage in a prophetic word:

> *"Woe is me, for I am undone! Because I am a man of unclean lips, And I dwell in the midst of a people of unclean lips; For my eyes have seen the King, The L*ORD *of hosts." Then one of the seraphim flew to me, having in his hand a live coal which he had taken with the tongs from the altar. And he touched my mouth with it, and said: "Behold, this has touched your lips; Your iniquity is taken away, And your sin purged." Isaiah 6:5-7, NKJV*

#saywhat: I thought I was already cleansed, right? Well, I am in my spirit as one with Jesus. But I was told that God wanted to take me to a higher level of purity and spiritual experience. I immediately assumed that I would have a dream or vision and get to visit the literal throne room. I soon learned that instead, I was to take a little trip through my heart. I visited my impure, deceitful heart, whose motives were found out by what came from my lips (#ouch). No, this prophetic word was not a rebuke. It was a wakeup call to my true identity, to where God wanted to take me. However, some things had to die. I had to put my heart on the altar and allow myself to be exposed and purged. This is *absolutely* necessary in order to be a living sacrifice; a vessel for honor prepared for His good works:

> *For You do not desire sacrifice, or else I would give it; You do not delight in burnt offering.* ***The sacrifices of God are a broken spirit,***

> ***A broken and a contrite heart** – These, O God, You will not despise.*
> *(emphasis added) Psalm 51:16-17, NKJV*

To offer sacrifices to God is to offer Him a broken and contrite heart. So, I willingly put my heart on the altar for months until I came out of the consecration with suffering. I began with the following prayer, "Search me, O God, and know my heart; Try me, and know my anxieties; And see if there is any wicked way in me." (Psalm 139:23-24, NKJV) I continued with repentance, brokenness, and tears until I was completely spent and humbled.

You will know you are doing this entire process "right" if you come out of the purging having suffered loss. Why? Because the vessel for honor is actually a *broken* vessel. When we are broken, His power (located in our spirits) can then be released through the cracks. In other words, the gold or treasure is uncovered within and begins to shine brightly (#thetreasureisChristinme). We become broken and humbled on the outside (the soul) because that is how the inside (the Spirit) gets released through ourselves and to others.

> *"In order for the inner life to be released, the outer life must suffer loss. If that which is outward is not broken, that which is inward cannot be released." Watchman Nee*

The purging humbles and breaks us in such a way that we realize the only good thing about us comes from God. There is no good thing in me, in my soul, or humanity apart from *Christ in me*. Likewise, I can do nothing without Him. I can't even love God without Him; I can't make myself a living sacrifice without Him; I can't lose weight without Him; I can't write without Him; I can't teach without Him; I can't love my husband and son without Him; I can't love others without Him; I can't have all my gifts without Him; the wisdom, the talents, the happy marriage, the healthy son, the nice house, the pug puppy, etc. You name it, there is literally nothing good about me apart from Christ! And, I don't know about you, but this revelation makes me want to burst into song as David did, "I will praise You, for I am fearfully and wonderfully made; Marvelous are Your works, And that my soul knows very well." (Psalm 139:14, NKJV)

David knew this truth, and now we can know this truth – we are fearfully and wonderfully made because the best thing about us is Jesus in us! Paul also received this same revelation, "…Therefore, I will all the more gladly boast in my weaknesses, so that the power of Christ [may completely enfold me and] may dwell in me." (2 Corinthians 12:9, AMP) We must be so poured out, emptied of our humanity and our independence, that we may be fully filled with His life and power. Job sums up his process in this way:

"I know that You can do everything, And that no purpose of Yours can be withheld from You.…Therefore I have uttered what I did not understand, Things too wonderful for me, which I did not know…I have heard of You by the hearing of the ear, But now my eye sees You. Therefore I abhor myself, And repent in dust and ashes."
(emphasis added) Job 42:2-3, 5-6, NKJV

Job was dealing with some major self-righteousness (#likeme). He kept presuming to know God's ways, but that all changed when He was confronted with the beauty and holiness of God. Purged of all he had, Job saw the true nature of his heart, humbled himself, and repented. The cleansing enabled his eyes to see the perfection of God and the weakness of man.

Practically speaking, and to better explain what this purging might look like, I will share some impurities that were revealed within *my* heart. These impurities were not blatant sins that you could see on the outside; they were impurities hidden within my soul: pride; independence; reputation; self-righteousness; the idol of worrying about God's timing; my lack of patience; the use of my words; withholding praise of His name; grumbling, complaining and critiquing; pursuing the resurrection power, the children, the American Dream more than God; attempting prophecy and words of knowledge without the motive of love; desiring "the approval of man" and my friend's approval; the need for acceptance; self-love and selfish motives; the comfort I had placed in fear and isolation; cowardice and fear of man; comfort in routines; my presumption to know God's ways; my own logic and opinion, etc.

#thatsalot: I know, right? Am I completely pure, and have I fully "arrived"? Of course not. But the new normal is to stay on the altar as a living sacrifice for the rest of my life. I love this quote from Jeremiah Johnson, *"We don't build a ministry or a platform; we build an altar of sacrifice."* It is only on this altar in a position of humility that we can keep His peace and feel His presence. It is only as a living sacrifice that the true purpose of our lives is simplified and made known.

1. A Priest

But you are a chosen generation, a royal priesthood, a holy nation, His own special people, that you may proclaim the praises of Him who called you out of darkness into His marvelous light.
1 Peter 2:9, NKJV

What is the true purpose of our lives? To love God, be a lover of Jesus, and be His priest. This is the highest and most worthy calling for every believer. In a previous chapter, I wrote about being queens and royalty in reference to this same scripture. As I have entered into further intimacy with Jesus, I have recently birthed revelation of what the priesthood actually means. After choosing to consecrate myself unto the Lord and allowing His fire to purge my soul, I have humbly stepped into my identity as His priest. In fact, we are *all* chosen to be priests before God:

*To Him who loved us and washed us from our sins in His own blood, and **has made us kings and priests to His God and Father**, to Him be glory and dominion forever and ever. Amen. (emphasis added)*
Revelation 1:5-6, NKJV

In the Old Testament, it was only the priests who could carry the Ark of the Covenant or the Presence of God; it was only the priests who could enter the Holy of Holies to minister before the Lord; it was only the priests who gave the sacrifices on behalf of the people. But it was also the priests who had to consecrate, cleanse, and prepare themselves before they could enter the inner courts.

Honestly, what makes us think we are any different? I mean, we know the Old Testament was literal. We can see that in literal sacrifice, circumcision, clean and unclean foods, the obedience of 613 laws, etc. In fact, the whole purpose for all of God's laws was to show us that we couldn't fulfill them without Him, to keep His people separate from sin, and, you guessed it, *holy* (#lightbulb #aha).

Jesus became the fulfillment of those 613 laws, and He freely gave us access into the Holy of Holies. Yes, but what if His finished work actually raised the bar? Think about it. We no longer sacrifice animals because *Jesus* became the sacrifice. We no longer physically circumcise for covenant because our *hearts* have been circumcised. What we eat is no longer unclean because it is our *hearts* that can defile us. We no longer obey each specific law because they are summed up in the first and second commandments to love. We no longer travel to worship solely in a temple because we *are* the temple. We no longer give an eye for an eye because we turn the other cheek. Even if we no longer commit adultery in the physical, we know we are adulterers by lustfully looking with our eyes. Even if we no longer commit murder in the physical, we murder if we hold anger in our *hearts* (#needisaymore).

Just in these examples alone, it is clear to see that because we have access to the Holy Spirit within us, God has raised the bar in our required level of holiness. We can be holy because He is holy and lives within us. It is no longer about the performance of outside rituals. Rather, it is about the inside condition of our hearts, and frankly, it always has been. "For the Lord sees not as man sees; for man looks at the outward appearance, but the Lord looks at the heart." (1 Samuel 16:7, AMP)

Jesus became our High Priest, the Sacrificial Lamb, enabling us to have both peace and relationship with God. Peter told us that we are priests, Paul told us that our bodies are temples and exhorted us to be living sacrifices. Just as Jesus did, we too become both the priest *and* the sacrifice of His temple:

> *Come and be his "living stones" who are continually being assembled into a sanctuary for God.* ***For now you serve as holy priests, offering up spiritual sacrifices*** *that he readily accepts through Jesus Christ. (emphasis added) 1 Peter 2:5, TPT*

Because of the finished work of Jesus, we know that we have tangible access to God's glory dwelling within us. What if we can receive and release this glory only *after* we become living sacrifices through the consecration and purifying of our hearts? What if this is why we renew our minds? What if this is what God has been after all along?

> ***Who may ascend into the hill of the Lord? Or who may stand in His holy place?*** *He who has* ***clean hands*** *and a* ***pure heart,*** *Who has not lifted up his soul to an idol, Nor sworn deceitfully. (emphasis added) Psalm 24:3-4, NKJV*

Who may ascend into the presence of God? Who may stand in His inner courts? The priest who has holy hands (actions, behavior) and a pure heart (thoughts, motive). Isaiah prophesied for the Lord, "I dwell in the high and holy place, With him who has a contrite and humble spirit..." (Isaiah 57:15, NKJV) James put it this way, "Draw near to God and He will draw near to you. Cleanse your hands, you sinners; and ***purify your hearts, you double-minded.***" (James 4:8, NKJV, emphasis added) Jesus simplified it this way, "Blessed are the ***pure in heart,*** For they shall see God." (Matthew 5:8, NKJV, emphasis added)

We shall see God *if* we are pure in heart. What does this mean? Because if we know that Jesus tore the veil and became the Way to our relationship with God, then we know we can come boldly to the throne of grace; we know anyone can believe and confess Jesus to become pure in spirit; we also know that we already have access to all that Jesus provided through His finished work located in that same spirit. However, I believe the above scriptures speak of a greater level of intimacy and knowledge of God's glory. In fact, this may be how we actually get what is inside of us (His power to heal, His fruitfulness, His faith, His love, His patience, etc.) to come *out* of us.

Interesting right? But it makes sense. He is holy, so we can be holy. And we can do it because we have the *Spirit of Holiness* empowering us to do so! The whole goal as a Christian is to be restored to the image of God, to become like Jesus, to become the vessel for honor so we can walk in His good works. But we can't imitate His good works and release His power in great measures unless we are pure in our soul realm; unless we continually place our hearts on that altar; unless we get rid of *all* mixture. Otherwise, the power can be blocked like a dam or become an impure, empty work, and we will eventually get burned out or caught up in religious performance (#beentheredonethat).

#disclaimer: If you have been around the body of Christ long enough, you will know that there have been many believers in various stages of sanctification who operate in gifts, signs, and wonders. They might be brand new Christians on fire for God, or they might have bad character but are extremely anointed. They might live compromised lives at the same time as operating in the gifts of healing and miracles.

To be honest, I don't understand how it all works. Maybe it simply reveals the goodness of God and His faithfulness to His Word; maybe it reveals how simplistic the gospel really is. I don't know. I know, however, that Jesus gave a warning to the ones who don't offer themselves fully on that altar to be transformed in intimacy:

> *"Many will say to Me in that day, 'Lord, Lord, have we not prophesied in Your name, cast out demons in Your name, and done many wonders in Your name?' And then I will declare to them, **'I never knew you; depart from Me, you who practice lawlessness!'"** (emphasis added) Matthew 7:22-23, NKJV*

#yikes! In other words, we are disobedient and wicked if we demonstrate the power of God without *knowing* Him. The Passion Translation says it this way, "...'Go away from me, you lawless rebels! I've never been joined to you!'" Lack of intimacy with God, not coming into the knowledge of the truth, and demonstrating the gifts of the Spirit is considered anarchy against the Kingdom.

When we come into the knowledge of the truth, when we enter into intimacy with Jesus, we take on who He is. We take on His character and nature, and it is *always* to be holy and *always* to love. Love is the only pure motive to do *anything* in the kingdom of God:

> *And **may the Lord increase your love until it overflows toward one another and for all people**, just as our love overflows toward you. Then your hearts will be strengthened in holiness so that you may be flawless and pure before the face of our God and Father at the appearing of our Lord Jesus with all his holy ones. Amen! (emphasis added) 1 Thessalonians 3:12-13, TPT*

#brokenrecord: Wow, that's so good! With all that said, however, how do we *enact* our priestly duties? What exactly *are* the priestly duties? Good question. Let's look at this incredible passage from Ezekiel:

> *"…they shall come near Me to minister to Me; and they shall stand before Me to offer to Me the fat and the blood," says the Lord God. "They shall enter My sanctuary, and **they shall come near My table to minister to Me, and they shall keep My charge**. And it shall be, whenever they enter the gates of the inner court, that they shall put on linen garments; no wool shall come upon them while they minister within the gates of the inner court or within the house. They shall have linen turbans on their heads and linen trousers on their bodies; **they shall not clothe themselves with anything that causes sweat… And they shall teach My people the difference between the holy and the unholy, and cause them to discern between the unclean and the clean**. (emphasis added) Ezekiel 44:15-18, 23 NKJV*

#inanutshell: We boldly access the throne room of God that dwells in our spirits. Here, we minister and serve Him. We stand before Him and offer Him our absolute best (the fat) and our life (the blood). How?

We give Him all of our heart, our soul, our mind, and our strength. We keep charge by obeying Him no matter what. We also stay in a position of rest by being clothed in the robe of righteousness and the garment of light. After we have ministered to Him and given Him our best, we are then equipped to teach others.

When we enact our priestly duties by keeping our eyes on the Word and souls on the altar, our hearts stay on loving God, receiving His love in return, and then becoming love to others; the glory will flow without us even trying. I believe the more we mature in love, the more we will release His glory, power, and anointing.

Although it may sound complicated, becoming a living sacrifice actually burns the complications away. It is simply about loving God, ministering unto Him. It is about being a lover of Jesus and coming into the knowledge of the truth. We are simply His priest. We make this the priority, and everything else will come. Healing in our bodies will come; power will come. But, to love Him with all our heart, soul, mind, and strength is what brings *Him* pleasure.

I want to bring Him pleasure. You see, I don't need the baby; I don't need the American Dream; I don't need the platform; I don't need the wealth; I don't need the power.

But I need God.

Yes. I need to know Him intimately. I need to worship Him and praise Him. I need to feed and meditate on His Word. Else, I starve. *He is the goal. He is my exceedingly great reward:*

A quiet time with You isn't for me; it's for YOU; to minister to You. To give You the attention, love, devotion, and worship due Your name. Because You are precious and merciful, You also minister to me. I can receive from You, but I must also give to You because You are worth it. You are worth it ALL. Everything else will come in time, but it is my honor to minister to You and to praise You. It is my honor to first minister to You before worrying about my book. You come first, not the people. I scale back, and I seek You. I repent and give you praise. You are first, not my assignment. My life's destiny is to minister to You. It's

> *a reward, and I thank You. (Journal entry from November 21, 2019)*
>
> *You are my reward; You are my inheritance. You are my victory. You are my exceedingly great reward. You! Everything else is just my cup overflowing with Your gifts and Your goodness. But You are the end result, the reward, the first place trophy.*
> *(Journal entry from December 3, 2019)*

I'll end this section with this simple statement of identity: we are Holy priests of a Holy temple that belongs to a Holy God.

A Clarion Call

#rabbittrail #propheticalert: Upon starting the writing of this section, our whole world was in various states of quarantine due to Covid-19 (the Coronavirus). I admit to being taken aback by this turn of events, considering the number of exciting prophecies tossed out at the beginning of 2020. Not to mention the prophetic sign of the Kansas City Chiefs winning the Super Bowl (#myhometown).

So yeah, this quarantine came as a shocker. The enemy was upping his game to take out a lot of what God had planned with a pandemic of fear and economic collapse. Of course, it's not going to work. If anything, the people of God are arising even more. Yes, it has been uncomfortable. And yes, anything not built by God is being shaken. But, a remnant of the church is re-evaluating, repenting, and getting cleansed of idols. Their hearts are being exposed, and they are crying out to the Lord. It is beautiful. And although my heart goes out to those who have lost loved ones and to those who are suffering, I can't wait to see what happens next. In fact, God is up to something amazing amidst the confusion; that is simply His nature.

#checkthisout: First let's look at the name Covid-19. As soon as this thing came around, my spiritual ears perked up because the number 19 has been significant; having had many dreams about this number throughout 2019. I came to learn that the nineteenth letter of the Hebrew alphabet is *kuf*, which signifies holiness. The gematria (numerical value) of the letter is 100, which signifies fullness. As the church begins to transition into her full measure of holiness, evil is attempting to make her unclean. Think about it, hygiene and cleanliness have been greatly emphasized in the physical. We are being told to wash our hands, cleanse our houses, and prevent any unclean thing from touching us (#whoasoundsfamiliar). Remember my vacuum, dishwasher, and washing machine? They were natural symbols of what was happening on the inside, as is this. God is glaringly leading His church into holiness! He is saying through natural circumstances to consecrate ourselves, cleanse our hands (actions, behavior) and purify our houses (temples, hearts).

Next, we were required to quarantine and stay home, which naturally forced us into communion with our families. We have been growing in intimacy with our families, so in the spiritual, we should be growing in intimacy with God and the *family* of God. Pretty cool, right? It is only those who have eyes to see and ears to hear that will respond to the call of purity, holiness, intimacy, and family in this hour.

Why do I include this rabbit trail in my book? Because I want to document this prophetic time in history. It is no coincidence that we are talking about the vessel for honor and a clarion call at the same time the Holy Spirit is leading His bride into consecration and holiness. In fact, The Barren Woman is actually symbolic of the barren and powerless church. Just as my journey has shown, The Barren Woman (the church) is transforming into The Joyful Mother of Children (the bride of Christ), so is the church transitioning into the fruitful bride of Christ to whom Jesus is returning. The fruitful bride is prepared, consecrated, and cleansed through intimacy:

> *"Let us rejoice and shout for joy! Let us give Him glory and honor, for the marriage of the Lamb has come [at last] and **His bride (the redeemed) has prepared herself.**" She has been permitted to dress in fine linen, dazzling white and clean – for the fine linen signifies the righteous acts of the saints [the ethical conduct, per-*

sonal integrity, moral courage, and godly character of believers].
(emphasis added) *Revelation 19:7-8, AMP*

#backtoaclarioncall: To recap, we have learned we are both the sacrifice *and* the priest of our temple. This leads us to become a vessel for honor prepared and useful for His good works. I originally had this section listed under the vessel for honor until I realized I was having another "baby." And ouch, this "birthing" hurt.

Why? Because I am weary.

Already, I am The Joyful Mother of children spirit and soul, but it has yet to manifest in the body. Frankly, I am so ready to move on. I am ready to complete this book and move on with my life as a mother and a vessel for honor. I cannot comprehend why I am still barren in the natural when I am so fruitful in the spiritual. It just doesn't make sense to me anymore. Each month, I am shocked that I am not pregnant. It feels like I keep getting bypassed. And each month, someone else in my life is getting pregnant or giving birth, and I have to keep my head above the water so as not to sink in the ocean of deception and despair. It. Is. So. Hard. This journey is very, very difficult, and I am never going to pretend otherwise (#truth).

Yes, I have come a long way. I am no longer in doubt or unbelief; my husband and I are no longer sick in our bodies; I am in the knowledge of the truth; I have received the revelation of Jesus as the answer; I believe that nothing is impossible, and my motherhood feels like it is already in existence. I seriously have no reason not to be pregnant! None! This is why it is so tough right now. It is past time; I know it is. And yet, I don't understand the holdup; at least I didn't until I gave birth to this revelation.

I am going to share something controversial, something that could be greatly misunderstood. But hopefully, by now, you know my heart to discover the truth even if it is uncomfortable or unpopular. This *is* my story and *my* journey. You may not be in the same place. What I share may be too difficult to wrap your mind around. I encourage you to seek the Lord, surrender to His leadership, and ask Him to lead you into His truth. He will in time.

After my recent season on the altar of sacrifice, I discovered that every circumstance is actually an invitation. What may originally be an attack from the enemy or come as a result of sin in the earth is ultimately an invitation. In other words, in every circumstance, we have a choice. We have a choice to either accept what comes our way and attempt to fix it our own way or we can ascend higher and contend for the ways of God; hence, this becomes a clarion call to action. For example, the barren womb was never intended to be a life sentence. It was always meant to be temporary. In fact, I believe it is actually a high calling to make history with God (#HIStory).

Why? Because *barren wombs make history*.

We can see this clearly in the lives of Sarah, Rebekah, Rachel, Manoah's wife, Hannah, and Elizabeth. Each child birthed from a barren womb had a very specific purpose on earth and went down in history. Think about it, why would all three Mothers of Faith be barren? Why would the lineage of Israel be birthed from barren wombs? What about Manoah's wife, Hannah, and Elizabeth? Why would God choose these three barren wombs to birth deliverers, prophets, forerunners, and history makers?

Furthermore, could it be that He is *still* doing this today? Could it be that with a barren womb comes the clarion call to impact history? Why not? Why *wouldn't* He redeem the pain and reproach with a story and a child to make the journey worth it all? Scripture proves this. Think about it; God never changes. He is good, and He is faithful to fulfill His Word; He restores and redeems; He works all things together for our good.

What would happen if, instead of accepting this circumstance with despair and shame, we saw the barren womb as an invitation to make history with God? Dear friend, whether it makes sense or not, *this* is reality! We have been seeing it all wrong. We have not been left out or forgotten; we have, in fact, been *chosen*.

#disclaimer: Please don't misunderstand me. God does not place sickness or disease-causing barrenness upon our bodies for His purposes. You already know where I stand on that. I am saying that with any circumstance that comes our way, we have a choice to look at it through the eyes of man or the eyes of God. Every circumstance is an invitation to partner with Him and His will.

Dear friend, we already know His will for us! We already know who we are, and we know the outcome of the finished work of the cross (#thejoyfulmotherofchildren). Does God actually see us as highly favored and chosen? (#yes) Man may see us as one to be pitied or reproached, but the truth is, God has issued this beautiful invitation to make history with Him.

We know God's ways are higher, and we know Jesus opened the door so we can partner with Him in those ways. But what are those higher ways? Well, before Jesus came to the earth, God actually had a historical solution for both natural and spiritual barrenness. This solution was recorded in Scripture not once, but three times. What is even more amazing is that this solution wasn't solely for the empty womb or the empty arms; this solution was also for the barren body of Christ, and *we* are invited to be a part of it!

#drumrollplease: God's solution to barrenness is to partner with an empty womb, issue a clarion call of action, and take up the mantle of a *Nazirite Family* (#saywhat). Let me explain. The Nazirite, or the *Nazir* in Hebrew, means to be consecrated and separated. Sound familiar? There was an option for those outside the Levitical order or Priesthood who wanted more of God but could not enter the Holy of Holies. These could voluntarily take a vow of separation and consecration unto the Lord:

> *Again the* Lord *spoke to Moses, saying, "Say to the sons of Israel, 'When a man or a woman makes a special vow,* **the vow of a Nazirite, that is, one separated and dedicated to the** Lord***,** he shall abstain from wine and strong drink; he shall drink no vinegar, whether made from wine or strong drink, nor shall he drink any grape juice nor eat fresh or dried grapes. All the time of his separation he shall not eat anything produced from the grapevine, from the seeds even to the skins. All the time of the vow of his separation no razor shall be used on his head.* **Until the time of his separation to the** Lord *is*

*completed, he shall be holy, and shall let the hair of his head grow long. All the time that he separates himself to the L*ORD *he shall not go near a dead body. He shall not make himself [ceremonially] unclean for his father, mother, brother, or sister, when they die, because [the responsibility for] his separation to God is on his head.* ***All the time of his separation he is holy to the L***ORD***.*** *(emphasis added) Numbers 6:1-8, AMP*

The whole goal of the vow was to abstain from anything that would make them unclean and separate from God. Sound pretty familiar? That is the choice we made at salvation. I mean, we were not mandated to join the "family business" with the Jewish people; we were grafted in, given an invitation. After He chose us, we chose Him. So, *all* true believers in Jesus are technically Nazirites. Think about it, our old man died, we became a new creation, we were made pure, no longer tainted with sin. We have died to ourselves, chosen to carry His cross and take on The New Man, Christ in me. We entered into sanctification and are daily abstaining from all that would make us unclean in our souls. Yep, it sounds like the Nazirite Vow to me!

What did the Nazirites vow to abstain from, then? The wine and grapes might have symbolized anything that was common or popular in the culture to even joy, celebration, and of course, excess. The hair might have symbolized the person themselves because it was some part of the person that could be placed on the altar. It could also have symbolized one's logic or reason. A dead body might have symbolized anything that would be dull or make one unclean or impure.

Now, if you would like this in New Testament lingo, Paul summed up the Vow of the Nazirite in a passage we have studied together:

Therefore I urge you, brothers and sisters, by the mercies of God, to present your bodies [dedicating all of yourselves, set apart] as a living sacrifice, holy and well-pleasing to God, which is your rational (logical, intelligent) act of worship. And do not be conformed to this world [any longer with its superficial values and customs], but be

> *transformed and progressively changed [as you mature spiritually] by the renewing of your mind [focusing on godly values and ethical attitudes], so that you may prove [for yourselves] what the will of God is, that which is good and acceptable and perfect [in His plan and purpose for you]. Romans 12:1-2, AMP*

Yes, the Nazirite Vow is equivalent to being a living sacrifice! Thus, the call to be a Nazirite Family is *anyone's* for the taking. However, what if this clarion call is unique to *us* because Nazirites are birthed from barren wombs? Seriously. Manoah's wife, Hannah, and Elizabeth gave birth to the Nazirites Samson, Samuel, and John the Baptist. Why do we know these names? Because they were history makers and world changers with specific purposes on the earth (#micdrop).

What if we, too, are called to birth Nazarites? What if, however, we are just one small part of the equation? What if God is raising up a whole generation of Nazirites? What if the Nazirite-holy-living-sacrifice-lifestyle is the answer to barrenness found all across the body of Christ? What if the prepared bride of Christ is a whole generation of Nazirites? What if revival, reformation, and power come through the Nazirite heart of consecration? What if the answer to the decay we see all across the earth is holiness and purity found in the Nazirite vessel for honor? What if the answer to the corrupt church is the holy Nazirite who walks in the full counsel of God and the fullness of Christ?

Think about it. We see the earth becoming eviler and more chaotic; we see the church as irrelevant, divided, more corrupt, and compromising. What is God's answer? A holy, separate people who fear the Lord. Paul confirmed this in his letter to the Corinthians:

> *"So COME OUT FROM AMONG UNBELIEVERS AND BE SEPARATE," says the Lord, "AND DO NOT TOUCH WHAT IS UNCLEAN; And I will graciously receive you and welcome you [with favor], And I will be a Father to you, And you will be My sons and daughters," Says the Lord Almighty. Therefore, since we have these [great and wonderful] prom-*

ises, beloved, **let us cleanse ourselves from everything that contaminates body and spirit, completing holiness [living a consecrated life – a life set apart for God's purpose] in the fear of God.** *(emphasis added) 2 Corinthians 6:17-18; 7:1, AMP*

This is the New Covenant, y'all! This is *after* the gospel of grace. As I said in the vessel for honor section, we are equipped with the Spirit of Holiness, which means that God has raised the bar. The Nazirite-holy-living-sacrifice-vessel-for-honor-lifestyle *is* that bar!

For some "red-letter proof," let's look at the Revelation of John. There, Jesus speaks to the churches of the last days. Of the seven churches, He rebukes five in their errors and tells them their judgment and reward if they overcome. Why is this significant to us today? Because we *are* those last days churches. And these warnings are for our benefit. They will give us a healthy dose of the fear of the Lord.

#speakingof: Nazirite families fear the Lord because they have come into the knowledge of God and the *entire* counsel of His Word. They know intimately both the kind, loving Jesus of the Gospels and the severe, loving Jesus of Revelation. Listen to these warnings. These are the words of our Bridegroom King who is soon returning:

- The Loveless Church. *"But I have this [charge] against you, that you have left your first love [you have lost the depth of love that you first had for Me]. So remember the heights from which you have fallen, and repent [change your inner self – your old way of thinking, your sinful behavior – seek God's will] and do the works you did at first [when you first knew Me]; otherwise, I will visit you and remove your lampstand (the church, its impact) from its place – unless you repent." (Revelation 2:4-5, AMP)*

- The Compromising Church. *"But I have a few things against you, because you have there some [among you] who are holding to the [corrupt] teaching of Balaam, who taught Balak to put a stumbling block before the sons of Israel, [enticing them] to eat things that had been sacrificed to idols and to commit [acts of sexual] immorality. You also have some who in the same way are holding to the teaching of the Nicolaitans. Therefore repent [change your inner self – your old way of thinking, your sinful behavior – seek God's will]; or else I am coming to you quickly, and I will make war and fight against them with the sword of My mouth [in judgment]." (Revelation 2:14-16, AMP)*

- <u>The Corrupt Church</u>. *"But I have this [charge] against you, that you tolerate the woman Jezebel, who calls herself a prophetess [claiming to be inspired], and she teaches and misleads My bond-servants so that they commit [acts of sexual] immorality and eat food sacrificed to idols. I gave her time to repent [to change her inner self and her sinful way of thinking], but she has no desire to repent of her immorality and refuses to do so. Listen carefully, I will throw her on a bed of sickness, and those who commit adultery with her [I will bring] into great anguish, unless they repent of her deeds. And I will kill her children (followers) with pestilence [thoroughly annihilating them], and all the churches will know [without any doubt] that I am He who searches the minds and hearts [the innermost thoughts, purposes]; and I will give to each one of you [a reward or punishment] according to your deeds. (Revelation 2:20-23, AMP)*

- <u>The Dead Church.</u> *"I know your deeds; you have a name (reputation) that you are alive, but [in reality] you are dead. Wake up, and strengthen and reaffirm what remains [of your faithful commitment to Me], which is about to die; for I have not found [any of] your deeds completed in the sight of My God or meeting His requirements. So remember and take to heart the lessons you have received and heard. Keep and obey them, and repent [change your sinful way of thinking, and demonstrate your repentance with new behavior that proves a conscious decision to turn away from sin]. So then, if you do not wake up, I will come like a thief, and you will not know at what hour I will come to you." (Revelation 3:1-3, AMP)*

- The Lukewarm Church. *"I know your deeds, that you are neither cold (invigorating, refreshing) nor hot (healing, therapeutic); I wish that you were cold or hot. So because you are lukewarm (spiritually useless), and neither hot nor cold, I will vomit you out of My mouth [rejecting you with disgust]. Because you say, 'I am rich, and have prospered and grown wealthy, and have need of nothing,' and you do not know that you are wretched and miserable and poor and blind and naked [without hope and in great need], I counsel you to buy from Me gold that has been heated red hot and refined by fire so that you may become truly rich; and white clothes [representing righteousness] to clothe yourself so that the shame of your nakedness will not be seen; and healing salve to put on your eyes so that you may see. Those whom I [dearly and tenderly] love, I rebuke and discipline [showing them their faults and instructing them]; so be enthusiastic and repent [change your inner self – your old way of thinking, your sinful behavior – seek God's will]." (Revelation 3:16-19, AMP)*

#woah: From just these passages alone, we see how a consecrated, holy people are the antidote for each warning of the last day's body of Christ. This is about a first commandment lifestyle, being holy and pure, repenting and letting our thinking be transformed, being all in and counting the cost, embracing His truth, not accepting a watered-down, impure message of immorality and idolatry. In other words, it is about being a holy, Nazirite people.

#checkthisout #Biblestudytime: At the time of Samson's birth and purpose on the earth, the Israelites (the people of God) were corrupt. Scripture records that they "did evil in the sight of the Lord, and the Lord delivered them into the hand of the Philistines for forty years." (Judges 13:1, NKJV) An angel of the Lord appeared to Manoah's wife and explained that she was to start the vow even before conception, "For behold, you shall conceive and bear a son. And no razor shall come upon his head, for the child shall be a Nazirite to God from the womb; and he shall begin to deliver Israel out of the hand of the Philistines." (Judges 13:5, NKJV) As Samson grew, it is said that the Spirit of the Lord came mightily upon him, so he moved in great strength and power as judge of Israel for twenty years.

Yes, Samson was chosen and did some pretty incredible feats, but he was also a good example of what can happen to a Nazirite when he breaks his vow and allows mixture and impurities to come into play. Likewise, his story is a good metaphor for what has happened in the modern-day church. Samson broke his vows multiple times without repentance. He eventually lost his strength, influence, and power, which led to his premature death. Could this same sort of unholiness and immorality have caused the death of the western church's influence and impact?

At the time of Samuel's birth and purpose to be on the earth, the priesthood was corrupt. In other words, the church was dry, barren, immoral, and lacking intimacy, "Now the sons of Eli were corrupt; they did not know the Lord." (1 Samuel 2:12, NKJV) and "... the word of the Lord was rare in those days; there was no widespread revelation." (1 Samuel 3:1, AMP) Even though Eli's sons were the ones committing the sinful atrocities, Eli was in error because he was passive in allowing it to go on in the temple. This same thing is happening in our western churches right now. Because the priesthood has been asleep, we have passively allowed sin to corrupt and infiltrate every area of the church. Because we have not corrected the ignorance, carnality, and blatant rebellion, much of the church is immature and lacking intimacy.

Remember, Hannah had made the Nazirite vow for Samuel and gave him to the Lord. He grew up right alongside the corruption in the temple. But Samuel knew he was born for a purpose even as a young boy, "Samuel ministered before the Lord..., wearing a linen ephod. Moreover, his mother used to make him a little robe and bring it to him year by year when she came up with her husband to offer the yearly sacrifice." (1 Samuel 2:18-19, NKJV) Each year, Hannah reminded her boy why he was born, so Samuel "grew in stature, and in favor both with the Lord and men." (1 Samuel 2:26, NKJV) Eventually, Samuel heard the word of the Lord and became one of the most renowned priests, prophets, and judges in Israel, the one who also so happened to appoint and usher in the kingdom of Israel through King Saul and King David.

Moreover, at the time of John the Baptist's birth and purpose to be on the earth, the priesthood was also corrupt (#surprisesurprise). Remember Jesus' severe rebukes recorded in the gospels? They were addressed to the Pharisees. The Pharisees *were* the priesthood! They were the church leaders, the ones who had intimate knowledge of the scripture, but they could not even recognize Truth when He was standing right before their eyes (#yikes). That gives us the fear of the Lord right there. We never want to miss Jesus and never want to miss out on what He's doing.

Between the ministry of Malachi (the last book of the Old Covenant) to the appearance of John the Baptist, there were approximately 400 years of prophetic barrenness. Whether it directly correlates to this same time frame or not, I find it interesting that Malachi prophesied about a corrupt priesthood:

> *"My covenant with Levi was [one of] life and peace, and I gave them to him as an object of reverence;* **so he [and the priests] feared Me and stood in reverent awe of My name.** *True instruction was in Levi's mouth and injustice was not found on his lips. He walked with Me in peace and uprightness, and he turned many from wickedness. For the lips of the priest should guard and preserve knowledge [of My law], and the people should seek instruction from his mouth; for he is the messenger of the* LORD *of hosts.* **But as for you [priests], you have turned from the way and you have caused many to stumble by your instruction [in the law]. You have violated the covenant of Levi,"** *says the* LORD *of hosts. "So I have also made you despised and abased before all the people, just as you are not keeping My ways but are showing partiality [to people] in [your administration of] the law."*
> *(emphasis added) Malachi 2:5-9, AMP*

Wow, it does sound just like the Pharisees, doesn't it? The priests turned from the way and caused many to stumble. How? By a lack of the fear of the Lord, an incorrect instruction of the law, and by showing partiality. Malachi then goes on to reveal the solution:

> *"Behold, I am going to send My messenger, and he will prepare and clear the way before Me. And the Lord [the Messiah], whom you seek, will suddenly come to His temple; the Messenger of the covenant, in whom you delight, behold, He is coming," says the* LORD *of hosts. But who can endure the day of His coming? And who can stand when He appears?* **For He is like a refiner's fire and like launderer's soap [which removes impurities and uncleanness]. He will sit as a refiner and purifier of silver, and He will purify the sons of Levi [the priests], and refine them like gold and silver,** *so that they may present to the* LORD *[grain] offerings in righteousness. Then the offering of Judah and Jerusalem will be pleasing to the* LORD *as in the days of old and as in ancient years. (emphasis added) Malachi 3:1-4, AMP*

The solution to a lack of the fear of the Lord is in the fire; refining, cleansing, and purifying. Wow, could that mean being a living sacrifice to become a vessel for honor (#soundslikeit)? "I will send My messenger." Guess who Malachi is speaking of? John the Baptist! I also find it interesting that Malachi goes on to prophesy the very words Gabriel told Zacharias about John the Baptist. Here is Luke's recording:

> *"For he will be great and distinguished in the sight of the Lord; and will never drink wine or liquor, and he will be filled with and empowered to act by the Holy Spirit while still in his mother's womb. He will turn many of the sons of Israel back [from sin] to [love and serve] the Lord their God. It is he who will go as a forerunner before Him in the spirit and power of Elijah,* TO TURN THE HEARTS OF THE FATHERS BACK TO THE CHILDREN, *and the disobedient to the attitude of the righteous [which is to seek and submit to the will of God] – in order to make ready a people [perfectly] prepared [spiritually and morally] for the Lord." Luke 1:15-17, AMP*

As we see, the Nazirite, John the Baptist, born of a barren womb, had a pretty significant role in redemptive history. I would venture to say that he had the most important role so far, preparing the way for Jesus. Guess what? This clarion call is the same assignment!

#saywhat: Yes, I am fully convinced that the clarion call to take up the Nazirite Family mantle is the action necessary to prepare the way of the Lord anew, to usher in the return of King Jesus, "Behold, I will send you Elijah the prophet before the coming of the great and dreadful day of the Lord." (Malachi 4:5, NKJV) Who is Elijah the prophet? We are! More to the point, the prophetic generation is moving in the spirit and power of Elijah. When is the great and dreadful day of the Lord? The day of Jesus' return!

#holdup: Didn't John the Baptist already fulfill this prophecy? Partially. However, prior to Jesus confirming the role of John the Baptist, He said, "Indeed, Elijah is coming first and will restore all things." (Matthew 17:11, NKJV) This means that another Elijah is coming. Now, this could be the literal Elijah, or this could be a generation of Nazirites moving in the Elijah spirit and power just as John did. We cannot know for a fact (#timewilltell).

Prophetically speaking, since the kingdom is all about multiplication and all disciples now have Jesus within, it makes sense to infer that the second Elijah would not be a lone individual but a whole generation of people. What if? What if John prepared the way for the Lamb, but this Nazirite generation prepares the way for the Lion? What if we are a part of this generation? What if the children coming from our wombs are a part of this generation? What if that is why they are not yet on the earth? Maybe, just maybe, you and your children play a vital role in this eternal clarion call of a Nazirite Family. (#whoa #selah).

Going Deeper:

- Put your heart on the altar in order to become the vessel for honor. Journal this process.
- List everything you cannot do or would not have without God. Then rejoice and praise Him that His Spirit dwells within you.
- What are your motives when serving and doing things for others? Search your heart.
- Journal your first reaction to this statement: "Barren wombs make history."
- Will you answer the clarion call to be a Nazirite Family? If so, write a statement of commitment to the Lord for your family and begin exercising your faith to believe for this reality.
- Scriptures to study: 2 Tim. 2:20-21; 2 Thess. 2:13-14; 1 Thess. 5:23-24; Rev. 19:7-8; 2 Cor. 11:2; Eph. 5:26-27; Lev. 19:2; 1 Pt. 1:13-16, 22-23; Rom. 12:1-2; 1 Cor. 3:9-14; Josh. 3:5; Jer. 17:9; Mt. 15:8, 10-11, 17-20; Is. 6:5-7; Ps. 51:16-17; Ps.139: 23-24; 2 Cor. 12:9; Job 42:2-3, 5-6; 1 Pt. 2:5, 9; Rev. 1:5-6; 1 Sam. 16:7; Ps. 24:3-4; Is. 57:15; Jas. 4:7-10; Mt. 5:8; Mt. 7:22-23; 1 Thess. 3:12-13; Ezek. 44:15-18, 23; Num. 6:1-8; 2 Cor. 6:17-18, 2 Cor. 7:1; Rev. 2; Rev. 3; Judg. 13; 1 Sam. 2:12, 18-19, 26, 1 Sam. 3:1; Mal. 2:5-9; Mal. 3:1-4; Lk. 1:15-17; Mal. 4:5-6; Mt. 17:11-12.

STAGE 3: THE DELIVERY OF THE PLACENTA

The Leaning Bride

> *Who is this **coming up from the wilderness leaning upon her beloved?** Under the apple tree I awakened you [to my love]; There your mother was in labor with you, There she was in labor and gave you birth. (emphasis added) Song of Solomon 8:5, AMP*

> *Who is this one? Look at her now! **She arises out of her desert, clinging to her beloved. When I awakened you under the apple tree, as you were feasting upon me, I awakened your innermost being with the travail of birth** as you longed for more of me. (emphasis added) Song of Songs 8:5, TPT*

#sighofrelief: The after-effects of giving birth to this precious "baby." Wow. Just as a new mother looks into her baby's eyes in awe and adoration, so do I look into my innermost being and marvel. After all this time of feasting upon Him (the Word), after all this time it's taken to give birth to this book, to give birth to each new identity in Him, to give birth to the previous eight "babies," I have been awakened. I have birthed the most important, lasting, eternal identity yet – The Leaning Bride:

And oh, how beautiful. She is mature, rooted, and deeply grounded in the Truth, bearing an abundance of good fruit. She is not leaning and clinging because she is weary of suffering. She is leaning because she knows that she is her best self and most victorious when she is weak in her humanity; when she leans her weak humanity onto her Beloved. She is clinging to her Beloved in heartsick love and intimacy. She is so fruitful and always pregnant, constantly giving birth to fruit that nurtures and feeds others. She is clinging to her Beloved because she is so overcome by His goodness. She is clinging to her Beloved because she is so at peace and rest. She is leaning on her Beloved because she is hidden in Him, and He is her shield. The leaning, clinging bride is awakened. Oh, how beautiful. (journal entry on January 6, 2021)

#happysigh: I am His mature and spotless bride, heartsick with love for my Beloved. I see Him, and I know Him intimately. I see His beauty and perfection. I see His goodness. I *know* His goodness. I am His leaning bride, clinging to Him unabashedly in love as I rest upon His chest. I am arising from my desert, and I have finally taken the land.

Ever since the chapters The Wilderness and The Promised Land, I have been learning how to defeat the enemies in my land. Whether I have known it or not, every chapter has been related to defeating my enemies, taking possession of the land, and learning how to *dwell* in the land. What is the land? The Kingdom, my inheritance, the promises of God that Jesus made available through His finished work of the cross, specifically, my motherhood.

My journey may have begun contending solely for the Land of Motherhood, but it was soon unveiled to be more about contending for the fullness of Christ in me. This whole chapter proves this, if not this whole book! And, although I don't feel like I have yet fully grasped the completeness of this identity, I do know the closure I feel is because I am officially dwelling in the land with rest all around:

So the Lord gave to Israel all the land of which He had sworn to give to their fathers, and they took possession of it and dwelt in it. **The**

Lord gave them rest all around, according to all that He had sworn to their fathers. And not a man of all their enemies stood against them; the Lord delivered all their enemies into their hand. (emphasis added) Joshua 21:43-44, NKJV

Just like the Israelites, I have taken possession of my land, and I am now dwelling in it. All of my enemies, which have been everything I had gone through and overcome through birthing this book, have been defeated. Because of this, the Lord has given me rest. This is the exact sense of closure I'm experiencing. I am at rest. I have stopped striving. I have ceased contending. I have finished my works and *finally* entered the rest of Jesus, "For he who has entered His rest has himself also ceased from his works as God did from His." (Hebrews 4:10, NKJV) Another way to say it is I am learning to lean my entire humanity on my Beloved:

Let us all come forward and draw near with true (honest and sincere) hearts in unqualified assurance and absolute conviction **engendered by faith (by that leaning of the entire human personality on God in absolute trust and confidence in His power, wisdom, and goodness)**, *having our hearts sprinkled and purified from a guilty (evil) conscience and our bodies cleansed with pure water.* (emphasis added) Hebrews 10:22, AMPC

Moreover, I am His *fruitful* bride because I cling to Him in intimacy. I can't get enough of Him, and He can't get enough of me. Because of this, we are constantly pregnant and giving birth. I know Him, and I keep longing to know Him more! We are intimate, and it never stops! I devour His Word, spend time learning who He is. This is how I know Him intimately. I know His nature, and His nature is encapsulated in His goodness. He really is good! And, I know Him! I *know* His goodness! When we plant His Word in the soil of our hearts, we conceive and bear fruit:

*"**The sower sows the word.** And these are the ones by the wayside where the word is sown. When they hear, Satan comes immediately*

> *and takes away the word that was sown in their hearts. These likewise are the ones sown on stony ground who, when they hear the word, immediately receive it with gladness; and they have no root in themselves, and so endure only for a time. Afterward, when tribulation or persecution arises for the word's sake, immediately they stumble. Now these are the ones sown among thorns; they are the ones who hear the word, and the cares of this world, the deceitfulness of riches, and the desires for other things entering in choke the word, and it becomes unfruitful.* **But these are the ones sown on good ground, those who hear the word, accept it and bear fruit: some thirtyfold, some sixty, and some a hundred."** *(emphasis added)* Mark 4:14-20, NKJV

God is the sower. This passage reveals that His Word can be tossed on the soil of our hearts all day long, but until we receive, or rather, *conceive* the Word, we will not bear fruit. In fact, we cannot truly conceive the Word unless we are intimate by knowing Him, trusting Him, and getting a revelation of His goodness for that specific promise. Once we become a living sacrifice allowing Him to renew our minds on that particular seed, our hearts will soften and make room for the seed. The seed, then, continues to take root and grow. As we meditate and keep getting to know Him, the seed will eventually and continuously bear fruit.

You see, I have discovered that all of the seeds of Truth (His promises) are *wrapped up* in God's goodness. The seed simply cannot mature and bear fruit without being unwrapped. And the unwrapping cannot occur unless we know Him. That is why believers who regularly read their Bibles can go their whole lives and never be transformed into the fullness of Christ nor display the power of His resurrection. Because they have seeds lying dormant on their hearts, seeds that can't go any further because they have never come into the knowledge of God and because they have never settled their hearts on His goodness, this unbelief hardens the heart and becomes like a weed that chokes the Word when it tries to bear fruit.

So, The Leaning Bride knows her Beloved is good. That is why she is clinging to Him; she is clinging to His goodness. Because of this, she bears much fruit in her old age:

> *The righteous shall flourish like a palm tree,* **He shall grow like a cedar in Lebanon.**
> **Those who are planted in the house of the Lord Shall flourish in the courts of our God. They shall still bear fruit in old age; They shall be fresh and flourishing,** *To declare that the Lord is upright; He is my rock, and there is no unrighteousness in Him. (emphasis added)*
> Psalm 92:12-15, NKJV

"He shall grow like a cedar in Lebanon... They shall still bear fruit in old age..." for The Leaning Bride bears fruit *because* she is old, *because* she is mature. She is compared to the ancient cedar of Lebanon, a majestically tall tree that didn't start bearing fruit until the age of 40 (Wikipedia) and then continued to bear fruit in its maturity, going on to live a long, fertile life. Why? Because The Leaning Bride has grown up! She is no longer a young, fresh bride trying to acclimate to her husband. She knows intimately the man she has married and is no longer immature in her knowledge.

In maturity, apostles, prophets, evangelists, pastors, and teachers equip the saints for the work of ministry and edify the body of Christ *until* the body comes to the unity of the faith and the *knowledge of the Son of God to a mature man*, and that measure is the fullness of Christ that we should no longer be children (Ephesians 4:11-14).

The job of the modern-day church is to grow us up! Think about it, siblings fight; young children argue and fight. It isn't until they mature that they begin to get along. The same is true for the body. We can't have true unity with our siblings until we mature. We won't value each other, and we won't see the best in each other until we see each other through mature eyes. Jesus even has answered prayer coming someday – that we will all be one just as He and the Father are one (John 17:11, 22). Not to mention the exhortation that the world will know who we are by our love (John 13:35).

This same concept is true for the way we see and know God. We lack understanding and knowledge of who He is when immature. We question His ways, doubt His good plans for us, and even accuse Him of the direction our lives have taken. But oh, when we mature and come into the knowledge of who He is, we can never go back! And we never want to. *God is good!* This is the foundation of our faith. Until we settle this truth in our hearts, we will lack maturity, thus lacking fruit.

Therefore, The Leaning Bride is mature; she knows her Beloved is good. Her heart is rich, fertile soil, and all the promises have been unwrapped and planted in her heart. Because of this, God is put on display and glorified in her life because she bears much fruit:

> *If you remain in Me and My words remain in you [that is, if we are vitally united and My message lives in your heart], ask whatever you wish and it will be done for you. My Father is glorified and honored by this, when you bear much fruit, and prove yourselves to be My [true] disciples. John 15:7-8, AMP*

The Passion Translation has verse 8, "When your lives bear abundant fruit, you demonstrate that you are my mature disciples who glorify my Father!" Maturity and fruitfulness go hand in hand. We simply cannot bring glory to God without bearing fruit. What is the fruit? The fruit of the Spirit, yes, but also the fruit of righteousness, the fruit of His resurrection power, and the fruit of our good works.

Think about it, when a tree bears fruit, that same tree doesn't partake of its own fruit, does it? No, that fruit feeds and nurtures others and continues to multiply by its seeds. That tree protects and guards others. Thus, so do we:

> *But now I have grown and become a bride, and my love for him has made me a tower of passion and contentment for my beloved.* **I am now a firm wall of protection for others, guarding them from harm.** *This is how he sees me – I am the one who brings him bliss, finding favor in his eyes. (emphasis added) Song of Songs 8:10, TPT*

The New King James reads, "I am a wall, and my breasts like towers," meaning I have a wall of protection for others. With my mature breasts, I become a nurturing life source. The Leaning Bride feeds and serves others with the fruit she bears in her maturity. In fact, it is almost as if she has a food pantry located within her spirit. The irony of this is that a friend and I actually birthed a food pantry in our city during the pandemic (#seriously). Just as this food pantry meets the needs of the city, so does the bride meet the needs of those who come to her. In the same way, The Leaning Bride serves and prepares others with rivers of living water that flow from her innermost being. She is a deep well from which they can partake. And because she believes God is good, she can walk in that goodness full of faith (John 7:38).

If you don't believe you have reached this identity yet, start contending for it. Start with receiving seed. Remember, that is how my whole journey began, this transformation journey, this healing journey, this amazing legacy I get to have on record for generations to come. It began with a seed, "The entirety of Your word is truth…" (Psalm 119:160, NKJV) The Holy Spirit asked me if I believed this. Even though, at the time, I was filled with so much doubt, unbelief, fear, and religion, I said yes and chose to go on this journey with Him. We must continue on together in the same way.

You see, The Leaning Bride is *coming up* out of her wilderness; she is *arising* from her desert. She is in motion, transforming and moving in a certain and specific direction. This is how our Beloved leads. He shepherds us and transforms us until we are a walking advertisement of His glory and His power; until we are His mature bride ready and eager for His return, full of His love and power and about His business on the earth, "…the people who know their God shall be strong, and carry out great exploits." (Daniel 11:32, NKJV)

Going Deeper:

- What enemies do you still need to defeat in your land (i.e., fear, doubt, unbelief, compromise, offense, jealousy, etc.)?
- Have you settled your heart on God's goodness with regard to your motherhood? Over any other promises/seeds (i.e., finances, peace, health, wisdom, joy, etc.)? Why or why not?
- Are you a nurturing life source for others? If not, keep contending for maturity by seeking intimacy and oneness with Jesus.
- Scriptures to study: Song of Songs 8:5; Josh. 21:43-44; Heb. 4:10; Heb. 10:22; Mk. 4:14-20; Ps. 92:12-15; Eph. 4:11-14; Jn. 17:11, 22; Jn. 13:35; Jn. 15:7-8; Song of Songs 8:10; Jn. 7:38; Ps. 119:160; Dan. 11:32.

Chapter twenty-four
A WALKING ADVERTISEMENT

I pray that you will continually experience the immeasurable greatness of God's power made available to you through faith. Then your lives will be an advertisement of this immense power as it works through you! Ephesians 1:19 TPT

I love how Paul summed up this portion of his prayer: "Then your lives will be an advertisement of this immense power as it works through you!" I desire so badly to bring glory to my Beloved. Thankfully, He reminds me often that I am bringing glory to Him by being His leaning bride, and I am in motion, moving forward in His love and power as a fruitful, walking advertisement of His resurrection. I mean, that's what bearing fruit is all about – putting Him on display, bringing Him glory, and making Him famous. In other words – being His witness.

That's beautiful, right? But what does it mean? To answer, let me ask you a question. Do you know Jesus as the Resurrection and the Life? "...I am the resurrection and the life. He who believes in Me, though he may die, he shall live.'" (John 11:25, NKJV) Yes, we know that one day, each of us will partake of a resurrected body. But have you personally experienced the resurrected Jesus? I am not speaking of a vision or a dream or even when the apostles got to see Him before He ascended to heaven. I am speaking of an unveiling, a revealing of Jesus as the resurrection in your own life. If not, then I would suggest that you haven't yet died to your humanity (#sorryouch).

Think about it. There has to be a death before there can be a resurrection. The resurrection is the whole foundation of our Christianity, right? The fact that Jesus defeated death and rose again is why we even worship Him. This truth sets Christianity apart from all other religions. Jesus is actually alive! But it's not enough to believe the truth of this matter; we must *experience* it, we must have the revelation of Him *in us* as the Resurrection and the Life.

We do this by experiencing and understanding the cross, by placing our souls on the altar, suffering with Him, knowing Him in intimacy, and being raised to life in Him. Similar to the apostles, we then become His witnesses, "And with great power the apostles gave witness to the resurrection of the Lord Jesus. And great grace was upon them all." (Acts 4:33, NKJV)

#checkitout: Almost immediately after the ascension of Jesus, the apostles understood that being a witness of the resurrection of Jesus was their primary role. They even cast lots to determine who would take Judas's position in this role, "…one of these must become a witness with us of His resurrection." (Acts 1:22, NKJV). Jesus, Himself, prophesied before He ascended, "But you shall receive power when the Holy Spirit has come upon you; and you shall be witnesses to Me in Jerusalem, and in all Judea and Samaria, and to the end of the earth." (Acts 1:8, NKJV) Furthermore, right after the infilling of the Holy Spirit, Peter stood as a witness and preached on the resurrection of Jesus:

> *…whom* **God raised up…** *"You have made known to me the ways of life; You will make me full of joy in Your presence." Men and brethren, let me speak freely to you of the patriarch David, that he is both dead and buried, and his tomb is with us to this day. Therefore, being a prophet, and knowing that God had sworn with an oath to him that of the fruit of his body, according to the flesh,* **He would raise up the Christ to sit on his throne, he, foreseeing this, spoke concerning the resurrection of the Christ,** *that His soul was not left in Hades,*

nor did His flesh see corruption. ***This Jesus God has raised up, of which we are all witnesses.*** *(emphasis added) Acts 2:24-32, NKJV*

"This Jesus God has raised up, of which we are *all* witnesses." All. We are *all* witnesses of His resurrection, whether we know it or not. Why? Because we have received the power of the Holy Spirit. And who is the Holy Spirit? The Spirit of the resurrected Jesus (#mindblown)! Jesus is alive, sister! He is not some mystical vapor or new age incense. He is a real person, and He is alive inside each one of us who call ourselves believers.

We are witnesses of His resurrection because He resurrects and activates our inner man with His very presence when we put ourselves on the altar, when we fellowship with Him in His sufferings, and when we know Him in intimacy. As our inner man becomes more active, and as we know Him more deeply in intimacy, we begin to experience and release the power of His resurrection, "...that I may know Him and the power of His resurrection, and the fellowship of His sufferings..." (Philippians 3:10, NKJV)

When I first read this passage and saw that we could experience the power of His resurrection, I cried out to the Lord and asked Him to show me how. I mean, let's face it. I am no longer content fellowshipping in His sufferings. I want *all* of Him! I want to know Him as my Resurrection and my Life. I want to spiritually and physically experience the power of His resurrection in every area that is lacking. Resurrection is all about redemption and restoration; it is about bringing life to that which is dead! *He is the Resurrection!* This is what He does because it is the very essence of His nature!

As it turns out, my Beloved in His goodness had already been at work answering this prayer. As I continued to surrender to His leadership (throughout this process), as I finally died to my soul, human logic, and effort (throughout the previous chapter), I realized I was actually sowing more seed. Although it appeared to be a death, I was actually planting for harvest. You see, nothing dies in the Kingdom. Jesus defeated death in all forms. So, even when a loved one dies on earth, he or she is still resurrected in Heaven, complete and whole; not to mention, Jesus will resurrect *all* of our bodies on the day of His return. No believer ever really dies!

#sidenote: What about those who experience grief and tragedy from the loss of loved ones here on earth? Well, there is still a resurrection and restoration available even then! Truly. There is comfort from the Comforter, and as we lean into Him and trust His nature in our brokenness, He will *always* bring good and *always* bring resurrection somehow or someway from any loss we have experienced. He can't help it. It is literally who He is.

With all of that said, I have been experiencing His resurrection life and power in almost every area that went into the ground (#ordied). The harvest is here. I can discern it spiritually, and I can see it tangibly; I am witnessing the glory of God, "Did I not say to you that if you would believe you would see the glory of God?" (John 11:40, NKJV)

This was Jesus' challenge to Martha after she questioned why He wanted to remove the stone from the grave of Lazarus. She was the same person He told previously that He was the resurrection and the life (verse 25). Remember, she agreed that Lazarus would rise again in the final resurrection, but she couldn't grasp that he could be raised at present. Because God never changes, this same principle is true today. If we *believe* Jesus is the resurrection and the life, we will *see* the glory of God in every area of our lives. It is already a done deal (#praisehandemojis).

Furthermore, you know that Spirit who dwells within us? Well, if you haven't gotten the picture just yet, the power He provides is none other than resurrection life, "But if the Spirit of Him who raised Jesus from the dead dwells in you, He who raised Christ from the dead will also give life to your mortal bodies through His Spirit who dwells in you." (Romans 8:11, NKJV)

Resurrection life has been at work since salvation. Salvation occurred because of His work on the cross; transformation occurs because of His resurrection. His Spirit is alive in us, bringing life to all that's dying and to all we let die. That's why Jesus said, "All who seek to live apart from me will lose it all. But those who let go of their lives for my sake and surrender it all to me will discover true life!" (Matthew 10:39, TPT) True life is resurrection life! Resurrection life is the abundant life, "...I have come that they may have life, and that they may have it more abundantly." (John 10:10, NKJV) The abundant life is the polar opposite of death and destruction because it is resurrection life! Resurrection life is alive! Why? Because Jesus is alive!

In a similar fashion, resurrection life is also the rivers of living water I was speaking of in the previous chapter, "He who believes in Me, as the Scripture has said, out of his heart will flow rivers of living water." (John 7:38, NKJV) What is living water? Water that is moving, active, and *alive*! If we believe in Jesus in His entirety, not solely as our Savior who died on the cross but also as our resurrected Lord dwelling within, we will have deep wells of living water overflowing from our innermost being. In other words, we will have deep wells of refreshing, resurrection life flowing effortlessly from our lips. Why from our lips? Because this is how we release His resurrection life into our own lives and to others.

The Spirit confirmed this when He said to me one day in prayer, "Mandi, resurrection life is in your command." Obviously, scripture backs this up with multiple examples like God using His voice to create/resurrect the world, Jesus resurrecting Lazarus from the dead, Jesus telling His disciples to speak to the mountain, Jesus healing the sick, etc. In fact, when I was writing a previous chapter about the decree, I was actually explaining this same principle of releasing resurrection life. I knew the power was there, even then, but I didn't have the power source fully unveiled just yet. Now I do. Resurrection life is the source of God's power working in us and through us.

And actually, this is really nothing new. God has been breathing His resurrection life into man since the beginning of time, "then the Lord God formed [that is, created the body of] man from the dust of the ground, and breathed into his nostrils the breath of life; and the man became a living being [an individual complete in body and spirit]." (Genesis 2:7, AMP) Another account is when God used Ezekiel to prophesy resurrection life to the army of dry bones:

> *Again He said to me, "Prophesy to these bones, and say to them, 'O dry bones, hear the word of the Lord! Thus says the Lord God to these bones: 'Surely I will cause breath to enter into you, and you shall live. I will put sinews on you and bring flesh upon you, cover you with skin and put breath in you; and you shall live. Then you shall know that I am the Lord.'... Also He said to me, "Prophesy to the breath, prophesy, son of man, and say to the breath, 'Thus says the Lord God: "Come from the four winds, O breath, and breathe on these slain, that they may live."' So I prophesied as He commanded me, and breath came into them, and they lived, and stood upon their feet, an exceedingly great army. Ezekiel 37:4-10, NKJV*

We *are* a spirit, we *have* a soul, and we *live* in a body. In our truest form, we are a spirit containing resurrection life. Without our spirits, our bodies would simply be flesh and bones, similar to this account in Ezekiel. Our true self is our spirit man, which became one with Jesus at Salvation. We were born again, resurrected, and made into a new creation. That's why salvation is called the new birth or being born again. Our spirit, our true self, was literally resurrected from the dead (#thenewman). Once we received the power of the Holy Spirit, He then began leading us through the process of sanctification in our souls. Remember, this transformation occurs by placing ourselves on the altar (#dying) and being transformed (#resurrected) in our minds through intimacy (Romans 12:1-3).

So then, a witness to the resurrection could also be equated with walking in a renewed and transformed mind with our faith working and active, thus displaying the perfect will of God by the fruitful manifestation in the natural realm. In other words, a walking advertisement.

#holdup: For those of you that need a simplified version or "formula," be of good cheer. I got you covered! Remember, there is no perfect formula to receive what Jesus made available. However, there are basic trends and principles in common with every believer on a similar journey. The reason we can't depend on another's formula or process is that we are each unique and have our own intimate relationships with Jesus. This is the way He likes it, which is evidenced in the gospels.

With that said, let us recall that all of God's promises are wrapped up in His goodness. We can't unwrap them into our hearts without knowing this truth, and we can't know this truth without knowing *Him*:

THE WORD +	MY BELIEF =	CONCEPTION =	FRUIT
The Truth; the promises Jesus made available for us through His finished work (of the cross and resurrection); the seed	My heart response after being renewed in my mind; my agreement and alignment; my confidence and trust which is transformed through intimacy and knowing His goodness	Faith becomes activated because I receive the Word sown in my heart; the Holy Spirit bears witness with my spirit from meditation of the Word and anchored hope in His goodness	Effortless manifestation of resurrection life and power to the physical/natural realms; a witness of the resurrection; harvest; a walking advertisement

THE WORD + MY BELIEF = CONCEPTION = FRUIT

#selah: Wow, so there we have it— the keys to being a witness of His resurrection and A Walking Advertisement of His resurrection power. However, I have to be real with you. There is a big difference between knowing something (even through revelation) and consistently seeing it physically manifest. I had all of the keys, you see. We were even seeing a major harvest in the area of our finances, things we prayed for and believed for supernaturally occurring. But, there still seemed to be a dam blocking the resurrection power from being released in me and through me on a consistent basis.

For example, I wasn't able to write or articulate what was being revealed, I still wasn't getting pregnant, and I began to experience the opposite of resurrection life within my body. I even began to experience sickness. Remember how I had decreed and received perfect cycles of 28-30 days with no spotting? Well, my cycles again turned wonky. I began to have weird spotting and insomnia. I began to have chronic sinus infections and colds (#saywhat). I know, right? Like, wasn't I healed from these already? How can these things come back when I was walking in faith more than ever before? When I was walking in intimacy with the Holy Spirit more than ever before? What's even worse is that I also began to have anxiety and panic attacks! Um yeah, talk about confusing!

But you know what? I now have revelatory answers to these questions because I didn't give up. I didn't quit or let my circumstances change my mind. I kept contending for what I knew to be true and for what I knew Jesus provided for me. Although my body was showing signs of regression, I knew in my heart that I was right on the cusp of a breakthrough. In fact, I think the enemy saw he was losing his influence over me, so that's why he upped his game with lies and deception. But it didn't work (#nowayjose). I am just way too convinced of God's goodness to believe otherwise. So why was I experiencing regression? Why did the resurrection power seem dammed up? Why did I still *feel* powerless even though I knew I wasn't?

Because I unknowingly became weak in faith.

My active faith became inactive; it literally stopped working because I began to look at my physical body as the evidence of my healing. Truly, I have done this for years, and we can see this mindset in all the previous chapters, wondering why I wasn't physically pregnant, thinking this journey was coming to an end, but *still* not getting the BFP (#bigfatpositive); committing to having faith and belief, then looking to my cycle, symptoms, or checking a HPT for final evidence, etc.

All the above is being weak in faith.

Why, right? I mean, when walking out a healing journey to receive physical healing and pregnancy, it makes perfect sense to look at our bodies as evidence of that healing. This *seems* perfectly logical. However, when walking out said journey in *faith*, scripture is very clear that faith alone is all the evidence we need, "Now faith is the substance of things hoped for, the evidence of things not seen." (Hebrews 11:1, NKJV) So *faith* is my evidence of what I hope for, not my symptoms or what my body is or isn't doing.

Additionally, because I was looking to my body as evidence of healing, I also became weak in faith because I unknowingly replaced that faith with my self-reliance and self-efforts. I asked the questions again, *What am I doing wrong? What am I missing? What am I supposed to do? Why do I feel so powerless?* I, I, I, me, me, me.

There I was, with all that truth and knowledge flowing within me, and it was blocked; the rivers of life and power could not be released no matter how much I was decreeing and speaking life. Until I restudied Paul's account of the faith of Abraham:

> ***And not being weak in faith, he did not consider his own body***, *already dead (since he was about a hundred years old), and the deadness of Sarah's womb. He did not waver at the promise of God through unbelief, but was strengthened in faith, giving glory to God, and being fully convinced that what He had promised He was also able to perform. (emphasis added) Romans 4:19-21, NJKV*

#ahamoment: Abraham did not consider his own body (or Sarah's) because he was not weak in faith. Weak faith considers the physical; inactive faith looks to the natural. Remember, the physical is anything we observe with our carnal/fleshly eyes. When looking at our bodies, bank accounts, or circumstances as evidence of God's healing and provision, faith becomes inactive/weak. Why? Because faith is the evidence of things *unseen*. In other words, faith is a *knowing* and a *receiving* with or without the natural circumstances changing (#boom).

Suddenly I had my lightbulb moment and could see all the ways I was damming up God's life and power. I could see the outline for this chapter, and I could finally see the end in sight! So then, A Walking

Advertisement has strong, active faith because she does not consider the following:

1. The past

Remember, weak faith looks to the physical. So, looking to the past, remembering all those times we thought it was going to happen, or paying attention to the timing of it all, can weaken our faith. Not only do we keep looking ahead in hopeful expectation, but we also come to the understanding that we really aren't *waiting* for anything.

Did you know that? We actually aren't "in the waiting" (#saywhat). Remember, dear sister, Jesus provided our healing and fruitfulness over 2000 years ago! We have His fruitfulness and fertility already in our bodies, not because we have all the equipment, but because we have *His Spirit*.

We are already The Joyful Mothers of children; we are already fruitful vines in the heart of our homes; we are already Mommies; we are already "fertile myrtles." Already! Because this is who Jesus already made us to be! This is the provision He already gave to us! It is already ours within our true selves – our spirits which are one with Jesus.

We don't look to the past. We don't consider the timing. We don't look through the lens of waiting for physical manifestation. If we do that, we are considering our bodies as the evidence of truth versus the Word of God and what Jesus already made available. Moreover, our faith becomes inactive because we automatically begin to waver and doubt. Why? Because we may not see any results! And if we are looking at those physical results as evidence that what we are praying is working, then wavering and unbelief will come.

Thus, we continue this vicious cycle of waiting and waiting for something to happen in the physical, not really knowing that our faith is inactive and the power is blocked from being released. Why? Because we have considered our body as evidence, thus entering into unbelief and weak faith. In fact, this revelation probably answers the question of why so many of us have had such extended seasons of barrenness even though we've thought we were in faith (#nocondemnation).

The solution? Let's look at what Abraham did, "And not being weak in faith, he did not consider his own body... he did not waver at the promise of God through unbelief, but was strengthened in faith...being fully convinced that what He had promised He was also able to perform." (Romans 4:19-21, NKJV) Faith is the evidence of things unseen, right? Strong faith is being fully convinced in what the Word has promised; active faith is being fully convinced of what Jesus made available through His finished work of the cross and resurrection.

Faith that produces results has nothing to do with what is seen, so it has nothing to do with our past, how long it's taken, the timing, and our physical bodies. In fact, the timing becomes a nonissue; the physical body becomes a nonissue. We keep our attention on Jesus and consider only what He already provided over 2,000 years ago.

2. The cares of this world

Now these are the ones sown among thorns; they are the ones who hear the word, and the cares of this world, the deceitfulness of riches, and the desires for other things entering in choke the word, and it becomes unfruitful. Mark 4:18-19, NKJV

A Walking Advertisement is strong in faith because she does not consider the cares of this world. Why? Because just as Jesus stated in this parable, worries can choke the Word and cause it to become unfruitful. If the Word is a seed unwrapped and planted within our heart, then it can't bear fruit if we are too distracted with the world and everything going on in it. Yes, I am speaking of the obvious distractions of the news, media, and social media. But I am also speaking of simply being too busy or distracted serving and caring for everybody else.

Wow, another contradiction, right? Like, aren't we supposed to spend our time serving others and investing in other people's lives? Isn't that the good "Christian" thing to do? Yes and no; it depends on the motives of the heart, the reasons for serving, and the seasons of life.

In my case, I began to almost become a "busybody." Why? Because my physical pregnancy just wasn't happening. I felt the need to fill up my time with good deeds, almost forcing my life to matter and mean something. Yikes, that was really difficult to admit, but it's the truth, and I am nothing if not honest and transparent.

You see, because I was looking to the physical and to what my body was or wasn't doing, I felt I was simply "waiting" for manifestation. In the meantime, and out of frustration, I filled up my time thinking of and serving everybody else when that was not at all what the Holy Spirit was leading me to do. Once I slowed down enough to listen, He revealed to me how all these cares and thoughts of others were choking the Word from bearing fruit. He revealed to me that even though it felt wrong or sounded wrong, I actually wasn't supposed to be serving all of these people. Instead, for this season, I was to be focused on aggressively receiving my primary call and assignment in life – motherhood; not just the son of my heart, but of the many children He has promised to me. He wanted me to aggressively receive for *me* what my pastor calls "sanctified selfishness."

I felt the Spirit keep asking me, "What do you want? What can I do for you?" Was He really telling me to stop worrying about everybody else and receive from Him? Absolutely He was! God is really that kind! It is His good pleasure to give us the desires of our hearts; it is His great joy to extravagantly give. Jesus confirmed this when He walked the earth "…for it is your Father's good pleasure to give you the kingdom." (Luke 12:32, NKJV) It is His good pleasure to give us the kingdom. Well, guess what? His kingdom includes fruitfulness, prosperity, and a big family or whatever it is you want that Jesus has already provided.

But first, we must learn to be good receivers.

If we're too busy running around, sticking our noses in everybody else's business, trying to serve and give to others, or even too involved in what's happening in society, we can't receive from Him; the Word is choked; the resurrection life and power is blocked.

Once I scaled back and planned my schedule to only seek the Lord and what He wanted to give me, a breakthrough came. That dam began to crack, and His life and power began to flow just a little more from within.

3. The facts

A Walking Advertisement is strong in faith because she does not consider the facts. What are the facts? The physical symptoms we see or feel with our five senses, i.e., spotting, the length of our cycle, pain, a negative HPT, test results, etc. In other words, the physical bodies of ourselves and our husbands, what they are doing or not doing. Also included in the facts are the thoughts, emotions, and feelings that derive from these physical realities. Yes, no matter how blaringly loud these physical symptoms and thoughts can become, we must stand strong in faith by not allowing our focus to remain on them.

Trust me; I know this is easier said than done. But it seemed the more I paid attention to my body and the facts of my body, the more my symptoms worsened both body and soul. Why? Because my physical body was what I was considering and focusing on. My physical body had my meditation, not the finished works of Jesus. My physical symptoms had my trust, not Jesus and what He has already given to me in my spirit man (#readthatagain).

Of course, my faith would become inactive! Of course, my faith would weaken! I began to place more emphasis on the natural realm than what is true in the spirit realm. And, because I was choosing to live carnally minded, it put me right back on the devil's playing field. I became deceived, tossed by the wind of my symptoms and what was happening and not happening in my body. What happens when we are no longer stable and rooted in what is true? Double mindedness, which leads to doubt and unbelief:

> *...for the one who doubts is like a billowing surge of the sea that is blown about and tossed by the wind. For such a person ought not to think or expect that he will receive anything [at all] from the Lord, being a double-minded man, unstable and restless in all his ways [in everything he thinks, feels, or decides]. James 1:6-8, AMP*

#yikes: So there I was, knowing that I needed to be a good receiver, but realizing I wouldn't be able to receive any of the provisions made available because I was double-minded. Why was I double minded? Because I was back to considering the facts. I was back to looking at my physical body. I was back to believing the lie that the BFP (#bigfatpositive) was the sole evidence of my fruitfulness (#morelikebigfatlie).

In fact, I can see now when it happened. I can vividly recall how I spiraled into the natural realm after another close person to me popped up pregnant at the exact same time I experienced a false alarm. I immediately succumbed to the lie that because she got the BFP and I didn't, that I was less-than and failing at this whole faith thing. Really? I was *still* struggling with this? Obviously, the Holy Spirit revealed to me that I had unknowingly put the BFP on a pedestal as proof of my fruitfulness.

So, when this person's baby was born, I grieved, more so than I had with any other friend or family member's birth. Why did this pregnancy and this baby hit me worse than all the others? Because my faith was entirely in the facts; my trust was in the physical outcome. And, because she was the one bringing home the baby, I believed the lie that she was better than me. Goodness, right? You'd think I would be past all of these thoughts and emotions. Technically, I was. But, because I considered the facts as the sole evidence of my faith in action, I regressed into double-mindedness and unbelief.

Trust me; I felt crazy. I couldn't believe I was fighting off some of the same lies and emotions I dealt with years ago. It was deeply disappointing. But as I grieved, it also felt different. It was almost as if I was grieving the loss of a mindset versus the grief of self-pity. And because I noticed this change and sought the Lord, He revealed to me that some giant weeds were being uprooted and *violently* yanked from my heart; weeds that had been choking the Word from bearing fruit for many, many years.

So, there He was, that amazing Teacher of ours, showing me His goodness in the midst of my disappointment and deception. Those monster weeds had to go! The weeds of putting the physical facts above the truth, of believing the best for everyone else and not receiving the best for me, of considering and focusing on the natural realm as evidence of healing, of idolizing the physical results of the BFP and the baby, and thinking that because I didn't have the physical results, I was less-than.

Well, I am happy to say that those weeds are officially gone! My doubting and double mindedness are gone. I became stable and deeply rooted in this truth: *the facts can change, but the truth cannot*. And shortly thereafter, I had another experience in which to practice this new way of operating in faith.

#storytime: Percy, my pug, came to us as a breeder release with only one good eye. One day, when he woke up, I noticed his good eye was swollen and squinty like he was in pain. I took him to the vet who diagnosed him with glaucoma, which is a death sentence to a dog's sight. He was a two-year-old, active, playful pug, and it was my worst nightmare for this little guy to lose his sight at such a young age. I kept having flashbacks of my old pug, Pollie, and how different she became when she lost her sight. To put it bluntly, I basically flipped a lid. My emotions were inconsolable. But I sought the Lord. He gave me the passage of Psalm 27:13, told me to keep speaking life and that I would see the goodness of the Lord in the land of the living.

My emotions remained a wreck, Percy's eye was getting worse, and I didn't trust this new vet, but I kept speaking life to his eye even in the midst of the snot and tears. I chose to obey and trust God even though my emotions and Percy's symptoms were screaming the opposite. Because I was standing on healing, I sought another opinion, found an animal eye doctor who didn't see *any* glaucoma, and diagnosed Percy with a simple eye ulcer that was perfectly treatable. I continued to speak life, and Percy's eye was completely restored!

So, what happened here? Well, after asking the Lord the same thing, He revealed to me that my emotions were indeed reacting off the physical facts. But my heart chose to trust in the rhema word God gave me and trust in the truth, which was remembering the authority I carried in my spirit man. I didn't have to accept the facts; I had another option. I could speak life and see the goodness of the Lord in the land of the living, which is what He promised me over this scenario (#andidid).

Thus, I discovered another valuable lesson in living a life of strong faith. Even if the facts are loud and even if our emotions react to those facts, we still don't have to consider them as the final outcome or truth of the scenario. It all comes back to the heart, and my heart belongs to Jesus. I love this passage, "The Lord is my strength and my shield; my heart trusted in Him, and I am helped…" (Psalm 28:7, NKJV) My heart believes in *Him*. What He has provided for me through His finished works is where I place my trust no matter how loud the facts are. I live and breathe His Words and His truth alone.

#speaking of: Practically, this is where the benefits of fasting can come into play. If you find that your physical body runs the show in your life, then let that be a good indicator you probably need to fast. Why? Because fasting trains your body to depend solely on the Word of God. Fasting is, in fact, the quickest way to crucify our carnal mindedness. It kills the patterns of the old man, it accelerates our transformation, and it breaks off doubt and unbelief, especially the kind we experience through our five senses. We can see this in the following passage:

> *"Lord, have mercy on my son, for he is an epileptic and suffers severely; for he often falls into the fire and often into the water. So I brought him to Your disciples, but they could not cure him."… Then the disciples came to Jesus privately and said, "Why could we not cast it out?" So Jesus said to them,* **"Because of your unbelief;** *for assuredly, I say to you, if you have faith as a mustard seed, you will say to this mountain, 'Move from here to there,' and it will move; and nothing will be impossible for you. However,* **this kind does not go out except by prayer and fasting."** *(emphasis added)*
> Matthew 17:15, 16, 19-21, NKJV

"This kind," meaning *this kind of unbelief,* does not go out except by prayer and fasting. Most likely, the disciples were intimidated by what they were seeing in the natural. Think about it. A demon was violently tormenting this little boy, throwing him in the fire and trying to drown him. Another account mentions he was foaming at the mouth and covered in bruises. I'm sure what they were witnessing was horrific, and they exhibited a normal, human response. However, they were no longer mere humans, just as we are no longer mere humans.

When we fast, and our bodies scream at us in ravenous hunger, by refusing to feed our bodies when they demand it, we are training them to submit. By denying them food, we retrain our bodies to remember that it's not the one in control. My body does not live off of bread alone, but by every Word that proceeds from the mouth of God (Matthew 4:4). My body does not call the shots. It is, in fact, the weakest link and has no choice but to respond and obey what I tell it. Even if it doesn't respond right away, I still refuse to consider the facts and give them my meditation. I consider only Jesus, and my faith remains strong.

4. Her self-efforts

For they did not gain possession of the land by their own sword, Nor did their own arm save them; But it was Your right hand, Your arm, and the light of Your countenance, Because You favored them. Psalm 44:3, NKJV

A Walking Advertisement is strong in faith because she does not consider her self-efforts. She does not strive; she does not try; she does not *do* anything in her own strength. She leans solely on her Beloved, on the finished works of Jesus, on the Holy Spirit within, and on God's favor that surrounds her as a shield (Psalm 5:12).

It is simply not about me. I don't have to *do* a darn thing in order to have my children; I don't. It is not about my self-efforts! It is not about my works or my words or the decree or how many times I pray or declare. It is not about my tone of voice or whether I speak to my body in boldness or through tears of pain. It is not about how confident I feel for one day or how weak I feel the next. It is not about whether or not I see results from my commands right away or after a month. What I do or don't do, what I see or don't see, proves absolutely nothing.

It all comes back to receiving.

Receiving the fullness of the gift of Jesus is all that's "required." Encompassed in this Gift is *all* we need and *all* we desire. Because God is really that good, He is really that kind, He really does have good plans in store for us and desires that we live the abundant life here on earth. What do we have to do to access these desires? Receive! It's really that simple. And yet, it can take time to overcome self-effort and pride that hinders us from doing so (#ouch).

That's the purpose of the transformation and renewal of our minds. The souls on the altar as a living sacrifice, the dying to self, the purging and refining, it *all* occurs so we can simply receive, so our hearts have *room* to receive and are no longer divided, so the mixture of self-righteousness and self-reliance is burned away to where all that's left is a pure heart, singularly focused on Jesus and fully receiving from His Spirit.

In fact, I have learned that the highest form of both worship *and* faith is to receive the fullness of Jesus, to receive absolutely everything He paid the highest price for. Yet again, because it is so simple and requires zero effort on our part, we struggle in our prideful humanity to receive. We choose the hard way of self-effort, striving, earning, trusting in our logic and opinions versus resting in what Jesus has already given.

All we have to do is receive!

All we have to do is lower ourselves before Him. It is a humble heart that receives the simplicity of the gospel of good news; it is a humble heart that receives the Gift of His undeserved, unearned grace and favor. It is childlike faith and humility that responds with, "Nothing is impossible with God, so let it be to me according to Your Word. Yes, nothing is impossible, even the all-encompassing-super-abundance-double-portion-more-than-all-I've-ever-asked-for-or-imagined-restoration. Yes, even the overflowing, overwhelming fruitfulness! Yes, to all of it! I receive it all. Every undeserved, unmerited bit of Your favor and grace. *You* made me worthy of it, Beloved. *Your* precious blood paid the price. To honor and worship *You* in thanksgiving, I open my heart to humbly receive it *all*."

#whatnext: There is then a release in the spirit realm. The resurrection life and power are free to flow within us and through us. We begin to walk in our true self, our spirit man, because we rely solely on the Spirit and not on our humanity. We partner our faith and expectation with the finished works of Jesus. We know His Spirit is the power source, and He has given us the authority to release that power. We know that the authority isn't in the tone of voice, but it's in the humility of receiving what's been given. We know that as we speak in His authority, it is His Spirit that goes to work on the outcome. And once we speak, we get to keep our eyes on Jesus – the Way, the Truth, the Door. We don't have to look at the outcome or worry about the outcome. Jesus provided what we are commanding, and we believe in Jesus. The Spirit has to respond and glorify Him, thus bringing glory to the Father, "And whatever you ask in My name, that I will do, that the Father may be glorified in the Son." (John 14:13, NKJV).

#practicallyspeaking: When I command a symptom to leave or when I command the outcome I want in my body (or someone else's), I trust the Holy Spirit to go to work bringing about what I have spoken, "…He who raised Christ from the dead will also give life to your mortal bodies through His Spirit who dwells in you." (Romans 8:11, NKJV) If the symptom doesn't leave right away or if thoughts of doubt try knocking on my door, I ignore them and say, "it's not my problem." Why? Because it's not! Jesus took care of what I am commanding, so I trust His Spirit to bring it to pass.

Remember, Jesus took all sickness and all disease on His body over 2,000 years ago. And His Spirit takes care of it now! The Holy Spirit provides the working power we have available within us when our faith is activated. Jesus is the Door, the access to the Kingdom here on earth. The more we lean on and depend upon Jesus, the more the Spirit can go to work. So, when I command what I want, I believe I have received what I have spoken. This is my posture, and I am sticking to it:

> *For assuredly, I say to you, whoever says to this mountain, 'Be removed and be cast into the sea,' and does not doubt in his heart, but believes that those things he says will be done, he will have whatever*

> *he says. Therefore I say to you, whatever things you ask when you pray, believe that you receive them, and you will have them.*
> *Mark 11:23-24, NKJV*

Does this mean I have stronger faith than others? No. In fact, those who walk in great favor, authority, and power don't necessarily have the strongest faith. They are simply the strongest receivers. They have allowed the renewing of their minds to transform their belief system into the fullness of receiving, into the fullness of trusting God. Because they know Him intimately, they can fully trust Him. Because they know Him intimately, they know who they are in Him – His witness.

Remember, that's why we put ourselves on the altar, to burn away all the mixture of self to the gold within. The altar helps us to receive. The transformation changes us from doers to receivers, from self-effort and works to rest and receiving, from sitting on the sidelines in exhaustion to joyfully becoming A Walking Advertisement of His resurrection power and life.

It really is that simple. And it works, y'all! I am walking in it. Resurrection life and power are beginning to flow in me and through me on a more consistent basis, and this section is the reason why. Healing in my body and healing in others is occurring more regularly. Why? Because I do not depend on myself, but I depend on God alone, I am receiving and releasing what *He* has put inside of me. It is *His* power and *His* authority I am releasing, all because I can fully believe and receive:

> *And these signs will follow those who believe: In My name they will cast out demons; they will speak with new tongues; they will take up serpents; and if they drink anything deadly, it will by no means hurt them; they will lay hands on the sick, and they will recover. Mark 16:17-18, NKJV*

We don't have to scream, yell, work, and strive when we command what we want. We just tell the mountain/obstacle to be removed and then speak life. And really, there is no right or wrong way to *do* any of this. There is no *doing* at all! We simply believe in Jesus and receive all He has provided as *His Spirit* does the work to bring it into the natural.

5. The limits

Lastly, A Walking Advertisement is strong in faith because she does not consider the limits. She does not consider her body's limitations. She does not consider how she thinks it all should look in her finite mind. She does not put God in a box. She does not limit His redemption by placing small expectations on the outcome. She does, in fact, dream big, she prays big, she hopes big, and she expects big.

In case you didn't realize it yet, dear sister, the babies are coming. And, they are coming with interest. Reward and honor are attached to this outcome because that is simply who God is. It is simply the way He does things, "...before honor is humility." (Proverbs 18:12, NKJV) And, "By humility and the fear of the Lord are riches and honor and life." (Proverbs 22:4, NKJV) A humble heart receives honor; a humble heart receives attention; a humble heart receives double:

> *Instead of your shame you shall have double honor, And instead of confusion they shall rejoice in their portion. Therefore in their land they shall possess double; Everlasting joy shall be theirs.*
> *Isaiah 61:7, NKJV*

A Walking Advertisement takes off the limits and surrenders to God's seven-fold restoration (Proverbs 6:31, Joel 2:25), she surrenders to God's twice-as-much-as-before-restoration (Job 42:10), she surrenders to the more-than-all-we-can-ask-for-or-imagine-restoration (Ephesians 3:20), and she prepares for it:

> *"For more are the children of the desolate Than the children of the married woman," says the Lord. "Enlarge the place of your tent, And let them stretch out the curtains of your dwellings; Do not spare; Lengthen your cords, And strengthen your stakes. For you shall expand to the right and to the left, And your descendants will inherit the nations, And make the desolate cities inhabited." Isaiah 54:2-3, NKJV*

This means we must take off the limits, make room, and *prepare for the more*. Likewise, if we haven't yet dealt with the fear of man, the fear of success, and the fear of notoriety, now is the time to do so. Remember, we have a story to tell, a testimony of the goodness and faithfulness of God. The babies we birth are not typical babies; they are not just another life here on earth to strive for the failing American Dream; they have a double mandate to prepare the way for the Lord's return and to reveal God's goodness from the womb to their grave. As their mothers, we cannot stay silent nor limit the amount of influence and attention He desires to bring to the fruit we bear.

With that said, we must also remember that bearing fruit is messy. Childbirth is messy. Here at the end of this journey, it's important to remember that we are still human. When imagining and dreaming about the manifestation of our family, it is so very easy to glamourize and fantasize the whole outcome. But, when it comes right down to it, family is simply messy. It always has been, and it always will be.

In fact, *everything* about humanity is messy, right? So, we must remove any unrealistic, rose-colored expectations we have put into place. For example, here at the end, I always imagined that my husband, my son, and I would be in faith at the same time, in perfect unity. We are not. Our son won't even talk about future siblings, and my husband is slowly but surely catching up with me, but not quite fast enough. We are not in perfect unity. We are not doing the "good Christian thing" and praying together as a family anymore (#beingreal). It is not where I expected to be, and it has been very disappointing at times.

But yet, the manifestation of these babies is still happening no matter what! Because it is not up to us; it is not dependent upon our religious traditions; it is not dependent upon our strengths or weaknesses; it is not dependent upon our perfect emotions. Time and time again, God has revealed His glorious way of entering into the utter mess and stink of humanity to bring life. He joyfully enters our mess and brings to life that which is dead and ugly; He loves it! He loves our humanity! He loves that we need Him!

Once I laid down those limits and expectations, I could finally see that this is what He's done for me, and in His kindness, He even gave me a dream to prove it. In the dream, I was watching myself, like an out-of-body experience. I noticed this shiny, dark, brown substance swirling around me. It was alive and beautiful. I watched as it broke into two separate substances, and each one entered my womb from both sides of my body at the same time.

When I woke up, I knew I had witnessed Romans 8:11 in action, "But if the Spirit of Him who raised Jesus from the dead dwells in you, He who raised Christ from the dead will also give life to your mortal bodies through His Spirit who dwells in you." I got to see the Spirit joining with my humanity and bringing life. The brown substance was earthy yet ethereal. It was a mixture of both the Spirit and my mortal body; it was resurrection life in action.

And friend, there was *nothing* ugly about it, just as there is nothing ugly about being in a place of weakness or chaos and still seeing the plans of God unfold. All you have to do is take off the limits and fully receive what He's already made available. There is no hindrance or limits to God's goodness other than what we place upon Him (#selah).

So, friend, may you walk perfectly imperfect as A Walking Advertisement of God's glory and power. May you freely receive all He has written for your life here on earth, starting with His love, grace, and goodness for you and your family. And may you, too, step into your identity as the Fruitful Bride of Christ and The Joyful Mother of Children in which you truly are.

Going Deeper:

- Have you received the revelation of Jesus in you as the Resurrection and the Life? Why or why not?
- Journal your thoughts on this statement: We are a spirit, we have a soul, and we live in a body. How can this truth change the way you walk in life?
- Are there any circumstances where you have become weak in faith? i.e., Are you looking to the physical realm as evidence of your healing and/or provision? Journal
- Journal your thoughts on this statement: We actually aren't in the waiting.
- Are there any changes you need to make in your life in order to "aggressively receive"? Journal and then answer God's question He is asking you, "What do you want? What can I do for you?"
- Journal your thoughts on this statement: The facts can change, but the truth cannot.
- Do you feel like you have received the fullness of the Gift of Jesus and all He purchased for you? Why or why not?
- Search your heart. Are you still striving and in self-effort? If so, place yourself back on the altar until all is burned away to the gold within – Christ in you.
- Are you prepared for the more that is coming with the birth of your children? Or do you still have limits in place?
- If you haven't already, lay down any fear of man, fear of success/notoriety, and/or any religious expectations you have placed on the outcome of the birth of your children.
- Meditate on this statement: There is no hindrance or limits to God's goodness other than what we place upon Him. Repent for putting any limits on God.
- Write a statement of faith to receive God's goodness and fullness He has planned for your family. You don't have to understand it; you just have to believe and receive, thus transforming into A Walking Advertisement of His power.

- Scriptures to study: Eph. 1:19; Jn.11:25; Acts 4:33, 1:22; 1:8, 2:24-32; Phil.3:10-11; Jn. 11:40; Rom. 8:11; Mt. 10:39; Jn. 10:10; Jn. 7:38; Gen. 2:7; Ezek. 37:4-10; Rom. 12:1-3; Heb. 11:1; Rom. 4:19-21; Mk. 4:18-19; Lk.12:32; Jas. 1:6-8; Ps.27:13; Ps. 28:7; Mt. 17:15-16, 19-21; Mt. 4:4; Ps. 44:3; Ps. 5:12; Jn. 14:13; Mk. 11:23-24; Mk. 16:17-18; Prov. 18:12; Prov. 22:4; Is. 61:7; Prov. 6:31; Joel 2:25; Job 42:10; Eph. 3:20; Is. 54:2-3.

The Capstone

#CLOSURE

Throughout this seven-year journey, I became resigned to the fact that God was doing something in me far more eternal than natural motherhood. You can see it all throughout this process. It was never solely about my motherhood here on earth. It was always about my identity in Christ. And my journey to motherhood just so happened to put me in the ideal circumstances of desire and desperation to seek God, to know Him, and to discover who I am in Him. Would I have sought Him this intently otherwise? I don't know. All I know is that conceiving my husband's child was the greatest hunger of my heart and the one thing I didn't yet have. The lack of it drove me to my knees, to the altar, and to His Word

So then, I write this with tears in my eyes as I look back and marvel. I marvel at His good leadership, His patience, and His kindness. I am in awe of what He has revealed to me and of the intimacy I now have with Him. I am in awe of His faithfulness to never give up on me and the way He never let me give up on Him and His promises. I am in awe of the way He transformed me and built me into a completely new person. Truly, I marvel and I weep. This has been the most difficult yet rewarding process of my life. But it has often felt like it would never end with the feeling of "closure" always just out of reach.

Until now. The closure is here. How do I know? Because the blueprints have come to an end and the house is finally complete. Yes, you read that right, the blueprints and the house are finished.

Just like this entire journey, my process has always been two-fold, both natural and spiritual. I came to understand and accept that the truths written in this book create blueprints; *natural* blueprints, in fact. They act as a how-to in transitioning The Barren Woman to The Joyful Mother of children, thus building her dream home, which is a house full of children, "God nests the once barren woman at home – now a joyful mother with children!" (Psalm 113:9, CEB) "Your wife shall be like a fruitful vine in the very heart of your house, your children like olive plants all around your table." (Psalm 128:3, NKJV) This should come as no surprise considering I knew going into this book that I was to tell my story and share *my* process in becoming The Joyful Mother of Children.

However, I eventually discovered that these same blueprints were also God's way of spiritually building *me* into *His* dream home:

> *"Come, I will show you the bride, the Lamb's wife." And he carried me away in the Spirit to a great and high mountain, and showed me the great city, the holy Jerusalem, descending out of heaven from God, having the glory of God. Revelation 21:9b-11, NKJV*

Yes, the Lamb's wife, the bride of Christ, is the great city, the holy Jerusalem. Why is she a city? Because she is a whole multitude of dwelling places! Remember, we are vessels for honor, we are His temple, and we are His home, "Jesus answered and said to him, 'If anyone loves Me, he will keep My word; and My Father will love him, and We will come to him and make Our home with him.'" (John 14:23, NKJV)

This has been God's heart from the beginning – to dwell in intimacy with man. He communed with Adam and Eve in the garden and He will one day dwell with us physically in the New Jerusalem. Spiritually, though, we already *have* this reality! The author of Hebrews wrote, "But you have come to Mount Zion and to the city of the living God, the heavenly Jerusalem…" (Hebrews 12:22). Spiritually, we are already in the city of the living God. This is why we are already seated in heavenly places with Christ (Ephesians 2:6).

All of us have received the Holy Spirit when we were born again. But remember, salvation is just the beginning; confessing Jesus is just the door. The whole purpose of our earthly lives is to die to ourselves and allow His Spirit to take up *complete* residence from the inside out. He goes to work, in fact, building His dream home within us through sanctification. The more we are sanctified and transformed by the renewing of the mind, the more we make room for the Spirit. The more we make room for the Spirit, the more mature and complete we become. The more mature and complete, the more we can steadily house His Presence, thus walking consistently in His glory and power to bring heaven to earth. Remember, all that Jesus is, so are we in this world (1 John 4:17). We don't have to wait until the next age; we can have His fullness *now*! We can live as His bride in intimacy with Him *now*!

So throughout the process, this is what He has ultimately built in me – His dream home, His house of glory, His mature bride. I haven't consistently produced the fruit of this identity, no, but I am closer than ever before! And really, gaining revelation and understanding of this spiritual reality is half the battle. For this assignment and for this journey, though, I have at long last attained a measure of closure.

You see, Jesus is a good Contractor. He doesn't just start jobs to never complete them. He is the Author *and* the Finisher; the Beginning *and* the End. But because this journey to motherhood became so increasingly extended, I couldn't *see* how it would ever come to a close. Yes, I could see it by dreaming and imagining, but I never felt fully released to experience the closure myself. Thankfully, God in His good leadership, let me witness the outcome through a friend's manifestation into motherhood.

#storytime: This friend is so precious to me; truly a Godsend. We have been friends since kindergarten and have always stayed close. After Christy married her wonderful husband they began trying to start their family. They tried on their own for a while and then attempted all the various fertility methods to no avail. Additionally, she was sick with diabetes, high blood pressure, PCOS and estrogen deficiency. But mostly, she was sick of soul and had partnered with the lies and the identity of The Barren Woman. She and her husband eventually gave up on ever having their own children until fourteen years later... when the Holy Spirit awakened in them the call to an unfulfilled assignment (#parenthood).

Right around this time on Christy's journey I formed a peer review group for this very book. Christy was one of the peers invited to pre-read it and something began transforming in her heart. As she got a hold of the foundational verse, "The entirety of Your word is truth" (Psalm 119:160), a seed was sown. As she continued reading and opening her heart to the Holy Spirit's leading, this seed was watered, her hope was resurrected, and her faith was strengthened. Likewise, she and her husband discerned something prophetically significant was happening so they said "yes" to the clarion call of the Nazarite Family. Then, within just a year's time, she accelerated through the exact same transformation in which I've written about all throughout this book. As she surrendered so beautifully to her sanctification, the Holy Spirit actually gave her the solution to the end of this process. It was a solution that I had not yet received; almost like I was blinded to it (#thankGodforthebody).

The solution? Knowing intimately Jesus, the Finisher:

> ..."*Not by might nor by power, but by My Spirit,*" *Says the Lord of hosts.* "*Who are you, O great mountain? Before Zerubbabel you shall become a plain! And he shall bring forth the capstone With shouts of 'Grace, grace to it!' Moreover the word of the Lord came to me, saying:* "*The hands of Zerubbabel Have laid the foundation of this temple; His hands shall also finish it. Then you will know That the Lord of hosts has sent Me to you.*" *Zechariah 4:6-9, NKJV*

Prior to Christy's revelation, I had been meditating on this passage for many months. In studying, I learned that the capstone, the finishing stone, was the last stone placed on various ancient Hebrew structures. In this passage, the structure is Zerubbabel's temple, the second temple in

Jewish history (with Solomon's being the first). I couldn't figure out why the Spirit led me here until it became fully clear that I had written transitional blueprints for The Joyful Mother of children *and* that something had been built: a completed temple; His dream home.

Likewise, Christy's revelation of Jesus, the Finisher made this passage even more clear. You see, Jesus completes what He starts. When He builds, He builds to fullness and completion; meaning from the spirit to the natural. Christy received this revelation and began walking in it.

She changed her prayers of asking and decreeing to prayers of thanksgiving for completing the work He began. Like Zerubbabel, who came with the finishing stone shouting, "Grace, grace!" Christy changed her songs of contention to songs of praise and deliverance; to songs of rejoicing in the goodness, grace, and favor of the Lord. To strengthen this revelation, God even gave her multiple confirmations through dreams and prophetic words.

As I watched this unfold, I finally had to admit that I just wasn't there yet. I couldn't be; not when my book was still so open-ended, lacking closure. As I observed her capstone faith in action, I had to ultimately acknowledge that my book and the fulfillment of my BFP were directly related. The reason I could not feel closure with my pregnancy was because I could not feel closure with my book. I could no longer deny it; they were one and the same, no matter how much I had wrestled with it for the entirety of this journey.

What happened next? Well, you guessed it. Shortly after Christy began standing on Jesus, the Finisher, she got her BFP for the first time *ever*! As you can imagine, when she shared the news with me, I was ecstatic! I mean, I got to witness this precious friend transform right before my eyes from The Barren Woman to The Joyful Mother of children. It was incredible!

Moreover, I rejoiced for another reason. I rejoiced because my prayer was abundantly answered, which has been that anyone who reads this book would be transformed spirit, soul, and body. I have also prayed that anyone reading this book would become The Joyful Mother of children both naturally *and* spiritually and that's exactly what happened. It worked! These transitional blueprints actually worked! And God, in His abundant goodness, allowed me a front-row seat (#happysigh).

Additionally, Christy and her husband revealed to me the way it's supposed to be. They showed me what happens when you take truths and receive them wholeheartedly. They showed me what happens when you choose to believe and receive the goodness of God; when you intentionally eliminate all distractions and strongholds to accelerate your sanctification; when you choose to say "yes" to the clarion call of God and His way of doing things; when you humbly allow Him to transform you and call you higher; and when you respond in obedience no matter how risky, no matter how much it doesn't make sense. They did all of this. And they did it quickly. In fact, I believe their fulfilled journey was accelerated for such a time as this.

Yes, I believe that Christy's children are among the generation who will usher in the second coming of Jesus. In fact, I think part of the reason I was blinded to the closure is because I wasn't yet ready. I wasn't yet ready to accept the high calling of the prophetic message in this book – which is the clarion call to the Nazarite Family; the invitation to be a part of God's prophetic plan on the earth for the preparation of the return of Christ.

#review: Remember, before God built the Kingdom of Israel through Kings Saul and David, He birthed Samuel the Nazarite from a barren womb. Before Jesus' arrival on the earth to display the Kingdom of heaven, He birthed John the Baptist, a Nazarite, from a barren womb. Now, here we are, nearing Jesus' second return and I sense God is issuing invitations to barren wombs once again. Who will hear the call? Who will respond?

Christy did, while at the same time confirming what I've prophetically sensed with her *own* discernment and her *own* intimacy with Jesus. (#thatiskey) Furthermore, she and her husband accelerated rapidly into their identities as the mature bride of Christ ready to prepare the way of the Lord. They are dream homes for God *and* the joyful parents of children spirit, soul, and body transformation – God's desire for us all.

So, what about me? Well, I happen to be deeply humbled and irrevocably transformed. My life has changed; I feel it and I see it. As I received this simple truth and began to acknowledge Jesus, the Finisher, I undoubtedly began seeing the Holy Spirit at work causing all my mountains to become a plain, bringing closure to open-ended circumstances, and fulfillment to deep desires and requests.

I like to call this movement of the Spirit, "repairing of the gap" (Isaiah 58:12). This is what He does, after all. The Holy Spirit repairs the breaches; He closes the gap and brings what's true in the spirit into natural manifestation.

For example, you know how in the last chapter, I confessed that my husband and son were not in the same place as me with their expectations? Well, that has since changed. Suddenly, it seemed, they were both accelerated into expectation and faith. My son explained how he simply just *knew* we were going to have more children and my husband and I were in unity of the faith for the very first time. All these years we had been allowing the Spirit to transform us individually and now here we were at the very end walking in unity. Only God can do something like that, friends! It is not by might nor by power, but by *His* Spirit!

Another fulfillment that took place was the legal adoption of my stepson. Yes, the son of my heart, whom I have chosen to love as my own since he was sixteen months old, has legally become my first born. Although we had planned for a different outcome, God showed up and surprised us again with His higher ways. This is a *very* big closure for our family. I mean, after a strenuous twelve-year journey, this was even more evidence of the Spirit at work closing the gap and making mountains a plain. Again, it is not by might, nor by power, but by *His* Spirit!

However, after extended journeys such as this one, it is only by knowing and trusting Jesus, the Finisher, that we give permission for His Spirit to bring closure. Jesus is always the Way. He is always the Door. We enter the Kingdom through Him, by Him, and for Him. He is the Finisher; He is the End. It is His very nature to bring closure. Why? Because He is our Kinsman-Redeemer and He has *already* redeemed us in full!

Like what Boaz did for Ruth, Jesus has taken us under His wing, married us, and given us His name. He has redeemed us from the curse, from sin, from any form of lack and given us back our land of inheritance (#motherhood). He fully accomplished this through the finished work of the cross. In other words, Jesus the Finisher completed His work by becoming the Avenging Lamb who was slain. We are avenged, dear friend (#enoughsaid).

Jesus is our Avenger! That's what a kinsman-redeemer would do – avenge their family member *and* their land. Everything the enemy has stolen from us, Jesus has already redeemed it back. Everything the locust has eaten, Jesus has already restored in full. And because I have *finally* made room in my heart for the simplicity of this truth and because I *finally* believe it, so do I then finally receive the closure that comes with it.

Simply stated, I have overcome.

My Redeemer has *made* me overcome. And the only possible completion of this journey is the natural fulfillment of the rest of my promised inheritance – *more children!* There is no other ending! Like Abraham, I am wholly and entirely convinced (Romans 4:21).

Just as *He* has made me overcome, so does *He* make me dwell in the house as The Joyful Mother of children. *He* does it. He already did it, in fact, and it is by His Spirit that He brings it to fruition. So that's what I continue to do – I dwell. I walk out life in intimacy with my Beloved and I dwell in fruitfulness within the heart of my home. It truly is a done deal and the rest of my children are a sure thing!

Dear reader, just like all truths contained in this book, this same reality is available to you. Your children are a sure thing! I pray you let the Spirit build His dream home within you and I pray you build your dream home through Him so that you may fully receive the desires of your heart as a lover of Jesus and The Joyful Mother of children. Trust me – there is no better way.

P.S. Remember that little girl from the beginning of the book? Well, she really did live happily ever after....

Do You Know Jesus?

If the answer is no, but you'd like to know Jesus as your Friend and Savior, then simply confess Him as Lord and ask Him to make you born again. Receive His love and His gift of salvation and all the goodness that includes. Simply say this prayer or something similar to it in your own words:

> Jesus, I repent and surrender my life to you. I choose you as the God I serve because I believe that you died on the cross for my sin and disease, and rose again so that I might be saved, healed, and delivered. Because of this decision, I believe that I am a new creation and beginning the journey of transformation in your truth and in your word. I commit my life to you, and my journey in your Kingdom starts today.
>
> In Jesus' name, Amen.

Congratulations! All of heaven is rejoicing over this decision you just made, including me (if you only tell me about it, that is). Please send me an email and let me know that you confessed Jesus so I can celebrate with you! thejoyfulmotherofchildren@gmail.com.

Also, please be sure to get plugged into a local spirit-filled fellowship of believers and definitely purchase a Bible or download a Bible app.

Would You Like Prayer?

I have some prayer warriors as part of my team and would love to take your prayer requests. Send any emails to:

thejoyfulmotherofchildren@gmail.com

with "Prayer Request" in the subject line.

Want to Connect?

If this book has touched you in any way, I'd love to hear from you! You can send me an email at thejoyfulmotherofchildren@gmail.com or find me on Facebook and Instagram.

ABOUT THE AUTHOR

Mandi Windsor is passionate about the Word of God! She loves discovering what it has to say regarding any trials and hardships we face in life. Her heart is to teach others the truth so they move forward in freedom as overcomers in Jesus. She and  her husband, Jonathan, have modeled and ministered this message for the entirety of their marriage in partnership with various churches, ministries, and social media platforms. As proud Missourians, they make their home in Kansas City along with their son, Jonathan Jr. (plus more kiddos to come), their two cuddle pugs, their two guinea pigs, and their twenty-five pound cat.

www.ingramcontent.com/pod-product-compliance
Lightning Source LLC
Chambersburg PA
CBHW030315100526
44592CB00010B/446